Law and the Relational Self

This book promotes a relational understanding of the self. It explores how law can be transformed by focusing on the promotion and protection of caring relationships, rather than individual rights. This offers a radical and profound re-imagining of what law is about and what it should be trying to do. It moves from the theoretical into offering practical examples of how the law could be developed to enhance relationships rather than undermine them.

Jonathan Herring is a fellow in Law at Exeter College, and a professor of Law in the Law Faculty at the University of Oxford. He has written on family law, medical law, criminal law and legal issues surrounding care and old age. His books include *Vulnerability, Childhood and the Law* (2018); *Human Thriving and the Law* (2018, with C. Foster); *Medical Law and Ethics* (2018); *Criminal Law,* (2018); and *Family Law* (2019).

The Law in Context Series

Editors: William Twining (University College London),
Maksymilian Del Mar (Queen Mary, University of London) and
Bronwen Morgan (University of New South Wales).

Since 1970 the Law in Context series has been at the forefront of the movement to broaden the study of law. It has been a vehicle for the publication of innovative scholarly books that treat law and legal phenomena critically in their social, political and economic contexts from a variety of perspectives. The series particularly aims to publish scholarly legal writing that brings fresh perspectives to bear on new and existing areas of law taught in universities. A contextual approach involves treating legal subjects broadly, using materials from other social sciences, and from any other discipline that helps to explain the operation in practice of the subject under discussion. It is hoped that this orientation is at once more stimulating and more realistic than the bare exposition of legal rules. The series includes original books that have a different emphasis from traditional legal textbooks, while maintaining the same high standards of scholarship. They are written primarily for undergraduate and graduate students of law and of other disciplines, but will also appeal to a wider readership. In the past, most books in the series have focused on English law, but recent publications include books on European law, globalisation, transnational legal processes and comparative law.

Books in the Series
Acosta: *The National versus the Foreigner in South America*
Ali: *Modern Challenges to Islamic Law*
Alyagon Darr: *Plausible Crime Stories: The Legal History of Sexual Offences in Mandate Palestine*
Anderson, Schum & Twining: *Analysis of Evidence*
Ashworth: *Sentencing and Criminal Justice*
Barton & Douglas: *Law and Parenthood*
Beecher-Monas: *Evaluating Scientific Evidence: An Interdisciplinary Framework for Intellectual Due Process*
Bell: *French Legal Cultures*
Bercusson: *European Labour Law*
Birkinshaw: *European Public Law*
Birkinshaw: *Freedom of Information: The Law, the Practice and the Ideal*
Brownsword & Goodwin: *Law and the Technologies of the Twenty-First Century: Text and Materials*
Cane & Goudkamp: *Atiyah's Accidents, Compensation and the Law*
Clarke & Kohler: *Property Law: Commentary and Materials*
Collins: *The Law of Contract*
Collins, Ewing & McColgan: *Labour Law*
Cowan: *Housing Law and Policy*
Cranston: *Legal Foundations of the Welfare State*

Darian-Smith: *Laws and Societies in Global Contexts: Contemporary Approaches*

Dauvergne: *Making People Illegal: What Globalisation Means for Immigration and Law*

Davies: *Perspectives on Labour Law*

Dembour: *Who Believes in Human Rights?: Reflections on the European Convention*

de Sousa Santos: *Toward a New Legal Common Sense*

Diduck: *Law's Families*

Estella: *Legal Foundations of EU Economic Governance*

Fortin: *Children's Rights and the Developing Law*

Garnsey: *The Justice of Visual Art: Creative State-Building in Times of Political Transition*

Ghai & Woodman: *Practising Self-Government: A Comparative Study of Autonomous Regions*

Glover-Thomas: *Reconstructing Mental Health Law and Policy*

Gobert & Punch: *Rethinking Corporate Crime*

Goldman: *Globalisation and the Western Legal Tradition: Recurring Patterns of Law and Authority*

Haack: *Evidence Matters: Science, Proof, and Truth in the Law*

Harlow & Rawlings: *Law and Administration*

Harris: *An Introduction to Law*

Harris, Campbell & Halson: *Remedies in Contract and Tort*

Harvey: *Seeking Asylum in the UK: Problems and Prospects*

Hervey & McHale: *European Union Health Law: Themes and Implications*

Hervey & McHale: *Health Law and the European Union*

Holder & Lee: *Environmental Protection, Law and Policy: Text and Materials*

Jackson & Summers: *The Internationalisation of Criminal Evidence: Beyond the Common Law and Civil Law Traditions*

Kostakopoulou: *The Future Governance of Citizenship*

Kreiczer-Levy *Destabilized Property: Property Law in the Sharing Economy*

Kubal: *Immigration and Refugee Law in Russia: Socio-Legal Perspectives*

Lewis: *Choice and the Legal Order: Rising above Politics*

Likosky: *Transnational Legal Processes: Globalisation and Power Disparities*

Likosky: *Law, Infrastructure and Human Rights*

Lunney: *A History of Australian Tort Law 1901-1945: England's Obedient Servant?*

Maughan & Webb: *Lawyering Skills and the Legal Process*

McGlynn: *Families and the European Union: Law, Politics and Pluralism*

Moffat: *Trusts Law: Text and Materials*

Monti: *EC Competition Law*

Morgan: *Contract Law Minimalism: A Formalist Restatement of Commercial Contract Law*

Morgan & Yeung: *An Introduction to Law and Regulation: Text and Materials*

Nicola & Davies: *EU Law Stories: Contextual and Critical Histories of European Jurisprudence*

Norrie: *Crime, Reason and History: A Critical Introduction to Criminal Law*

O'Dair: *Legal Ethics: Text and Materials*

Oliver: *Common Values and the Public–Private Divide*

Oliver & Drewry: *The Law and Parliament*

Picciotto: *International Business Taxation*

Probert: *The Changing Legal Regulation of Cohabitation, 1600–2010*
Reed: *Internet Law: Text and Materials*
Richardson: *Law, Process and Custody*
Roberts & Palmer: *Dispute Processes: ADR and the Primary Forms of Decision-Making*
Rowbottom: *Democracy Distorted: Wealth, Influence and Democratic Politics*
Sauter: *Public Services in EU Law*
Scott & Black: *Cranston's Consumers and the Law*
Seneviratne: *Ombudsmen: Public Services and Administrative Justice*
Seppänen: *Ideological Conflict and the Rule of Law in Contemporary China*
Siems: *Comparative Law, 2nd Edition*
Stapleton: *Product Liability*
Stewart: *Gender, Law and Justice in a Global Market*
Tamanaha: *Law as a Means to an End: Threat to the Rule of Law*
Turpin & Tomkins: *British Government and the Constitution: Text and Materials*
Twining: *General Jurisprudence: Understanding Law from a Global Perspective*
Twining: *Globalisation and Legal Theory*
Twining: *Human Rights, Southern Voices: Francis Deng, Abdullahi An-Na'im, Yash Ghai and Upendra Baxi*
Twining: *Jurist in Context*
Twining: *Rethinking Evidence: Exploratory Essays*
Twining & Miers: *How to Do Things with Rules*
Ward: *A Critical Introduction to European Law*
Ward: *Law, Text, Terror*
Ward: *Shakespeare and Legal Imagination*
Wells & Quick: *Lacey, Wells and Quick: Reconstructing Criminal Law*
Zander: *Cases and Materials on the English Legal System*
Zander: *The Law-Making Process*

International Journal of Law in Context: A Global Forum for Interdisciplinary Legal Studies

The *International Journal of Law in Context* is the companion journal to the Law in Context book series and provides a forum for interdisciplinary legal studies and offers intellectual space for ground-breaking critical research. It publishes contextual work about law and its relationship with other disciplines including but not limited to science, literature, humanities, philosophy, sociology, psychology, ethics, history and geography. More information about the journal and how to submit an article can be found at http://journals.cambridge.org/ijc

Law and the Relational Self

JONATHAN HERRING

University of Oxford

CAMBRIDGE
UNIVERSITY PRESS

CAMBRIDGE
UNIVERSITY PRESS

University Printing House, Cambridge CB2 8BS, United Kingdom

One Liberty Plaza, 20th Floor, New York, NY 10006, USA

477 Williamstown Road, Port Melbourne, VIC 3207, Australia

314–321, 3rd Floor, Plot 3, Splendor Forum, Jasola District Centre, New Delhi – 110025, India

79 Anson Road, #06–04/06, Singapore 079906

Cambridge University Press is part of the University of Cambridge.

It furthers the University's mission by disseminating knowledge in the pursuit of education, learning, and research at the highest international levels of excellence.

www.cambridge.org
Information on this title: www.cambridge.org/9781108425131
DOI: 10.1017/9781108348171

© Jonathan Herring 2020

First published 2020

Printed and bound in Great Britain by Clays Ltd, Elcograf S.p.A.

A catalogue record for this publication is available from the British Library.

Library of Congress Cataloging-in-Publication Data
Names: Herring, Jonathan, author.
Title: Law and the relational self / Jonathan Herring, University of Oxford.
Description: Cambridge, United Kingdom ; New York, NY : Cambridge University Press, 2019. |
Series: The law in context series | Includes bibliographical references and index.
Identifiers: LCCN 2019018391 | ISBN 9781108425131 (hardback : alk. paper) |
    ISBN 9781108441209 (pbk. : alk. paper)
Subjects: LCSH: Law–Philosophy. | Jurisprudence–Philosophy.
Classification: LCC K231 .H49 2019 | DDC 340/.1–dc23
LC record available at https://lccn.loc.gov/2019018391

ISBN 978-1-108-42513-1 Hardback

Contents

Acknowledgements   *page* ix
Table of Cases   x
Table of Legislation   xii

1   The Concept of the Relational Self   1
  1.1 Introduction   1
  1.2 The Traditional Individualised Understanding of the Self   1
  1.3 Theories of the Individual Self   4
  1.4 A Rejection of the Individual Self   7
  1.5 The Relational Self   11
  1.6 Autonomy   16
  1.7 Disability   19
  1.8 Conclusion   23

2   Law and the Vulnerable Self   24
  2.1 Introduction   24
  2.2 Introducing Vulnerability   24
  2.3 Defining Vulnerability   25
  2.4 Who Is Vulnerable?   28
  2.5 All the Time or Some of the Time?   33
  2.6 The Significance of the Claim That We Are All Vulnerable   35
  2.7 Criticisms of the Claim   44
  2.8 Conclusion   45

3   Law and the Caring Self   46
  3.1 Introduction   46
  3.2 The Definition of Care   49
  3.3 Care Ethics   57
  3.4 The Disability Critique of Care Ethics   62
  3.5 Care Ethics and the Law   66
  3.6 State Support of Care   68
  3.7 Conclusion   72

4 **Law and the Abused Self**   74
   4.1 Introduction   74
   4.2 Statistics   74
   4.3 Defining Intimate Abuse   76
   4.4 Developing a Definition   79
   4.5 Intimate Abuse and Children   95
   4.6 Developing a Legal Response   96
   4.7 Conclusion   98

5 **Medical Law and the Relational Self**   99
   5.1 Introduction   99
   5.2 Bodies and Body Ownership   99
   5.3 Capacity   109
   5.4 Best Interests   123
   5.5 Personhood   128
   5.6 Conclusion   140

6 **Family Law and the Relational Self**   141
   6.1 Introduction   141
   6.2 The Family of Family Law   141
   6.3 Remedying Unequal Distribution of Relational Advantages or
        Disadvantages   148
   6.4 Parenthood   155
   6.5 Parental Responsibility   158
   6.6 Disputes over Children   162
   6.7 Conclusion   165

7 **Criminal Law and the Relational Self**   167
   7.1 Introduction   167
   7.2 Relational Harms   167
   7.3 Consent and the Criminal Law   178
   7.4 Exploitation   182
   7.5 Relational Blame and Joint Enterprise   185
   7.6 Conclusion   194

8 **Concluding Thoughts**   196

   Index   198

Acknowledgements

There would be something very wrong if a book on the relational self did not include an acknowledgements section! Book writing is as good an example of a communal endeavour as any other. All of the material here is a result of engaging with and thinking about the writing of others; discussing it with friends; and simply noticing everyday life. I can hardly claim it as 'mine' in any serious sense.

I am enormously grateful for the support, ideas and fun of many colleagues and friends including Alan Bogg, Shazia Choudhry, Michelle Madden Dempsey, Charlotte Elves, Charles Foster, Stephen Gilmore, Imogen Goold, Tessa Roynan and Rachel Taylor.

During the final stages of writing this book, I had a series of health issues and will be always grateful to the teams of NHS staff for their remarkable work and care.

I am grateful too to the team at Cambridge University Press, especially Marianne Nield for her support of the project.

Kirsten, Laurel, Joanna and Darcy are a constant source of joy and conclusive proof that relationships are at the core of well-being.

Table of Cases

A, B, C and Others v. Leeds Teaching Hospital [2004] EWHC 644
  (QB)   107
A Local Authority v. Mr and Mrs A [2010] EWHC 1549 (Fam)   113, 120
A Local Authority v. TZ [2013] EWHC 2322 (COP)   109
A NHS Trust v. Dr A [2013] EWHC 2442 (COP)   113
AB v. Leeds Teaching Hospitals NHS Trust [2003] EWHC 1034   156
Ahsan v. University Hospitals Leicester NHS Trust [2006] EWHC 2624
  (QB)   3
Attorney-General's Reference (No 90 of 2009) [2009] EWCA Crim 2610
  89

B (A Child), Re [2009] UKSC 5   3
B-H, Re [2015] EWCA Civ 389   159

Dawson v. Wearmouth [1999] 1 FLR 1167   162
DL v. A Local Authority [2012] EWCA 253   36
Doodeward v. Spence (1908) 6 C.L.R. 906   100

Evans v. UK (2006) 43 EHRR 21   108

G (Children) (Residence: Same-Sex Partner), Re [2006] UKHL 43   162
G(T), Re [2010] EWHC 3005 (COP)   126
Gillick v. West Norfolk Area Health Authority [1985] 3 WLR 830   158

JS v An NHS Trust [2002] EWHC 2734 (Fam),   125

Miller v Miller [2006] 2 FCR 213   150

P (Contact: Supervision), Re [1996] 2 FLR 314   162
PC v. York [2013] EWCA 478   109, 120

R v. Brock and Wyner [2001] 2 Cr App Rep 31   186
R v. Chan Fook [1994] 1 WLR 698   170
R v. Dica [2004] EWCA 1103   174

R v. Dhaliwal [2006] EWCA Crim 11   169, 170
R v. Emmett [1999] All ER (D) 641   174
R v. Hassan [2005] UKHL 22   187
R v. Hinks [2000] UKHL 53   179
R v. Howe [2014] EWCA Crim 114   89
R v. Kennedy 2007] UKHL 38   189
R v. Khan [2009] EWCA Crim 2   189
R v. M (1995) 16 Cr App R (S) 770   171
R v. Meachen [2006] EWCA Crim 2414   175
R v. Millberry [2002] EWCA Crim 2891   171
R v. Pagett (1983) 76 Cr App R 279   189
R v. PH [2001] 1 Cr App R (S) 52   172
R v. Powell and English [1997] UKHL 45   185
R v. R [1992] 1 AC 599   171, 172
R v. Secretary of State for Education and Employment ex parte Williamson
    [2005] UKHL 15   158
R v. Stone and Dobinson [1977] QB 354   187
R v. Sullivan [1984] AC 156   113
R v. Wilson [1997] QB 47   174
R (Macdonald) v. Kensington and Chelsea [2011] UKSC 33   73
R (N) v. Dr M, A NHS Trust [2002] EWHC 1911   113
Radmacher v. Granatino [2010] UKSC 42   154

State of North Carolina v. Norman 366 SE 2d 586 (NC App 1988)   91

The Mental Health Trust v. DD [2014] EWCOP 11   114

Y (Mental Patient: Bone Marrow Donation), Re [1997] 2 FCR 172   124
Yearworth v. North Bristol NHS Trust [2009] EWCA Civ 37   101, 106
Yemshaw v. London Borough of Hounslow [2011] UKSC 3   79

Table of Legislation

Children Act 1989
  s.1   162
  s. 3   158
  s.8   162
  s. 31   158

Domestic Violence Crime and Victim Act 2004
  s.5   188

Human Fertilisation and Embryology Act 1990   106, 156
Human Fertilisation and Embryology Act 2008   156
Human Rights Act 1998   97, 121
Human Tissue Act 2004   106

Inheritance (Provision for Family and Dependents Act) 1975
  s. 1A   142

Mental Capacity Act 2005   36, 109, 118, 119, 123
  s. 2   109
  s. 3   109–110
  s.4   123
Legal Aid, Sentencing and Punishment of Offenders Act 2012   77
  Sch 1   77
Marriage (Same Sex Couples) Act 2013   142, 144
Misuse of Drugs Act 1971
  s. 8   187

Offences Against the Person Act 1861   168

Protection from Harassment Act 1997   176

Serious Crime Act 2015
  s. 76   176
Sexual Offences Act 2003   96

Theft Act 1968
  S. 4   103

1

The Concept of the Relational Self

1.1 Introduction

Who am I? That most profound of questions has troubled humans from the time people first began to think. The nature of the self raises complex and puzzling questions. It is not an issue which is only of interest to insomniacs, daydreamers or philosophers. It is of central importance for lawyers. The law's understanding of the nature of the self determines the way legal rights and responsibilities are understood; what goals are set for legal intervention; and the nature of legal proceedings.

It is not the aim of this book to provide a fully argued answer to the question of the self. Not least because the author lacks the ability to do so! Rather, it will explore one particular concept of the self: the relational self. In recent years there has been a growing body of literature on the concept. Sociology,[1] theology,[2] ethics,[3] anthropology,[4] philosophy[5] and disability studies[6] have all explored this understanding of the self. This book will start by explaining the concept of the relational self, and its primary aim is to consider the implications for the law if it were adopted.

1.2 The Traditional Individualised Understanding of the Self

Lawyers tend not to spend much time contemplating the nature of the self. Yet it is a concept at the heart of the law. It is found in the names we give our

---

[1] P. Donate and M. Archer, *The Relational Subject* (Cambridge University Press, 2015); N. Crossley, *Towards Relational Sociology* (Routledge, 2011).

[2] M. Pagis, 'Religious Self-Constitution: A Relational Perspective' in C. Bender, W. Cadge, P. Levitt and D. Smilde (eds.) *Religion on the Edge: De-centering and Re-centering the Sociology of Religion* (Oxford University Press, 2012), 92; J. Herring, 'The Vulnerability of God and Humanity' (2018) 180 *Law and Justice* 5.

[3] H. Lindemann, *Holding and Letting Go: The Social Practice of Personal Identities* (Oxford University Press, 2014).

[4] L. Shults, *Reforming Theological Anthropology: After the Philosophical Turn to Relationality* (Eerdman, 2003).

[5] C. Sedikides, L. Gaertner, and E. O'Mara, 'Individual Self, Relational Self, Collective Self: Hierarchical Ordering of the Tripartite Self' (2011) 56 *Psychological Studies* 98.

[6] S. Reindal, 'A Social Relational Model of Disability: A Theoretical Framework for Special Needs Education?' (2008) 23 *European Journal of Special Needs Education* 135.

cases: *Smith* v. *Jones* indicates there is a person called Smith who is claiming against another called Jones. In criminal cases the whole process is based on the idea the defendant is a self who can be held to account for what they have done in the past: that they are the same person in court and when they are punished as they were when they committed the crime. The law assumes that there are individual human beings who can be given legal rights and responsibilities. Further, the nature of those rights, interests and responsibilities reveals our understanding of what is important about the self. The understanding of what a person is, what is important to people and how people flourish will powerfully influence what we consider to be good law. This book will argue that understanding the self in relational terms means a very different set of rights, values and interests will be at the heart of the law, compared with more individualised understandings of the self.[7]

I will start by exploring features of the traditional understanding of the self, before exploring the relational understanding.

1.2.1 The Self as Unique

Hans Joas[8] refers to the self as one of social science's greatest discoveries. The separation of human beings into separate individual selves means that we recognise the different interests, claims and personalities of each one. It recognises each person is unique. Martha Nussbaum[9] explains why she believes the individual should be the basic unit for political thought:

> It means, first of all, that liberalism responds sharply to the basic fact that each person has a course from birth to death that is not precisely the same as that of any other person; that each person is one and not more than one, that each feels pain in his or her own body, that the food given to A does not arrive in the stomach of B.

Someone's personal identity in this sense consists of those features she takes to 'define her as a person' or 'make her the person she is'.[10] Crucially, it identifies those features that make her different from others. By the law taking seriously the nature of the unique self it avoids a person being seen as merely part of a group, with no regard for what makes them different. It means, for example, when a court in a family case decides what order will promote a child's welfare, it can consider the interests, character, family situation and relationships of the particular child before it, rather than rely on generalisations about what is

[7] E. Olson, 'Self: Personal Identity' in W. Banks (ed.) *Encyclopaedia of Consciousness* (Elsevier Academic Press, 2009).
[8] H. Joas, *The Genesis of Values* (Polity Press, 2000).
[9] M. Nussbaum, *Sex and Social Justice* (Oxford University Press, 1999), 62.
[10] E. Olson, 'Personal Identity' in E. Zalta (ed.) *Stanford Encyclopaedia of Philosophy* (Stanford University, 2015), 1.

generally good for children.[11] Treating people without regard for their individual situations and characteristics will exacerbate the disadvantages that exist in society for those who differ from the norm. The feminist literature on the male norm is a good example of how a law that fails to recognise difference perpetuates inequality.[12]

1.2.2 The Self over Time

The traditional concept of the self captures the idea that there is a significant link between the entity that existed in the past and the entity that exists now. The Jonathan who acted a year ago, the Jonathan who acts now and the Jonathan who acts in the future have a morally significant connection. We certainly live as if that is true. We save now to spend later; exercise now to keep healthy later; even create now a legacy for when we die. Similarly, we feel ourselves responsible for our past acts. We apologise, seek to compensate or take credit for past actions. This all reflects a belief in the self which exists over time.

Clearly, the concept of self over time is significant for lawyers. Criminal law punishes the person today for acts they did in the past. Under contract law the person today is bound by the promise they made a month ago. And a person who produces an advance directive is seeking to influence how they will be treated in the future if they lose capacity.[13] Similarly, when a decision has to be made about a person who is no longer able to make decisions for themselves, a particular focus on the values that the person used to have is generally seen as appropriate. For example, if a lifelong ardent vegetarian has now lost capacity, it seems appropriate to respect their earlier wishes and not feed them meat.[14] In all these examples, we see the person in the present as responsible for and linked to the person they were in the past, and as having some rights to determine what will happen to them in the future. That is because they are sufficiently morally connected: they are the same (or essentially the same) self.

1.2.3 The Self, Property and Bodies

The concept of the self is also used to explain a separation between things which are mere 'property' and things which are our 'self'. Those things that relate to the self have particular importance and value. For example, if someone ran off with my slippers, it would be different from them running off with my hand. That is because the latter is more closely connected to the self. The right to bodily integrity is one of the most strongly protected

---

[11] *Re B (A Child)* [2009] UKSC 5.
[12] For example, N. Naffine, *Criminal Law and the Man Problem* (Bloomsbury, 2019).
[13] Olson, 'Self: Personal Identity'.
[14] *Ahsan* v. *University Hospitals Leicester NHS Trust* [2006] EWHC 2624 (QB).

rights that one can have. Jesse Wall and I have argued that the right to bodily integrity

> is non-reducible to the principle of autonomy. Bodily integrity relates to the integration of the self and the rest of the objective world. A breach of it, therefore, is significantly different to interference in decisions about your body. This explains why interference with bodily integrity requires justification beyond what will suffice for an interference with autonomy.[15]

This leads to a broader consideration of the relationship between the self and the body. The kind of thought experiment commonly used to encourage people to start thinking about the nature of the self is to imagine that persons A and B have their brains removed and person A's brain is put into person B's body. The resulting person will have the memories and values of person A but the body of person B. Are they person A or person B? Should the new person be responsible for the crimes or debts of person A or B or both or neither? Which person should own the property that previously belonged to A or B? If either A or B had issued an advance decision about what should happen to them does this bind the new person?

Many people struggle with these questions. The theory of Cartesian Dualism, that the self was located in the mind, which used the body as a machine, or that the self was a pearl seated inside a shell (the body), has few supporters today.[16] Our bodies are commonly seen as having a close connection to our identity. Neuroscience shows that the mind cannot be seen as simply a thing living in a body.[17] Our minds, consciousness and emotions react to and reflect changes throughout the body. Bodies reflect and partly constitute the self, although quite how this is understood varies greatly. This explains why we struggle with the switching head issue raised in the previous paragraph. The self involves both mind and body. The weight the law attaches to bodily integrity, as discussed in the previous section, reflects the law's acceptance of the special connection of the self to the body.

1.3 Theories of the Individual Self

1.3.1 The Bodily Self

One understanding of the individual self is to conceive of it in bodily terms. Your body is the same now as it was then, maybe with a bit of extra fat or a little less hair! Your body now is similar to the body you will become. This theory is sometimes called animalism: that we should be understood as

---

[15] J. Herring and J. Wall, 'The Nature and Significance of the Right to Bodily Integrity' (2017) 76 *Cambridge Law Journal* 566.

[16] H. Robinson, 'Dualism', https://plato.stanford.edu/entries/dualism [accessed 1 February 2019].

[17] B. Hood, *The Self Illusion* (Constable, 2012).

biological organisms.[18] The continuity of the self is found in terms of biological continuity. Aristotle is perhaps the best known holder of this view.[19]
But it is not convincing. Our bodies are constantly changing. Prosthetics and
organ transplants offer replacement parts, without surely changing the essential nature of the self. Old bits of us fall off and new pieces grow. In purely
biological terms, little of us exists now that did so at the time of our birth.[20]
Our bodies contain countless non-human organisms that are crucial to our
being.[21] The image of the constant body is a false one. Further, most people
would want to see there being more to their sense of identity than their
biological material.

1.3.2 The Psychological Self

'I think therefore I am,' Descartes famously declared.[22] This reflects a more
popular theory in contemporary thought than the bodily self, namely, that
psychological constancy constitutes the self. This view emphasises that our values,
memories and personalities persist over time. While these will change and
develop, there is a degree of consistency about these things which creates a unique
sense of identity and self. Hume argued that we are 'bundles of mental states and
events'.[23] We are made not of cells or atoms, but memories. We are processes and
events, rather than substances: more like a theatre production than a static entity.

This approach has its appeal, but it is not without its difficulties. Were
Dr Jekyll and Mr Hyde two persons or one?[24] Is a person who undergoes a
religious conversion (or complete loss of faith) and has an utter change in
behaviour and values a different person or the same? These questions show the
problems with relying on psychological continuity for the essence of the self.
The emphasis on memory can have some strange consequences. Eric Olsen
gives this example:

> Suppose Charlie's memories are erased and replaced with accurate memories (or
> apparent memories) of the life of someone long dead – Guy Fawkes, say. Ought
> we to conclude, on the basis of memory evidence, that the resulting person is not
> Charlie but Guy Fawkes brought back to life, or ought we instead to infer from
> the absence of physical continuity that he is simply Charlie with memory loss?[25]

---

[18] P. Snowdon, 'Persons, Animals, and Ourselves' in C. Gill (ed.) *The Person and the Human Mind* (Clarendon Press, 1990).

[19] E. Olson, *The Human Animal: Personal Identity without Psychology* (Oxford University Press, 1997).

[20] J. Herring and P.-L. Chau, 'My Body, Your Body, Our Bodies' (2007) 15 *Medical Law Review* 34.

[21] J. Herring and P.-L. Chau, 'Interconnected, Inhabited and Insecure: Why Bodies Should Not Be Property' (2014) 40 *Journal of Medical Ethics* 39.

[22] R. Descartes, *Discourse on Method* (1637).

[23] D. Hume, *Treatise of Human Nature* (Clarendon Press, 1978, original work 1739).

[24] E. Olsen, 'Was Jekyll Hyde?' (2003) 66 *Philosophy and Phenomenological Research* 328.

[25] E. Olson, 'Self: Personal Identity'.

There is also a concern that the psychological self over-emphasises the mental aspect of our identity. It makes no reference to our bodies. This seems to enforce Cartesian Dualism, which draws a sharp distinction between the body and mind, and sees the body as simply a tool for the self. This approach is, as already mentioned, very unpopular in much contemporary thought. Our sense of self and the nature of our bodies are closely entwined.[26] Our bodies dictate how we are treated, disadvantaged, benefited and categorised by society. Disability, looks, sexuality, age, physical shape and race all have profound impacts on the choices we have open to us and that we can make.[27]

The emphasis on psychological continuity is also problematic for cases where a person has a cognitive impairment. Quite clearly, there can be problems with its application in a case where a person's condition means they do not have a coherent set of memories, values and beliefs. But more significantly, it also appears to elevate cognition as a core element of the human self. And a particular form of cognition: one based on rationality, coherence and belief. This sends an implied message that those incapable of these forms of cognition are not properly human selves.

1.3.3 The Soul

One can begin to see why religious writers have developed the concept of a soul as an eternal self.[28] This much discussed concept is somewhat opaque. It is generally seen as the essence of the self. It is not restricted to the body, but is more than mere thoughts and memories. It is not necessarily a religious concept, but most of the writing on the soul is found in theology. Plato, Descartes and Leibniz all supported concepts of the soul outside of a formal theological context.[29] Plato suggested the soul should be seen as having three parts:

1. The logos (reason), which directs and balances the competing desires in the self with reason.
2. The thymos (emotion), which drives us to act for emotional reasons in acts of bravery or love.
3. The pathos (carnal appetites), which drives people to meet bodily needs and passions.

Under this model, things go wrong for a soul when their logos fails to control either the thymos or pathos and the person becomes out of control through emotions or bodily desires. As can be seen, this understanding of the soul involves the integration of the mind and the body.

---

[26] Herring and Wall, 'The Nature and Significance of the Right to Bodily Integrity'.
[27] D. Rhodes, *The Beauty Bias* (Oxford University Press, 2011).
[28] R. Swinburne, *The Evolution of the Soul* (Oxford University Press, 1984), 21.
[29] Ibid.

Capturing a definition of the soul in modern terminology has proved problematic. The soul has been defined as 'the inner essence of a being comprising its locus of sapience (self-awareness) and metaphysical identity'.[30] Generally, it is taken that souls are immortal and survive death. Hence, they are regarded as incorporeal and can be separated from bodies. Clearly, the concept of the soul has significance in the hope it offers for those who believe in an afterlife. It can also have significance to the present, as it offers an idea there is an 'essential you' and that wrongful acts can be dismissed as an aberration not reflecting the true self (the soul). It also offers coherence to one's life: despite all the ups and downs, changes and similarities, there is an essential you which is at the core of it all.

Although presented as three models (the self as the body, the self as mind and the soul), it is possible to combine these approaches.[31] There is an extensive literature on the individual self. As the focus of this book is on developing the theory of the relational self, I will not develop these theories further, but rather focus more on the objections to these traditional models and developing the concept of the relational self.

1.4 A Rejection of the Individual Self

A significant body of writing rejects the conception of the individual self. Ngaire Naffine writes:

> We can think of human beings as discrete individuals, fully independent of one another and preferring it that way, because others cause worry: they pose a threat to property and personal security. Such nervous, self-isolating beings need law to keep others at bay. They do best – are most autonomous, even happy – when left to their own devices. This way of thinking about persons may seem quite natural because it has been so influential in our Western liberal legal and political tradition.[32]

However, she explains that image of the self is a caricature. No one can, in fact, survive without the practical, emotional and psychological support of others.

One powerful line of critique of the concept of the individual self has come from feminist writing. Simone de Beauvoir boldly declares: 'He is the Subject, he is the Absolute – she is the Other.' The claim is that the assumptions about the self in law, politics and wider culture are based on a male norm.[33] Cynthia

---

[30] New World Encyclopaedia contributors, 'Soul'. *New World Encyclopaedia*, www.newworldencyclopedia.org/p/index.php?title=Soul&oldid=1007531 [accessed 31 January 2019].

[31] C. Sedikides and M. Brewer, 'Individual Self, Relational Self, and Collective Self Partners, Opponents, or Strangers?' in C. Sedikides and M. Brewer (eds.) *Individual Self, Relational Self, Collective Self* (Psychology Press, 2002), 1.

[32] N. Naffine, 'The Liberal Legal Individual Accused: The Relational Case' (2014) 29 *Canadian Journal of Law and Society* 123.

[33] D. Meyers (ed.) *Feminists Rethink the Self* (Westview Press, 1997).

Willett, Ellie Anderson and Dianna Meyers[34] argue that 'the self is a free, rational chooser and actor – an autonomous agent' and that those who do not live up to this are seen as not being real people. They explain:

> Since women have been cast as lesser forms of the masculine individual, the paradigm of the self that has gained ascendancy in U.S. popular culture and in Western philosophy is derived from the experience of the predominantly white and heterosexual, mostly economically advantaged men who have wielded social, economic, and political power and who have dominated the arts, literature, the media, and scholarship. As a result, feminists have not merely perceived the self as a metaphysical issue but have also drawn attention to its ethical, epistemological, social, and political imbrication.

The privileged white male-dominated influence mentioned in the quote is not explicitly acknowledged in definitions of the individual self. However, it is apparent in many practical manifestations of these definitions. The highly influential Kantian writing on the self imagines a person who finds absolute moral values through the power of rational thought. Similarly, the 'homo economicus' of mainstream economics is driven by reason to rank and maximise desire satisfaction. These highly influential understandings of the self do reflect a particular understanding of what a self is. They imagine a self free from relationships and society who strives for moral or economic perfection through rationality. There is no discussion of relationships; indeed, if anything, these are seen as threatening objectivity. For example, Kant expressed concern that social and emotional bonds could undermine a rational commitment to duty. They could cause a person to defy their rational obligations by focusing on their caring responsibilities. Similarly, the person who complies with their relational responsibilities fails to act in line with self-interest and self – wealth maximisation. That undermines the expectations that underpin traditional economic analysis. These individualistic models also play down the role of emotions and ignore the 'complexity of the dynamic, intrapsychic world of unconscious fantasies, fears, and desires'.[35] The focus on rationality underplays the worries, prejudices, unwanted desires, ambivalences and fears that are central to human experience.

So, the definition of the individual self presupposes and privileges a particular class of humans. As Willett, Anderson and Meyers put it:

> Although represented as genderless, sexless, raceless, ageless, and classless, feminists argue that the Kantian ethical subject and homo economicus mask a white, healthy, youthfully middle-aged, middle- or upper-class, heterosexual, male citizen.[36]

[34] C. Willett and E. Anderson, 'Feminist Perspectives on the Self' (*Stanford Encyclopaedia of Philosophy*) https://plato.stanford.edu/entries/feminism-self/ [accessed 1 February 2019].
[35] C. Willett and E. Anderson, 'Feminist Perspectives on the Self' (*Stanford Encyclopaedia of Philosophy*) https://plato.stanford.edu/entries/feminism-self/ [accessed 1 February 2019].
[36] Ibid.

The image of the self as in its nature governed by rationality, self-direction and self-sufficiency meant that caring work and relating to others were subservient aspects of the self. As Willet et al. put it: 'To identify the self with the rational mind is, then, to masculinize the self.'[37] They go on to explain:

> The masculine realm of rational selfhood is a realm of moral decency – principled respect for others and conscientious fidelity to duty – and of prudent good sense – adherence to shrewd, fulfilling, long-range life plans. However, femininity is associated with a sentimental attachment to family and friends that spawns favoritism and compromises principles. Likewise, femininity is associated with immersion in unpredictable domestic exigencies that forever jeopardize the best-laid plans and often necessitate resorting to hasty retreats or charting new directions. By comparison, the masculinized self appears to be a sturdy fortress of integrity. The self is essentially masculine, and the masculine self is essentially good and wise.[38]

Further, the individualised notion of the self, as bounded and self-contained, encourages the promotion of self-reliance and independence. The self should be directing his efforts to doing all he can do to maximise personal gain. As Lorraine Code writes:

> His independence is under constant threat from other (equally self-serving) individuals: hence he devises rules to protect himself from intrusion. Talk of rights, rational self-interest, expediency, and efficiency permeates his moral, social, and political discourse.[39]

The problems with this individualised conception of the self can be summarised as follows. First, they fail to recognise the reality that relationships and caring responsibilities, far from being impediments to the self, are core to people's identity. As Willett and Anderson ask:

> Who models this free, rational self? Although represented as genderless, sexless, raceless, ageless, and classless, feminists argue that the Kantian ethical subject and homo economicus mask a white, healthy, youthfully middle-aged, middle- or upper-class, heterosexual, male citizen. On the Kantian view, he is an impartial judge or legislator reflecting on principles and deliberating about policies, while on the utilitarian view, he is a self-interested bargainer and contractor wheeling and dealing in the marketplace. It is no accident that politics and commerce are both domains from which women have historically been excluded. It is no accident, either, that the philosophers who originated these views of the self typically endorsed this exclusion. Deeming women emotional and unprincipled, these thinkers advocated confining women to the domestic sphere where their vices could be neutralized, even transformed into virtues, in

---

[37] Ibid.
[38] Ibid.
[39] L. Code, *What Can She Know?: Feminist Theory and the Construction of Knowledge* (Cornell University Press, 1991), 77–78.

the role of empathetic, supportive wife, vulnerable sexual partner, and nurturant mother.[40]

We will explore this further when developing the concept of the relational self.

Second, the model of the individual self privileges male interests and diminishes or denies women's sense of self. There is a long history of women being presented as weaker or inadequate versions of men, and these differences being used to justify subordination of women.[41] Indeed, the caring and relational values are used to produce legal structures which oppress women. Hence, we can see pregnant women treated as 'fetal container'[42] and forced to have medical procedures solely to benefit the foetus. Similarly, legal doctrines assume a wife's identity is subsumed with her husband's on marriage.[43]

Third, more broadly, the traditional visions of the self promote an ablest, classist and racist vision of the white able-bodied male as the norm around which to develop an understanding of the self. As Clifford Geertz, a renowned anthropologist, notes:

> The Western conception of the person as a bounded, unique, more or less integrated motivational and cognitive universe, a dynamic center of awareness, emotion, judgment, and action organized into a distinctive whole and set contrastively both against other such wholes and against a social and natural background is, however incorrigible it may seem to us, a rather peculiar idea within the context of the world cultures.[44]

Fourth, there are concerns about the consequences of taking the individualised version of the self. Kenneth Gergen writes:

> If what is most central to me is within me – mine and mine alone – then how am I to regard you? At the outset, you are fundamentally "other" – an alien who exists separately from me. I am essentially alone; I come into the world as an isolated being and leave alone. Further, you can never fully know or understand my private world, for it is never fully available to you, never fully revealed.[45]

As he argues, the image of the individualised self leads to self-doubt, distrust of others and a crisis of self-esteem. Worse still, 'If the self is the centre of one's existence, and one can never fully know or trust another, then our primary mission must be to "look out for number one"!'[46] This can lead to what

[40] C. Willett and E. Anderson, 'Feminist Perspectives on the Self' (*Stanford Encyclopaedia of Philosophy*) https://plato.stanford.edu/entries/feminism-self/ [accessed 1 February 2019].

[41] Ibid.

[42] L. Purdy, 'Are Pregnant Women Fetal Containers' (1990) 4 *Bioethics* 273.

[43] J. Herring, 'No More Having and Holding: The Abolition of the Marital Rape Exemption' in S. Gilmore, J. Herring and R. Probert (eds.) *Landmark Cases in Family Law* (Hart, 2011), 212.

[44] C. Geertz 'From the Native's Point of View: On the Nature of Anthropological Understanding' (1974) 28 *Bulletin of the American Academy of Arts and Sciences* 26.

[45] K. Gergen, *An Invitation to Social Construction* (Sage, 2015), 94.

[46] Ibid., 95.

Christopher Lasch has called 'the culture of narcissism'[47] with the instrumental use of other people and the environment for one's own ends. As Kenneth Gergen puts it:

> There is a substantial dark side to constructing a world of individual and agentic selves. When a fundamental distinction between self and other is established, the social world is constituted in terms of differences. The individual stands as an isolated entity, essentially alone and alienated.[48]

Fortunately, there is better way of understanding the self: the relational self.

1.5 The Relational Self

Out of these criticisms of the traditional models of self come arguments about a relational understanding of the self.[49] At the heart of this approach is the claim that the self emerges out of our relationships with each other: that the self is constituted by and through our relationships. As the novelist Elena Ferrante puts it, 'It's the people who love us or hate us – or both – who hold together the thousands of fragments we are made of.'[50] These relationships are also found in the form of communal forces and constructions which provide the background for relationships with others. Hence social identities connected with gender, disability, race, sexual orientation, class, age, ethnicity etc., and intersections between these identities, interface with our personal relationships and generate the self. It is not through gazing at our navels that we gain an insight into who we are. It is by talking, touching, teaching, and caring with each other.

Nagaire Naffine sums up the case for the relational self, saying we should

> think of human beings as inseparable from their relations. The guiding idea is that we are formed through relations – the mother-child bond provides an obvious one – and that we move through life within, and more importantly as , a great shifting constellation of relations. Within relations we become what we are as persons; here, we must make sense of our lives, which in turn must be understood by scholars who wish to explain us. There is never a full separation between persons, and indeed, human beings draw their very identity from their relations. When they work well, relations are not only formative (and unavoidable) but also conducive to human autonomy and to the flourishing of the individual. It follows that the role of law is to regulate relations rather than to ward them off . Law's job is to ensure that they run smoothly and that they neither oppress nor harm us.[51]

[47] C. Lasch, *The Culture of Narcissism* (W. W. Norton & Co, 1991).
[48] K. Gergen, 'The Social Construction of Self' in S. Gallagher (ed.) *The Oxford Handbook of the Self* (Oxford University Press, 2011).
[49] M. Emirbayer, 'Manifesto for a Relational Sociology' (1997) 103 *American Journal of Sociology* 208.
[50] E. Ferrante, *Frantumaglia: A Writer's Journey* (Penguin, 2016), 305.
[51] Naffine, 'The Liberal Legal Individual Accused: The Relational Case', 123.

The theory of the relational self argues that the self is created by our relationships with others. When children first interact with the world, they do so through their relationships with their caregivers. These relationships give them words, gestures and facial expressions to describe what they see and experience.[52] The relationships give ways of looking at the world and language to express it. It is from these that an understanding of self emerges.[53] As Kenneth Gergen explains:

> Our ability to share symbols also benefits from our innate capacities for role-taking. That is, as we watch others respond to our gestures, we take their role; we begin to experience their responses within us and we are able to gain a sense of what the other's gesture symbolizes for him or her ... By taking the role of the other, as he or she responds to my actions, I come to understand who and what I am.[54]

Hilde Lindemann[55] writes of the process by which the self is created in childhood:

> It requires children to engage with others in all kinds of language games, in the course of which they are brought into the space of reasons. They have to learn what words mean and the rules for using them correctly. They have to get the hang of the shared sensibilities that undergird rule following, rationality, and social life in general. They have to form a self-conception and a sense for who others are, both singly and together. They have to become storytellers. They have to appreciate the patterns of expression, recognition, and response in which their own and others' identities play a key role. They have to try on the moral values and attitudes they are taught and come either to question them or to claim them as fully their own. They have to act out of their sense of who they are and become aware that others will identify them by how they act.

Annette Baier[56] has described people as 'second persons' to capture the sense that through childhood we come to know ourselves through care and relationships. She writes: 'My first concept of myself is as the referent of "you", spoken by someone whom I will address as "you" ... The second person, the pronoun of mutual address and recognition, introduces us to the first and third.'[57]

Of course, the sense of self develops from childhood, but this is through interactions with others and the wider social forces mentioned previously. Our understanding of the world and our place in it may change but these occur as a result of our interactions with others. As Suzanne Kirschner[58] puts it:

---

[52] G. Mead, *Mind, Self and Society 1934* (University of Chicago Press, 1934).
[53] Gergen, *An Invitation to Social Construction*.
[54] Ibid.
[55] Lindemann, *Holding and Letting Go: The Social Practice of Personal Identities*, 203.
[56] A. Baier, *Postures of the Mind: Essays on Mind and Morals* (University of Minnesota Press, 1985), 180
[57] Ibid., 186.
[58] S. Kirschner, 'Subjectivity as Socioculturally Constituted Experience' in J. Martin (ed.) *The Wiley Handbook of Theoretical and Philosophical Psychology* (Wiley, 2015).

Our identities (the labels and categories by which we are identified or identify ourselves) are ascribed, and thus our subjectivities are formed, through our immersion in particular languages, relationships, cultural symbols, social practices, and institutional trajectories.

We are now what our relationships with our parents, siblings, school friends, nursery assistant, neighbour, teacher etc. were. Each gives us an understanding of ourselves and the world. As Mead[59] put it 'No hard-and-fast line can be drawn between our own selves and the selves of others, since our own selves exist and enter as such into our experiences only in so far as the selves of others exist and enter as such in our experience also.' It is those relationships which give us the structure on which to understand ourselves.[60] It is for these reasons that abusive and neglectful childhoods can have such profound impacts on the whole of a person's life.

As we grow up and in adulthood, we define ourselves in relational terms. If I was to ask you who you were, you would inevitably reply in terms that our relational: be that as a member of a community; a family; a sports supporters club; or religion. Time and again when people are asked what is most important to them they state families and friends.[61] This is why bereavement and relationships breakdown have such profound psychological effects. In a real sense a bit of us has died. What marks out the human species from other animals is our social nature and in particular the capacity for love, friendship and cooperation.[62]

Intersectional analysis provides some useful insights into the concept of the relational self. This analysis emerged from African American feminists challenging the traditional emphasis on race and gender in determining a person's legal status. They argued that race and gender and class do not operate independently from each other but interact in complex ways.[63] So that the experience of, for example, a black woman was not captured by adding together the disadvantages of being black or being a woman, but rather the experiences of black women created further distinct disadvantages. Similarly, once class, disability, sexuality and so forth are added in, the picture becomes all the more complex.[64] For the purposes of this book, this rich literature shows that the complex relationship between an individual and different

---

[59] Mead, *Mind, Self and Society*, 164.
[60] Donate and Archer, *The Relational Subject*.
[61] A. Bowling, 'What Things Are Important in People's Lives? A Survey of the Public's Judgements to Inform Scales of Health Related Quality Of life' (1995) 41 *Social Science and Medicine* 1447.
[62] C. Willett, *Maternal Ethics and Other Slave Moralities* (Routledge, 1995); C. Willett, *The Soul of Justice: Social Bonds and Racial Hubris* (Cornell University Press, 2001).
[63] K. Crenshaw, 'Demarginalizing the Intersection of Race and Sex: A Black Feminist Critique of Antidiscrimination Doctrine, Feminist Theory, and Antiracist Politics' in K. Bartlett and R. Kennedy (eds.) *Feminist Legal Theory* (Westview Press, 1991), 57.
[64] C. Willett and E. Anderson, 'Feminist Perspectives on the Self' (*Stanford Encyclopaedia of Philosophy*) https://plato.stanford.edu/entries/feminism-self/ [accessed 1 February 2019].

groups they belong to and interact with can have powerful influences on their identify and sense of self. The powerful influence that patriarchy, racism, disablism, classism etc. exert within society shape the experience of the self and the identity that goes with it.

The link between the self and society is a two-way process. As Stets and Burke[65] argue:

> The self influences society through the actions of individuals thereby creating groups, organizations, networks, and institutions. And, reciprocally, society influences the self through its shared language and meanings that enable a person to take the role of the other, engage in social interaction, and reflect upon oneself as an object. The latter process of reflexivity constitutes the core of selfhood.

This picture of the relational self changes the image presented by the individual self of individual atoms fighting for success or survival. Under an individualistic definition of the self, the emphasis is on distinctions between the self and others. We are separated from and distinct from others because that is the nature of the self. It follows from this understanding that autonomy and self-sufficiency are core values. If our nature is dependent on defining for ourselves who we are and developing our own comprehension of our values, then being able to make decisions for ourselves and being free from responsibilities to others is key. Under the individualistic model, conflict and competition become the standard behaviour. By contrast, under the relational model 'the foundation of human society [is] derived from nurturance, caring attachment, and mutual interestedness'.[66]

And that is one of the great positives of the relational understanding of the self. As the self is not self-generated, we are not stuck with who we are. As the self emerges through interactions with others, we can generate new perceptions, experiences, values and interest through interacting with others. The self becomes inevitably dynamic. Our value is not precariously left in our own sense, but through others. As Hilde Lindemann[67] argues, this gives our lives moral significance as it means we are held in personhood by others who recognise our personhood and respond accordingly. As we have to 'let go' (e.g. by leaving home to go to college, going through a divorce or suffering a bereavement) the stories grow and develop. The self changes in response to the differing holdings and acquires new values and new meanings. As one set of relationships may fall away, they can be replaced by others. By contrast, where

---

[65] J. Stets and P. Burke, 'A Sociological Approach to Self and Identity' in M. Leary and J. Tangney (eds.), *Handbook of Self and Identity* (The Guilford Press, 2003), 128.

[66] M. Friedman, 'Feminism and Modern Friendship: Dislocating the Community' (1989) 99 *Ethics* 275.

[67] H. Lindemann, *Holding and Letting Go: The Social Practice of Personal Identities* (Oxford University Press, 2014).

the value and identity is only found in ourselves when mental ill health or loss of self-confidences challenges ourselves we have nowhere to go.[68]

A particularly helpful example of the relational identity theory can be the experiences of those with dementia.[69] Some people argue that if dementia deprives a person of their memory and rationality then the self has been lost or changed. An extreme version of this view has been expressed by David Smith:

> [A]lthough cancer kills you … it doesn't remove your very humanity … It doesn't turn you into a vegetable … All diseases are depersonalizing to some extent. But you're still human. But a person with a serious dementia is no longer human. He's a vegetable. That's devastating. Fearsome. Terrifying, to anyone who's ever seen it – the thought that it could happen to you.[70]

However, the theory of the relational self offers us a way to avoid that somewhat unpalatable conclusion. The person may have dementia and there may be a loss of psychological identity but they are still treated by their family members and friends as the previous self. Family members will discuss past experiences with them and try to ensure their values are respected. The relational construction of the self survives even profound personality and psychological selves.

I will now explore some of the concerns that might be expressed about the relational understanding of the self. First, there is a danger of relational self theory appearing to glamorise relationships. That, however, would be to misunderstand the theory. It is not claiming that all relationships are good. It fully accepts that through bad relationships significant harm can be caused. We shall emphasise this in Chapter 4. Indeed, as that chapter explains, it is the relational theory of the self which is best able to explain the harms that abusive relationships cause and offer the hope of finding positive relationships to overcome those harms. In Chapter 7 we will see how criminal law's approach to harms based on the individualised understanding of the self has missed some important wrongs which are well recognised by an approach based on the relational self.

Second, it might be said that the relational self model makes it too easy for an individual's interests to be lost in the name of promoting relationships. However, as Jennifer Nedelsky aptly puts it, the 'relational approach does not stand in opposition to the importance of individuality; it is an account of what makes it possible'.[71] The relational model produces a richer account of an individual's interests as emerging in and through their relationships. As argued in the previous paragraph, it is better able to account for harms to an individual which occur within relationships than the idea of the individualised self.

[68] I. Burkitt, *Emotions and Social Relations* (Sage, 2014), 208

[69] C. Malabou, *The New Wounded: From Neurosis to Brain Damage* (Fordham University Press, 2012).

[70] D. Smith, 'Seeing and Knowing Dementia' in R. Binstock and S. Post (eds.) *Dementia and Aging: Ethics, Values, and Policy Choices* (John Hopkins University Press, 1992), 51.

[71] J. Nedelsky, *Law's Relations* (Oxford University Press, 2011).

Third, while much of the challenge to the concept of the individualised self has come from feminist writing, the alternative of the relational self is not unproblematic for feminists. The greater the emphasis on social construction around the self, the greater the danger that patriarchy can create the self. Then the only escape could be to emphasis a 'true self' (in an individualised sense) which is being assaulted by patriarchal forces.[72] In other words, a highly relational understanding of the self, combined with an appreciation of the power of patriarchy, can lead to the self being inevitably overwhelmed by patriarchy. But, that may be the correct conclusion: that patriarchy does enormous damage to the self. This just makes the demands to break down patriarchy all the more important. I think it is important to emphasise, as Nkiru Uwechia Nzegwu[73] does, that the self emerges out of negotiations and struggles. The relational self offers hope that through drawing on communal, relational and social forces the self can escape from oppressive social pressures. Only then can patriarchy be challenged and a different understanding of what it is to be a woman or a mother be offered.[74]

Fourth, many of those sympathetic to the concept of the relational self as outlined in this chapter believe that we need to combine both relational and individualistic readings of the self. For example, Rosie Harding emphasises the relational sense of self: 'Our social interconnections always help make us who we are, shape our decisions and influence our well-being',[75] but then goes on to say that, 'we cannot, in all good conscience, think of anyone ceasing to exist without their relational context'. She sees the relational aspect as an important dimension of the self, but not the sole dimension.

As these points show, as with any higher level theory, there are dangers with the concept of the relational self being misunderstood in a way which produces harmful results and there are tensions within it. However, there are serious dangers, as illustrated earlier, with the concept of the individualised self. I have argued here that the relational self offers a more accurate and powerful account of our values and interests.

1.6 Autonomy

As will already be apparent, one of the key aspects of an understanding of the relational self is a rejection of a traditional conception of autonomy.[76] In short,

---

[72] Willett and Anderson, 'Feminist Perspectives on the Self' https://plato.stanford.edu/entries/feminism-self/ [accessed 1 February 2019].
[73] N. Nzegwu, *Family Matters: Feminist Concepts in African Philosophy of Culture* (State University of New York Press, 2006).
[74] P. Hill Collins, *Black Feminist Thought: Knowledge, Consciousness and the Politics of Empowerment* (Hyman, 1990).
[75] R. Harding, *Duties to Care* (Cambridge University Press, 2017).
[76] R. Haliburton, *Autonomy and the Situated Self* (Lex, 2015)

the traditional understanding of autonomy is that a person should be the 'author of their life'. Life should be self-determined. As Isiah Berlin put it:

> I wish my life and decision to depend on myself, not on external forces of whatever kind. I wish to be the instrument of my own, not of other men's act of will. I wish to be a subject, not an object; to be moved by reasons, by conscious purposes, which are my own, not by causes which affect me, as it were from outside.[77]

Or as Philip Pettit puts it;

> We want to be the authors of our own stories, to be able to look on our works and say:
> "this bears my signature, this is me".[78]

There is a vast literature that unpacks the concept of autonomy, and even within its traditional forms there are disagreements over the extent to which decision making should be made within the context of a moral law and can be independent of it. For lawyers, the key argument is that a person's decisions about their lives should be respected. That is subject to two key caveats. The first is that a decision which harms another, or impedes the autonomy of another, does not require respect. So, obviously, A may wish to marry B, but if B does not wish for that marriage, A cannot rely on an autonomy claim that B marry them. The second is that this only applies in relation to decisions about a person's capacity to make the decision. There are, as we shall see in Chapter 5, considerable debates as to what 'capacity' to decide means in this context. Broadly, the capacity conditions fall into two categories: conditions which are cognitive and volitional competencies required, ensuring the person has the information and freedom to make the choice; and those which focus on the authenticity conditions, ensuring the decision is a person's own.[79] These requirements are important because if the basis of autonomy is enabling a person to direct their lives then if their decision is based on a misunderstanding or is not genuinely their own then respecting that 'decision' will not be enabling them to direct their lives. Once we are persuaded the decision is an autonomous one and does not impact on the autonomy of others, the decision cannot be interfered with on the basis that it is immoral or improper. This is seen as ensuring there is pluralism in society in terms of ways of life, values, religion, sexual preference and traditions.[80]

---

[77] I. Berlin, *Two Concepts of Liberty* (Oxford University Press, 1969).

[78] P. Pettit, *A Theory of Freedom: From the Psychology to the Politics of Agency* (Oxford University Press, 2001), 6.

[79] C. Mackenzie, 'Three Dimensions of Autonomy. A Relational Analysis' in A. Veltman and M. Piper (eds.) *Autonomy, Oppression and Gender* (Oxford University Press, 2014), 15.

[80] J. Christman and J. Anderson (ed.) *Autonomy and the Challenges to Liberalism* (Cambridge University Press, 2005).

It is easy to see how this kind of presentation of autonomy fits in with the individualist concept of the self. If our values and meaning are found within ourselves then it is important that our decisions are respected and others prevented from impeding them. That model of autonomy fits with concepts of self-sufficiency, independence and freedom, which are the heart of the concept of the individual self. But the relational self offers a very different vision. Relational autonomy is not based on the concepts of free will and self-sufficiency. The ideal of relational autonomy is not the self-contained, independent, rational being. Rather, true autonomy is found within relationships. Where our decisions are made with and supported by others. Where our goals are mixed up with the decisions of others. The ideal autonomous person is not the lone businessman striving off to work protected by his suit and briefcase, but the mother changing the nappy. John Lawless argues[81]

> As social beings, our agency emerges from our relationships with the other members of our communities—relationships that necessarily limit our options and render us subject to others' choices. The attendant limitations and vulnerabilities do not threaten our agency, but give it determinate form.

He uses the analogy with a game of chess. The rules of the game constrain both players and the moves one person makes restrict what another person may do. However, those rules and limitations are essential for the game to be a success. They limit choice, but are needed to enable chess to be played. He goes on:

> intrapersonal autonomy requires that one take oneself to have the authority to make one's own choices, and that one take oneself to have capacities to make those choices well. And (the argument goes) we do not come by self-respect, self-trust, and self-esteem in a social vacuum. Rather, we acquire these attitudes in the course of interactions with others who treat us as beings possessed of the relevant authorities and capacities. Deprived of these interactions, we may not learn to see ourselves as the authors of our own stories, and so might passively accept the circumstances in which we find ourselves and the decisions that others make for us.

Relational autonomy recognises that emotions and feelings play a key role in decision makers and that we need advice and encouragement of others to reach decisions. It flows from this that relational autonomy tends to reject a clear binary autonomy/non-autonomous distinction and rather recognises there is a scale of autonomy. For example, it has become common to support the idea of 'supported decision making' so that those of questionable capacity might be given the assistance and support they need to make decisions. Typically, this will involve the input of friends, family members and professionals to facilitate the decision-making process. The argument here is that all of us need that kind of framework of support in making decisions. Indeed, if a

---

[81] J. Lawless, 'Agency in Social Context' (2017) 94 *Res Philosophica* 471.

person makes an important decision with no form of consultation with others, this might indicate a lack of capacity.

As Catriona Mackenzie and Natalie Stoljar[82] explain:

> Relational autonomy perspectives are premised on a shared conviction, the conviction that persons are socially embedded and that agents' identities are formed within the context of social relationships and shaped by a complex of intersecting social determinants, such as race, class, gender, and ethnicity. Thus the focus of relational approaches is to analyze the implications of the inter-subjective and social dimensions of selfhood and identity for conceptions of individual autonomy and moral and political agency.

An important aspect of relational autonomy is, therefore, a recognition of the impact of patriarchal and other social forces on the decision-making of women and men. It can mean that internalised oppression can cause people to have alienated desires. A danger of this argument is that it can be seen to undermine the importance of autonomy, a theme we will return to in Chapter 5. However, it also shows the particular wrong of patriarchy, racism, disablism etc.: that it impacts on the social and relational context in which people make decisions and their understanding of themselves.

1.7 Disability

The theory of the relational self has much to say about disability.[83] The traditional view is that disability reflects a flaw with someone's body. John Harris,[84] a highly influential bioethicist, has argued that a disability is a 'harmed condition'. He is aware of the potential dangers with this claim and emphasises that a disabled person can live a good life, and he is also absolutely clear that he sees a disabled life as being as valuable as any other. However, he sees those statements as not inconsistent with a claim that a disabled person would have improved chances of a better life if he or she were not disabled. The example he uses is the deaf person, who by virtue of their deafness is denied the opportunity of hearing beautiful music or the voices of loved ones. That he suggests must be a harmed condition and hence a disability. However, here are three reasons why I believe that view to be misguided or at least over-simplistic.

First, as many disability rights scholars have argued, very often the social environment in which the disabled person has to live turns a physical

---

[82] C. Mackenzie and N. Stoljar, *Relational Autonomy: Feminist Perspective on Autonomy, Agency, and the Social Self* (Oxford University Press, 2000), 12.

[83] J. Herring, 'Health as Vulnerability: Interdependence and Relationality' (2016) 22 *The New Bioethics* 18.

[84] J. Harris, 'Is There a Coherent Social Conception of Disability?' (2000) 26 *Journal of Medical Ethics* 95, 99.

difference into a disadvantage.[85] The Union of the Physically Impaired Against Segregation[86] explains:

> In our view, it is society which disables physically impaired people. Disability is something imposed on top of our impairments by the way we are unnecessarily isolated and excluded from full participation in society. Disabled people are therefore an oppressed group in society. To understand this it is necessary to grasp the distinction between the physical impairment and the social situation, called "disability", of people with such impairment. Thus we define impairment as lacking all or part of a limb, or having a defective limb, organism or mechanism of the body and disability as the disadvantage or restriction of activity caused by a contemporary social organisation which takes little or no account of people who have physical impairments and thus excludes them from participation in the mainstream of social activities. Physical disability is therefore a particular form of social oppression.

The social model of disability demonstrates that it is wrong to assume that the root cause of disadvantages flows from a particular body and that the solution is to correct the 'misfit' body. The root cause may be in the way society has chosen to position and allocate its resources. The terminology of 'disabled people' is therefore appropriate: they are disabled by the fact that social spaces, services and provisions are modelled around certain kinds of bodies to the disadvantage of others.

The theory of the relational self is significant here. As argued in Chapter 2, we are all vulnerable, and societal provisions can make some differences in reducing disadvantages. But, it is wrong to identify particular bodies as more vulnerable. Further, and significantly, because our self is found in our relationships it is the response of others and society that determines whether a body is perceived to be able or disabled.

The second issue is that Harris makes assumptions about what makes a good life. Let us take the view that to be disabled is to hinder or limit flourishing.[87] It is commonly assumed that a disability is a disadvantage because one cannot partake in certain activities and so one flourishes less. It is said the deaf person cannot hear the soothing beauty of Bach's suites for unaccompanied cello; the unsighted cannot enjoy the delicacy of a Rembrandt portrait. This kind of argument has several problems. The first is that the selected list of joys is notable: only a minority of people in fact do enjoy Bach's suites or Rembrandt's portraits. It is true, of course, that while a deaf person cannot enjoy these things, while many others could, in theory, hear the music,

---

[85] A. Silvers, 'Reprising Women's Disability: Feminist Identity Strategy and Disability Rights' (1998) 13 *Berkeley Women's Law Journal* 81.

[86] Union of the Physically Impaired Against Segregation, *Policy Statement* (University of Leeds, 1975), 3–4.

[87] S. Wilkinson, *Choosing Tomorrow's Children: The Ethics of Selective Reproduction* (Oxford University Press, 2011).

they simply choose not to. But, it may, then, be questioned whether they are 'missing out' or at least 'missing out' to any extent that is notable. There are dangers here of ability privilege, that is, 'the advantages enjoyed by those who exhibit certain abilities and the unwillingness of these individuals to relinquish the advantage linked to the abilities especially with the reason that these are earned or birth given (natural) abilities'.[88] It may also reflect the reluctance, mentioned earlier, to acknowledge the limitations we all have.

Third, Harris's approach does not put into the equation the benefits that may come from a disability. In Andrew Solomon's remarkable book, *Far From the Tree*,[89] the author looks at families raising disabled children and describes the mixed pictures of disability. For example, on deafness he writes:[90]

> Most hearing people assume that to be deaf is to lack hearing. Many deaf people experience deafness not as an absence, but as a presence. Deafness is a culture and a life, a language and an aesthetic, a physicality and an intimacy different from all others. This culture inhabits a narrower mind-body split than the one that constrains the rest of us, because language is enmeshed with the major muscle groups not just the limited architecture of the tongue and larynx.

Andrew Solomon's book discusses many examples of disabled people who could be treated or cured and yet prefer their lives with the disability. Often, it is the social interactions and community ties which are important in those decisions. As Solomon's book shows, it is the lack of able-bodied imagination that things could be done otherwise that assumes a disability is a harm. For example, the assumption is that the loss of hearing a loved one's voice is a harm, but if hearing a loved one is just one developing a relationship with another, and there are other ways of establishing intimacy that may be just as good, there is no reason to see the loss of that method as being a harm. There is no evidence that deaf people have less close relationships because they cannot hear. The theory of the relational self shows that it is our interactions with others that create our identity and this involves the mixing together of skills, bodies and interests. So, within a relationship, who has 'the disability' disappears as a question.

Eva Feder Kittay's daughter Sesha has cerebral palsy. She is profoundly cognitively and physically impaired. She will always be dependent on others for life's basics. Feder Kittay[91] writes:

> Sometimes I wonder if Sesha is a special being sent to us from elsewhere, for there is an impossible to – articulate sweetness, graciousness, and emotional openness about her qualities we rarely find in others.

---

[88] G. Wolbring, 'Ability Privilege: A Needed Addition to Privilege Studies' (2014) 12 *Journal for Critical Animal Studies* 118, 119.

[89] A. Solomon, *Far from the Tree* (Vintage, 2012).

[90] Ibid., 62.

[91] E. Feder Kittay, 'Forever Small: The Strange Case of Ashley X' (2011) 26 *Hypatia* 610, at 621.

Much modern legal and ethical thought is premised on the norm of an autonomous self-contained self. This is problematic for disability, as Myrian Winance[92] writes:

> The difference between disabled people and able-bodied people lies in the fact that, for the latter, their "standard" body matches the construction standards of the heterogeneous networks that make up our society; it is therefore easier for them to acquire the status of autonomous and independent subject. Disabled people, for their part, must face many gaps and therefore have a harder time making themselves into autonomous subjects.

If we are all vulnerable, as Chapter 2 claims, and we all need care, as Chapter 3 claims, then we are all profoundly dependent on others for our physical and psychological wellbeing. Part of our vulnerability leads from our embodiment. Our bodies are insecure and vulnerable. Our society has built up a wide range of structures and forms of assistance which disguise our vulnerability. Indeed, we are forced by a wide range of societal pressures to disguise or mitigate our vulnerability so that we can behave in an acceptable way in the public realm. This understanding of the self challenges assumptions, which are harmful for the valuing of both disability and care, about the normal body and what is a productive citizenship. As Rosemarie Garland-Thomson[93] argues:

> I would argue that disability is perhaps the essential characteristic of being human. The body is dynamic, constantly interactive with history and environment. We evolve into disability. Our bodies need care; we all need assistance to live. An equality model of feminist theory sometimes prizes individualistic autonomy as the key to women's liberation. A feminist disability theory, however, suggests that we are better off learning to individually and collectively accommodate bodily limits and evolutions than trying to eliminate or deny them.

Vulnerability and dependence are not only inevitable parts of humanity: they are to be greatly welcomed. They are virtues, not vices. Self-reliance has become a dominant theme in social policy. But this ignores the fact that as humans we are interdependent. No one can be truly independent.

The anti-vulnerability narrative tends to promote disablist approaches to the issue. As many writers from disability studies have written, there is great pressure on disabled people to be perceived as being independent and lacking vulnerability. Success for a person with a disability is measured by the extent to which they may be able to be (or present themselves as being) independent and autonomous – in short, to be 'normal'. As Jayne Clapton[94] puts it:

[92] M. Winance, 'Rethinking Disability: Lessons from the Past, Questions for the Future' (2016) 10 *European Journal of Disability Research* 99, 102.

[93] R. Garland-Thomson, 'Integrating Disability, Transforming Feminist Theory' (2002) 14 *Feminist Disability Studies* 1, 2. See also R. Garland-Thomson, 'Misfits: A Feminist Materialist Disability Concept' (2011) 26 *Hypatia* 591.

[94] J Clapton, 'Tragedy and Catastrophe: Contentious Discourses of Ethics and Disability' (2003) 47 *Journal of Intellectual Disability Research* 540, 540.

Such a construction, which privileges a particular understanding of personhood, assumes a prototypical disembodied person – that is, typically a male characterized by independence and the presence of rationality and reason; or in other words, that which constitutes, in the philosophical sense, 'normal'.

1.8 Conclusion

W. H. Auden reminds us:

> ... no one exists alone
> Hunger allows no choice
> To the citizen or the police;
> We must love one another or die.[95]

This chapter has advocated for an understanding of the self as emerging and interacting through our relationships. It rejects an image that sees the self as self-contained, self-generated and self-sufficient. It has argued that our relationships give us the language we speak; the words we use to make sense of the world; ways of interpreting what we see and what others do; and an understanding of the self as constructed through our relationships with others.

The chapter has argued that this has a crucial impact for law. The law tends to reflect the values that are suitable for an individualised understanding of the self: autonomy, privacy and bodily integrity. The law undervalues or ignores relational values: trust, mutuality and interdependence. The law tends to pitch the rights of one individual against the rights of another rather than seeing the relationship between two people as being the core object of legal concern.

As this book develops, we will explore further the understanding of the relational self and consider specifically how this will impact on law in practice. In the next two chapters I will unpack two core concepts connected with the idea of the relational self: universal human vulnerability and the importance of care. I will then go on to examine how such an understanding impacts on particular areas of the law: abuse; family law; medical law and criminal law.

---

[95] W. H. Auden, 'September 1, 1939' *Another Time* (Random House, 1940), 34.

2

Law and the Vulnerable Self

2.1 Introduction

This chapter explores the concept of the vulnerable self.[1] We are all vulnerable ... and we should be thrilled about that. First I will explore the ways in which we are vulnerable. Second, I will explore the significance for the law of the vulnerability of the self. Finally, I will explain why we should rejoice in our vulnerability.

The concept of the vulnerable self is closely tied to the concept of the relational self. If we are all vulnerable then our relationships are essential to our survival. Yet similarly, our relationships are part of what makes us vulnerable. The concept of universal vulnerability is, therefore, integral to the claim of the relational self.

2.2 Introducing Vulnerability

The claim we are all vulnerable is, in legal circles, most closely associated with the writing of Martha Fineman, and she has championed universal vulnerability theory.[2] This chapter will seek to build on her work, although my approach differs from hers in some minor respects.

Vulnerability is commonly discussed in the media and by politicians. But when it is discussed in political circles, it comes with heavily negative connotations. Particular groups are defined as vulnerable and in need of protection. They become an object of concern. Charities often describe themselves as being designed to protect the most vulnerable. Vulnerability, we are told, is something to be avoided or remedied. We are encouraged to be independent, self-sufficient, autonomous and free from reliance on others. We should avoid becoming dependent on state benefits, we should not be a burden to others, but rather be self-supporting. We are to save now so that we can fund our old

---

[1] This chapter draws on earlier work, particularly J. Herring, *Vulnerable Adults and the Law* (Oxford University Press, 2016) and J. Herring, *Vulnerability, Childhood and the Law* (Springer, 2018).

[2] M. Fineman, 'The Vulnerable Subject: Anchoring Equality in the Human Condition' (2008) 20 *Yale Journal of Law & Feminism* 1.

age and do not become a drain on our children or the rest of society. David Cameron, the then British Prime Minister, captured this attitude well:

> We will look after the most vulnerable and needy. We will make the system simple. We'll make work pay. We'll help those who want to work, find work. But in return we expect people to take their responsibilities seriously too.[3]

The claims of universal vulnerability theory, which I will develop later, have a very different take on the significance of vulnerability to the popular one. It argues that everyone is vulnerable. Vulnerability is an inevitable part of the whole human condition.

2.3 Defining Vulnerability

Vulnerability is a notoriously vague term and its precise definition is problematic. The notion of vulnerability is used in many disciplines and without a consistent meaning.[4] According to the New Oxford Dictionary of English, to be vulnerable means 'to be exposed to the possibility of being attacked or harmed, either physically or emotionally'.[5] That seems an extremely broad understanding. You would need to stay in bed very firmly wrapped up in your duvet to escape the possibility of being harmed! However, it does capture a core idea about vulnerability: that it is about being exposed to risks. Tom Beauchamp and James Childress, writing in a bioethics context, write:[6]

> In biomedical ethics, the notion of vulnerability often focuses on a person's susceptibility, whether as a result of internal or external factors, to inducement or coercion, on the one hand, or to harm, loss, or indignity, on the other.

This definition seems to posit a risk to 'inducement' as equivalent to harm. That seems surprising. We are all susceptible to inducements, which is why advertisers have jobs. And it seems that without knowing what one is being induced to do it is hard to see the link to harm. It would not seem a natural understanding of vulnerability to be susceptible to inducement to eating healthily or undertaking exercise. It seems better to secure the concept of vulnerability to harm.

The uncertainty over the definition of vulnerability is, in part, because it is used for different purposes in different disciplines. It might be designed to designate a person who is in need of especial attention; or a group who are

---

[3] Press Association, 'David Cameron Unveils Welfare Reform Bill' *The Guardian* 17 February 2011, www.theguardian.com/politics/2011/feb/17/david-cameron-welfare-reform-bill [accessed 1 February 2019].

[4] M. Dunn, I. Clare and A. Holland, 'To Empower or to Protect? Constructing the "Vulnerable Adult" in English Law and Public Policy' (2008) 28 *Legal Studies* 234.

[5] *Oxford English Dictionary* (Oxford University Press, 2010).

[6] T. Beauchamp and J. Childress, *Principles of Biomedical Ethics* (Oxford University Press, 2009), 254.

entitled to protection; or define those who may not participate in certain activities. Nevertheless, there are sufficient similarities to produce a definition in broad terms.

I would suggest that a person (P) is vulnerable if the following three factors are present:

1. P faces a risk of harm.
2. P does not have the resources to be able to avoid the risk of harm materialising
3. P would not be able to respond adequately to the harm if the risk materialised.[7]

Harm in this context should be understood broadly. Daniel Engster[8] has argued that vulnerability refers to a risk of more than just harms:

> the concept of vulnerability encompasses a range of undesirable conditions and events that are only obliquely referenced by notions of need and harm. We are vulnerable to discrimination, humiliation, disrespect, loss of persons we love, loss of objects or things that are important to us, bodily and mental deterioration, mental illness, and many other undesirable states.

There are two aspects of vulnerability which it is worth developing.

2.3.1 Internal and External Elements

We can separate two elements of vulnerability: external elements (being exposed to the possibility of harm) and internal elements (being substantially unable to protect oneself from the possibility of harm). External elements are forces from outside that threaten harm to the individual. They may come from other people or be natural forces, such as weather. Internal elements are the ability to protect oneself from these forces. This element means that someone may be vulnerable to an external element, but be able to protect themselves from it or respond to it. There may, therefore, be a range of resources a person can draw on to be resilient to a threat or to be able to avoid the threat.[9] Doris Schroeder and Eugenijus Gefenas[10] capture these two elements of vulnerability in this way, 'To be vulnerable means to face a significant probability of incurring an identifiable harm while substantially lacking ability and/or means to protect oneself.' The distinction between external risks and internal capabilities to respond to risks is helpful, but it is not a watertight distinction.

---

[7] Herring, *Vulnerable Adults and the Law*, chapter 1.
[8] D. Engster, 'Care Ethics, Dependency, and Vulnerability' (2019) 13 *Ethics and Social Welfare* 100.
[9] S. Hurst, 'Vulnerability in Research and Health Care: Describing the Elephant in the Room?' (2004) 7 *Medicine, Health Care and Philosophy* 281.
[10] D. Schroeder and E. Gefenas, 'Vulnerability Too Vague and Too Broad' (2009) 18 *Cambridge Quarterly of Healthcare Ethics* 113.

An individual characteristic can only be a source of vulnerability in the context of particular social circumstances. Being unable to walk might, or might not, render one at greater risk of being mugged depending on a wide range of social circumstances.[11] There being a high level of pollen in the air might not create a risk of harm to most people, but it will for those whose bodies are particularly sensitive to pollen. Catriona Mackenzie, Wendy Rogers and Susan Dodds[12] draw a similar distinction between 'inherent' vulnerabilities (those intrinsic to the human condition such as thirst or tiredness); situational vulnerabilities (which are context specific and exacerbated by social, political or environmental factors); and pathogenic vulnerabilities (which result from dysfunctional relationships or socio-political oppressions).

2.3.2 Subjective/Objective Understanding of Vulnerability

A second distinction which can be helpful in understanding vulnerability concerns whether the vulnerability is understood in a subjective or objective way. Michael Dunn, Isobel Clare and Anthony Holland distinguish 'etic' and 'emic' understandings of vulnerability:

> "Etic" approaches equate vulnerability with risk, and assess an individual's vulnerability in terms of the risk facing that person, justifying intervention as a means of managing that risk with regard to objectively determined standards.[13] "Emic" approaches, in contrast, are based on the experiential perception of "exposure to harm through challenges to one's integrity ... [It] places vulnerability in a psycho-socialcultural context"[14], and focus on the subjective reality of a person's everyday life ... [V]ulnerability exists as lived experience. The individual's perception of self and challenges to self, and of resources to withstand such challenges, define vulnerability.[15]

This distinction is helpful because it opens up the possibility of recognising that what might be regarded as vulnerability from the outside perspective might not be so regarded by the individual. Similarly, a person might perceive themselves to be vulnerable to a risk, which they are not, objectively, facing. The benefit of this recognition is that it requires listening to the voice of the person that is said to be disadvantaged to ascertain what it means to be vulnerable. A good example might be the hearing of voices by someone with

---

[11] Hurst, 'Vulnerability in Research and Health Care: Describing the Elephant in the Room?' 281.

[12] C. Mackenzie, W. Rogers and S. Dodds, 'Introduction: What Is Vulnerability, and Why Does It Matter for Moral Theory' in C. Mackenzie, W. Rogers and S. Dodds (eds.) *Vulnerability* (Oxford University Press, 2014), 1.

[13] See, for example, L. Aday, *At Risk in America: The Health and Health Care Needs of Vulnerable Populations in the United States* (Jossey-Bass, 2001).

[14] J. Spiers 'New Perspectives on Vulnerability using Emic and Etic Approaches' (2000) 31 *Journal of Advanced Nursing* 715, 718.

[15] See, for example, Aday, *At Risk in America: The Health and Health Care Needs of Vulnerable Populations in the United States.*

Schizophrenia. To an external observer this might be a source of risk, but to the individual the voice might be seen as a source of comfort and even a resource to cope with life.[16]

2.4 Who Is Vulnerable?

2.4.1 Particular and Deficient Vulnerability

In the current public discourse, vulnerability is used to identify a particular group of people who are at risk of suffering harm or behaving in a way deemed undesirable. Typically, this group is seen as needing intervention or surveillance to protect them from harm. Vulnerability is seen as undesirable because the vulnerable need help from others and cannot live up to the ideals of independence and self-sufficiency. Steps may also be required to prevent those in danger of becoming vulnerable from falling into that category. Vulnerable people may also be deemed unable to participate in certain activities. For example, a medical researcher may be prohibited from using a volunteer from a member of a 'vulnerable group'. As Rosie Harding[17] points out, the particular and deficient understanding of vulnerability draws 'our attention to deficit, rather than potential; to loss rather than strengths'. The notion that there are particular groups of people who are vulnerable and that vulnerability is an undesirable characteristic I will describe as the 'particular and deficient theory of vulnerability'.

England now has a Secretary of State for Vulnerability. Revealingly, the full title is Parliamentary Under Secretary of State for Crime, Safeguarding and Vulnerability.[18] The grouping of these three topics in the title is revealing. It reinforces the 'particular and deficient theory'. It requires particular people to be safeguarded from harm because they cannot look after themselves. It can also be linked to moral harm: vulnerable people are at risk of becoming extremists or engaging in other undesirable activity. At a local level, Oxfordshire County Council, for example, has a group designed to 'protect vulnerable people'.[19] It explains that the council can offer support to maintain 'personal safety and security'. Again, this emphasises that the authority has in mind a group of vulnerable people who are at risk of abuse or being taken advantage of. Indeed, my search of gov.co.uk found 8,933 hits[20] for government programmes particularly aimed at groups of vulnerable people, covering everything from oral health needs to the dangers of nitrates.

---

[16] Living with Schizophrenia, *Understanding Voices* (Living with Schizophrenia, 2017).

[17] R. Harding, *Duties to Care* (Cambridge University Press, 2017), 19.

[18] www.gov.uk/government/ministers/parliamentary-under-secretary-of-state–62 [accessed 1 February 2019].

[19] www.oxfordshire.gov.uk/residents/social-and-health-care/adult-social-care/keeping-safe/protecting-vulnerable-people [accessed 1 February 2019].

[20] As at 1 February 2019.

It is not just at a political level that we can see the 'particular and deficient theory of vulnerability in operation'. Children are educated to prevent them becoming 'vulnerable' online and sexual consent and education classes teach how to avoid being 'vulnerable to sexual assault'. Parents, schools or colleges which did not enable students to escape these vulnerabilities would be seen as failing in their task. Isiah Hankel, a popular psychologist, gives online advice with fifteen strategies on 'How to stop being a weak and vulnerable man.[21] He argues that men must learn to take control of their lives. He quotes Frederick Douglas:

> The lesson taught at this point by human experience is simply this, that the man who will get up will be helped up; and the man who will not get up will be allowed to stay down. Personal independence is a virtue and it is the soul out of which comes the sturdiest manhood ... this virtue cannot be bestowed. It must be developed from within.[22]

As this quote indicates, the 'particular deficient vulnerability' model relies on a contrast with the independent, autonomous, self-contained individual who is able to maintain themselves and protect themselves from danger. This is the norm and the desirable state from which vulnerable people fall short.

2.4.2 Universal Beneficial Vulnerability

I would argue for a very different view: that everyone is vulnerable and that is a really good thing. I will call this the 'universal and beneficial theory of vulnerability'. It is important to appreciate that universal vulnerability rejects the common approach of identifying vulnerable populations (such as the elderly, children or single parents). Rather, it argues that being vulnerable is in the nature of all people. Martha Fineman has done more than anyone to develop the concept of universal vulnerability, and she explains the theory in this way:

> The vulnerability approach recognizes that individuals are anchored at each end of their lives by dependency and the absence of capacity. Of course, between these ends, loss of capacity and dependence may also occur, temporarily for many and permanently for some as a result of disability or illness. Constant and variable throughout life, individual vulnerability encompasses not only damage that has been done in the past and speculative harms of the distant future, but also the possibility of immediate harm. We are beings who live with the ever-present possibility that our needs and circumstances will change. On an individual level, the concept of vulnerability (unlike that of liberal autonomy)

---

[21] I. Hankel, 'How to Stop Being a Weak and Vulnerable Man' www.isaiahhankel.com/vulnerable-man [accessed 18 February 2019].
[22] F. Douglas, 'My Bondage and My Freedom', available at www.artofmanliness.com/articles/manvotional-self-made-men-by-frederick-douglass/ [accessed 18 February 2019].

captures this present potential for each of us to become dependent based upon our persistent susceptibility to misfortune and catastrophe.[23]

Vulnerability is an inherent part of being human.[24] As Emmanuel Lévinas puts it: 'The I, from head to foot and to the bone-marrow, is vulnerability.'[25] Or as Catriona Mackenzie, Wendy Rogers and Susan Dodds explain 'To be vulnerable is to be fragile, to be susceptible to wounding and to suffering; this susceptibility is an ontological conditional of our humanity.'[26] Admittedly, this is not how people generally understand themselves. We emphasise our capacity, independence and autonomy. But we puff ourselves up with such talk. In reality, we are all vulnerable because we are all profoundly dependant on others for our physical and psychological well-being.

Society has built up a wide range of structures and forms of assistance which disguise our vulnerability. We rely on others and social provision for survival. In a powerful article, Kate Lindemann contrasts the emphasis that is paid to the 'accommodations' that are put in place for disabled people, with the lack of appreciation of the accommodations for the able bodied:

> Colleagues, professional staff members, and other adults are unconscious of the numerous accommodations that society provides to make their work and life style possible. ATM's, extended hours in banks, shopping centres and medical offices, EZpass, newspaper kiosks, and elevators are all accommodations that make contemporary working life possible. There are entire industries devoted to accommodating the needs of adult working people. Fast food, office lunch delivery, day time child care, respite care, car washing, personal care attendants, interpreters, house cleaning, and yard and lawn services are all occupations that provide services that make it possible for adults to hold full time jobs.[27]

We thus highlight the facilities used to deal with the vulnerabilities of others, while overlooking the accommodations 'we' need to deal with our vulnerabilities. No one can get up to the second floor of a building without an accommodation. You might need stairs or you might need a lift, but we need something to assist us to get up there. You might think that you, unlike a baby, can feed yourself, but you rely on shops, farmers, transporters, health inspectors etc. to provide you with food.

Few of us could, and fewer seek, utterly independent lives. Yet with interdependence comes vulnerability. Others might let us down in the provision of

---

[23] Fineman, 'The Vulnerable Subject: Anchoring Equality in the Human Condition', 1.

[24] M. Shildrick, *Embodying the Monster: Encounters with the Vulnerable Self* (Sage, 2002); A. Beckett *Citizenship and Vulnerability* (Palgrave, 2006).

[25] E. Lévinas (1993) *Humanismo Del Otro Hombre* (Caparros, 1993), 3.

[26] W. Rogers, C. Mackenzie and S. Dodds, 'Why Bioethics Needs a Theory of Vulnerability' (2012) 5 *International Journal of Feminist Approaches to Bioethics* 11, 12.

[27] K. Lindemann, 'The Ethics of Receiving' (2003) 24 *Theoretical Medicine and Bioethics* 501.

what we need; we might let others down and fail to provide them with what they need.[28] Mary Neal puts it this way:

> I am vulnerable because I am penetrable; I am permanently open and exposed to hurts and harms of various kinds. These two sources of vulnerability – reliance on others for co-operation, and openness to positive harm – are simply two means by which I might come to experience suffering; thus, it is suffering, and the capacity for suffering, that is definitive of this negative aspect of vulnerability. The extent and intensity of my vulnerability at a particular moment, or with regard to a particular need or harm, may be affected by my age, my sex, my degree of capacity, my health, my social status, my wealth, and a variety of other factors. Nevertheless, even the least vulnerable human being is still fundamentally, and inescapably, vulnerable in the negative sense, since none of us can meet her basic needs and satisfy her core desires without the co-operation of others; and even the most capable adult is vulnerable to hurt and harm, both physical and emotional.[29]

Consider, for example, the work of Samia Hurst.[30] In examining international guidelines of research ethics and setting out who might be regarded as vulnerable she produces a list of vulnerable groups, which include the following:

- Racial minorities
- The economically disadvantaged
- The very sick
- The institutionalised
- Children
- Prisoners
- Pregnant women and foetuses
- Incompetent persons
- Persons susceptible to coercion
- Persons who will not derive direct benefits from participation
- Persons for whom research is mixed with clinical care
- Junior or subordinate members of a hierarchical group ... [such as] medical and nursing students, subordinate hospital and laboratory personnel, employees of pharmaceutical companies, and members of the armed forces or police
- Elderly persons
- Residents of nursing homes
- Patients in emergency rooms
- Homeless persons

---

[28] S. Whitney, 'Dependency Relations: Corporeal Vulnerability and Norms of Personhood in Hobbes and Kittay' (2011) 26 *Hypatia* 554.

[29] M. Neale, '"Not Gods but Animals": Human Dignity and Vulnerable Subjecthood' (2012) 33 *Liverpool Law Review* 177, 187.

[30] Hurst, 'Vulnerability in Research and Health Care', 191, 187.

- Refugees or displaced persons
- Patients with incurable disease
- Individuals who are politically powerless
- Members of communities unfamiliar with modern medical concepts
- Patients with incurable diseases.

No doubt more could be added to this list.[31] But notice how lengthy the list is. There must be few people who do not fall into one category or another. And her list is not unusual. The Declaration of Helsinki states that vulnerable groups include 'the economically and medically disadvantaged'; 'those who cannot give or refuse consent for themselves'; 'those who may be subject to giving consent under duress'; 'those who will not benefit personally from the research'; and 'those for whom the research is combined with care'.[32] Again the vast majority of the population could fit in with this description of vulnerability.

I will now explain more precisely some of the ways that we are in our nature vulnerable.

First, our embodied nature creates vulnerability. Experience teaches us that our bodies are vulnerable to sickness, illness and accidents.[33] Our health is frail. As Martha Fineman puts it: 'we are born, live, and die within a fragile materiality that renders all of us constantly susceptible to destructive external forces and internal disintegration?'[34] Our bodies are 'profoundly leaky'.[35] They are constantly changing, with new material being added to them and old material being discarded. Inside, our bodies are dependent on a wide range of non-human material to survive, and outside they are constantly interacting with the environment.[36] All of this means our bodies are mutable, porous and vulnerable.

Second, as argued in Chapter 1, in a radical sense our relationships constitute our selves.[37] We primarily understand ourselves in terms of how we relate to and are understood by others. We define ourselves in terms of how others understand us. It is only in response to others that our selves have meaning. The language we use; the way we look at the world; and the sense of self in the world are generated through these early relationships and develop and change

---

[31] C. Coleman 'Vulnerability as a Regulatory Category in Human Subject Research' (2009) *Journal of Law, Medicine and Ethics* 12.

[32] World Medical Association, *Declaration of Helsinki* (WHO, 2008), A(9).

[33] S. Matambanadzo, 'Embodying Vulnerability: A Feminist Theory of the Person' (2012) *20 Duke Journal of Gender Law & Policy* 45.

[34] M. Fineman, 'Feminism, Masculinities and Multiple Identities' (2013) 13 *Nevada Law Review* 619.

[35] M. Shildrick, *Leaky Bodies and Boundaries* (Routledge, 1997).

[36] P.-L. Chau and J. Herring, 'My Body, Your Body, Our Bodies' (2007) 15 *Medical Law Review* 34.

[37] K. Gergen, *Relational Being* (Oxford University Press, 2009); K. McLaughlin, *Surviving Identity: Vulnerability and the Psychology of Recognition* (Routledge, 2012).

through subsequent relationships. This understanding of the self means we are in constant danger of our self being challenged by others rejecting us; not accepting us as members of a group; not providing the support we expect; or using our relationships to harm us.

Third, we are dependent on others to meet our needs.[38] There will be times during our lives, in a very obvious way, that we will be dependent on others for our most basic needs. In early years and in times of sickness, perhaps, particularly towards the end of life, we will need care. In such a dependency, we must rely on others to survive and this inevitably creates vulnerability. That care may cease or may be inadequate. Of course, for most people there will be times when this overt kind of dependency will not be apparent. However, often others will be dependent on us to meet their needs, either as parents or carers for others. This itself creates a vulnerability. Our responsibilities to meet the needs of others in one sense limit our lives. We are on constant call to meet others. As Fiona Williams argues, we need to recognise 'us all as interdependent and as having the potential and responsibility to be caring and cared for'.[39] If care is an essential part of what it is to be a person and care produces vulnerability then vulnerability is an essential part of being a person.

Martha Fineman[40] refers to four elements of vulnerability: universality, constancy, complexity and particularity. Universality refers to vulnerability being part of the human condition and is shared by all. The reference to constancy is that we are constantly dependant on others and our relationships. There is a constant state of risk of harm that 'cannot be hidden'. She refers to the complex nature of vulnerability. Complexity results from the fact vulnerability 'can manifest itself in multiple forms'. For example, a physical harm could ripple out to harm relationships with other people or harm institutions, which could then cause economic or social harm, or create harm for others. Her fourth element is particularity, and we shall return to this now in more detail because it is more controversial among vulnerability theorists, and that is the particularity of the experience of vulnerability.

2.5 All the Time or Some of the Time?

We are now in a position to address a fierce debate within the vulnerability literature. Is it correct to claim that we are all equally vulnerable or do we need to recognise there are some groups that are particularly vulnerable and so need special protections in law?

---

[38] J. Herring, *Caring and the Law* (Hart, 2013).

[39] F. Williams, 'The Presence of Feminism in the Future of Welfare' (2002) 31 *Economy and Society* 502, 503.

[40] M. Fineman, 'The Vulnerable Subject and the Responsive State' (2011) 60 *Emory Law Journal* 251.

There is some disagreement among vulnerability theorists on how to respond to the fact that even though we may all be inherently vulnerable, this is experienced to a different extent by different people in different contexts. Martha Fineman accepts that in a typical lifespan there will be times of different capacity and strengths. But, the typical 'adult liberal subject' focuses on just one part of that life span (middle age) and essentialises this as the standard. That means the vulnerable nature can get overlooked. She argues:

> Throughout our lives we may be subject to external and internal negative, potentially devastating, events over which we have little control – disease, pandemics, environmental and climate deterioration, terrorism and crime, crumbling infrastructure, failing institutions, recession, corruption, decay, and decline. We are situated beings who live with the ever-present possibility of changing needs and circumstances in our individual and collective lives. We are also accumulative beings and have different qualities and quantities of resources with which to meet these needs of circumstances, both over the course of our lifetime and as measured at the time of crisis or opportunity.[41]

Other writers have suggested that we are equally valuable throughout our lives and it is the provision of social resources which grants some people greater resilience to their vulnerability than others. Hence I have argued, taking this line:

> It is true that at different times and in different circumstances we may be more overtly in use of societal resources should not disguise the fact that we are in need of communal and relational support for all our lives. We may be differently positioned within a web of economic and social relationships and this will impact on our experience of vulnerability and the resources at our disposal.[42]

In some of her writings, Fineman seems to take a similar line, observing that '[v]ulnerability . . . is both universal and particular; it is experienced uniquely by each of us . . . our individual experience of vulnerability varies according to the quality and quantity of resources we can command'.[43]

One way of understanding the issue is to consider it in terms resilience.[44] Fineman and Grear[45] argued, 'While vulnerability is universal, resilience is particular, found in the assets or resources an individual accumulates and dispenses over the course of a lifetime and through interaction with and access to society's instructions.'

---

[41] M. Fineman, '"Elderly" as Vulnerable: Rethinking the Nature of Individual and Societal Responsibility' (2012) 17 *Elder Law Review* 23.

[42] J. Herring, *Vulnerability, Childhood and the Law* (Springer, 2018), 65.

[43] Fineman, 'The Vulnerable Subject and the Responsive State', 251, 269.

[44] H. ten Have, *Vulnerability* (Routledge, 2016).

[45] M. Fineman and A. Grear, 'Introduction' in M. Fineman and A. Grear (eds.) *Vulnerability* (Ashgate, 2014), 1.

Resilience can take a range of forms, as Martha Fineman and Silas Allard[46] explain:

> There are different types of resilience-producing resources, accumulated across different social sites. For example: material resources are produced in employment and financial arrangements; social resources are gained when we act with others, as we do in unions and by taking political or civic action; "human capital" is accumulated through educational institutions or other skill-generating sites like apprenticeships; relational resources are formed in families and friendships; and existential resources can come from interaction within religious institutions or through aesthetic experiences.

There is clearly a tension here between the solidarity provided by the claims of universal vulnerability and an acknowledgement that different levels of resilience can impact on lived experiences. Phil Bielby finds a way through this:

> while our unique experience of vulnerability is contingent on the resilience to withstand what happens to us during our life, what we are vulnerable to is not contingent, as it is rooted in our universal vulnerability, which is constant. The recognition that aspects of universal vulnerability are experienced more acutely or onerously due to limitations on resilience that we all encounter further entrenches a solidarity understanding of vulnerability ... the right question to ask is how constraints on one's resilience to cope with universal vulnerability are causing one's lived experience of vulnerability to be more acute or onerous than that of someone else, rather than whether one is vulnerable or not, or how vulnerable one is.

This perhaps then clarifies the apparent disagreement. Insofar as the resilience is provided by sources external to the self (e.g. by social provision; societal resources) we can acknowledge universal vulnerability and locate different experiences in different levels of social provision. However, for those who see reliance as a personal resource one can develop for oneself, this challenges universal vulnerability. I see resilience as residing in social provision, but this is not the place to seek to resolve that debate and there is no need to do so for this particular chapter.[47]

2.6 The Significance of the Claim That We Are All Vulnerable

Let us now explore the significance of the claim that we are all vulnerable. It might legitimately be asked whether vulnerability is a particularly helpful concept if it is simply an aspect of the human condition. As we have seen, many supporters of the view that we are all vulnerable would want to go on to

[46] M. Fineman and S. Allard, 'Vulnerability, the Responsive State, and the Role of Religion' in J. Springhart and G. Thomas (eds.) *Exploring Vulnerability* (Vandenhoeck & Ruprecht GmbH & Co KG, 2017), 185.
[47] See also D. Engster, 'Care Ethics, Dependency, and Vulnerability' (2019) 13 *Ethics and Social Welfare* 100.

say that although we have a shared vulnerability there may be particular situations where individuals are super-vulnerable; or our inherent vulnerability has particular significance. But if so, we should be seeking to define these and the observation that we are all vulnerable is not particularly helpful. I disagree. I think the view that we are all vulnerable has significant repercussions for the law in a range of ways.

2.6.1 Our Image of the Legal Self

The legal conception of the self profoundly affects the kinds of legal rights we have. As adults, we like to emphasise our independence, capacity for rational thought and autonomy. Hence in our legal system autonomy and liberty are emphasised as key rights, whose interference requires strong justification.[48] Our right to be able to make our own choices over how to act, to only be subject to those responsibilities we choose to take, is seen as a central pillar of economic, social and legal structures. The law's role is, under that image of the self, to protect the individual from unwanted intrusions and to protect liberty to pursue one's goal for one's life. We are portrayed as independent self-interested people. Those who most obviously fall outside the paradigm are described as 'vulnerable' and that terminology is used to monitor, supervise and discipline them. They lack those essential skills to direct their own lives and protect themselves and so need others to do that for them. The Mental Capacity Act 2005 authorises others to make decisions for those who lack capacity to make decisions, based on an assessment of their best interests. Even those who have capacity, if they have impaired autonomy, are deemed to be 'vulnerable adults' and in need of protection under the inherent jurisdiction.[49] Children are seen as being vulnerable and hence in need of special protection under the law.[50]

If, however, we start with a norm of vulnerable, relational, interdependent, caring people then the nature of legal intervention becomes different. The importance of upholding and maintaining those relationships becomes key. The law does not emphasise independence, liberty and autonomy but rather seeks to uphold relationships of care.

Rethinking the law from this fundamentally different starting point has profound impacts on the legal approaches. To take one example, rather than starting from the assumption that each person is free to negotiate their own contracts and that the law should respect liberty of contract, in fact we should start from the image of vulnerable contractors liable to manipulation and exploitation. For example, I have promoted a contract law:

[48] C. Foster, *Choosing Life, Choosing Death: The Tyranny of Autonomy in Medical Ethics* (Hart, 2009).
[49] *DL* v. *A Local Authority* [2012] EWCA 253.
[50] J. Herring, *Childhood, Vulnerability and the Law* (Springer, 2018).

> Where all contracting parties are encouraged to recognize each other's vulnerability and act in good faith towards each other, providing them with the information they need, doing what they can to ensure the other is not mistaken or entering a clearly unfair bargain. Where the values promoted are honesty, mutuality and interdependence.[51]

How different from our current contract law, which seems designed to enable people to exploit the weakness of the other party; squeeze a high price as possible; and ensure neither contracting party will ever want to speak to the other again!

Susan Dodds[52] explores the impact more broadly, arguing:

> Attention to vulnerability ... changes citizens' ethical relations from those of independent actors carving out realms of rights against each other and the state, to those of mutually-dependent and vulnerability-exposed beings whose capacities to develop as subjects are directly and indirectly mediated by the conditions around them.

Susan Dodds[53] also argues that we need a legal and social system which is premised not on individualistic conceptions of autonomy but on an acceptance of our vulnerability:

> A vulnerability-centred view of the self and of persons is better able to capture many of our moral motivations and intuitions than can be captured by an autonomy-focused approach. We are all vulnerable to the exigencies of our embodied, social and relational existence and, in recognizing this inherent human vulnerability, we can see the ways in which a range of social institutions and structures protect us against some vulnerabilities, while others expose us to risk. We do not have to view our obligations towards those who lack the capacity to develop or retain autonomy as having a different source from our obligations towards those whose autonomy is made vulnerable due to a degree of dependency. It may be easier to recognize the social value of provision of care if it is viewed as something on which we all have been dependent and on which we are all likely to be dependent at different points in our lives, rather than altruistic behaviour extended to those who lack full personhood.

The acknowledgement of universal vulnerability also creates a different image of the legal relationship between the individual and the state. Rather than seeing the obligations of the state as owed towards a few particularly vulnerable citizens to meet their needs, it acknowledges that the institutions and provision of the state are used to meet the needs of all. The question then becomes the extent to which the state meets all of our needs and which needs it chooses not to meet.

---

[51] Herring, *Vulnerable Adults and the Law*, 221.
[52] S. Dodds, 'Depending on Care: Recognition of Vulnerability and the Social Contribution of Care Provision' (2007) 21 *Bioethics* 500, 507.
[53] Ibid.

2.6.2 Autonomy

In Chapter 1 I highlighted the elevated place given to autonomy in standard presentations of the law. As Robert Stevens says: 'The starting position of the common law is based upon a premium placed upon our freedom to choose how we live our lives.'[54] I argued there that the concept of the relational self challenges the emphasis on autonomy. There are strong links between autonomy and vulnerability. Alison Diduck[55] argues that:

> autonomy cannot exist without its "other", which in current rhetoric has become vulnerability. In the same way that autonomy may be the "friendly face" of individual responsibility, vulnerability may be the friendly face of dependence.

She argues that autonomy is closely linked to the claim that people are responsible for the choices that they make. Vulnerability is seen as the antithesis of this. Vulnerability is a state for which an individual is not to be blamed and is not accountable. Diduck argues that vulnerability 'implies disability, lack of capacity, of competence or victimhood, rather than the irresponsibility which tended to pervade dependency discourse'. The vulnerable person in this regard is to be treated as grateful for the protection and services of the state, which an autonomous person is normally spared. Vulnerability provides the language to account for the blatantly non-autonomous, and leaves the norm of autonomy possible.

I suggest that Diduck is entirely right to question the extent to which we are autonomous. In fact, we are all too aware of our own limitations in decision-making. Very few people consenting to medical treatment or people making financial decisions are in fact able to make a fully informed decision or to act on the basis of a rational decision-making process. Unsurprisingly, we often delegate such decisions to others or at least involve others in our decision making. Further, an exploration of how decisions are made suggests that people are typically influenced by forces and motivations of which they are unaware. The typical presentation of an unencumbered, free, rational decision maker is simply a fiction. We will explore this further in Chapter 5.

2.6.3 Duties to the Vulnerable

In Robert Goodin's significant work *Protecting the Vulnerable*,[56] he argues that the vulnerability of other people is the source of our responsibility to them. Hence vulnerability is key to law because it is the source of responsibility. To him, the extent of these duties depends on the details of our relationship with

---

[54] R. Stevens, *Torts and Rights* (Oxford University Press, 2007), 9.
[55] A. Diduck, 'Autonomy and Vulnerability in Family Law: The Missing Link' in J. Herring and J. Wallbank (eds.) *Vulnerabilities, Care and Family Law* (Routledge, 2013), 104.
[56] R. Goodin, *Protecting the Vulnerable* (University of Chicago Press, 1985).

the person. We have special responsibility towards the vulnerability of friends and families, but also have a duty towards vulnerable people at large. He argues 'we have an obligation to act so as to prevent harm to, or protect the interests of, those who are especially vulnerable to our actions and choices'. The greater the needs a person has and the better position the other is in to meet those needs, the greater the responsibility. Hence a parent has specially strong responsibilities to a baby, but less so as the child matures.

An important aspect of his thinking is that it rejects the traditional liberal approach, which suggests that obligations must be agreed or chosen. Indeed, for Robert Goodin, 'duties and responsibilities are not necessarily (or even characteristically) things that you deserve. More often than not, they are things that just happen to you.'[57] Notably, Goodin's obligation does not even require that one person is in any way responsible for causing another's vulnerable state. Nor does it need to be shown that the responsibility is chosen. All of this is inimical to traditional autonomy-based approaches.

Daniel Engster,[58] building on the work of Goodin and others, sets out the arguments leading from vulnerability to the duty to provide care:

(A) All human beings can be assumed to value their own survival, development, functioning, ability to avoid harm and suffering, capacity to exercise some control over their lives, opportunity to pursue projects and plans without interference and domination, and being treated with respect;

(B) All human beings are vulnerable to not achieving some or all of these goods largely because of human actions and rely on other human beings to help them mitigate this vulnerability;

(C) All human being can therefore be assumed to claim, at least implicitly and in normative terms, that others should help them to mitigate their vulnerability to various harms, losses, needs, and blights. We all act in ways that imply our commitment to this principle through daily actions that call on others to help us sustain an orderly and mutually beneficial social existence;

(D) Because every human being who can affect us plays some role in determining how vulnerable we are to various harms, losses, and needs, we must direct our claims toward all others in seeking to reduce our vulnerability. Implicitly, we claim that all capable human beings ought to do what they reasonably can to help us to reduce our vulnerability to various harms, losses, and needs consistent with their own self-interested desire to limit their vulnerability;

---

[57] Ibid., 27.
[58] D. Engster, 'Care Ethics, Dependency, and Vulnerability' (2019) 13 *Ethics and Social Welfare* 100.

(E) Because we have all implicitly made use of this moral principle in seeking
    to limit our own vulnerability, we ought (out of consistency) to recognise
    and honour it when others direct it toward us in order to limit their
    vulnerability.

This would have a wide-ranging impact on legal responses in nearly every area
of law. These will be explored in this law. Key themes for the law would be as
follows: first, caring would become a central activity of importance to the law.
If we are relational, vulnerable and interconnected, it is clear that care is
essential to human survival. Our legal system would put the sustenance of
caring relationships at its heart.[59] We will explore this in Chapter 3. Second,
essential to the promotion of caring relationships is protection from abusive
relationships. This is discussed in Chapter 4. Third, we would recognise that
we all need social provision and support for survival. These are not only
required for 'vulnerable people' or failing people but are needed by us all.
Fourth, our interactions with each other would be governed by responsibilities
to ensure we do not exploit each other's vulnerability. This is discussed in
Chapter 6.

   Overarching all of this, it becomes clear that the state has responsibilities to
respond to the needs of all people and provide resources and social institutions
to enable people to live with their vulnerability.[60] Traditionally, the state has
delegated this duty to families. The problem with this is that families may not
have the resources to meet all the needs of their members and/or may do so in
an abusive way. Crucially, it means that the burdens of meeting needs falls
disproportionately on women who have undertaken the vast majority of care
work within families. The vulnerability perspective highlights the needs of all
that must be met. It shines light on the unequal way that some people are
given resources for resilience to respond to their vulnerability and others are
not; and the unequal sharing of the costs and burdens of meeting needs. This
ties into the next point about the significance of the claim we are all vulnerable.

2.6.4 The Goodness of Vulnerability

Not only is vulnerability universal but I believe it is a desirable characteristic.
Vulnerability is often seen in a negative light. As Margrit Shildrick noted that,
'in western modernity at least, vulnerability is figured as a shortcoming, an
impending failure'.[61] However, I would argue vulnerability carries with it a
range of benefits.

---

[59] Herring, *Caring and the Law.*
[60] N. Kohn, 'Vulnerability Theory and the Role of Government' (2014) 26 *Yale Journal of Law &
Feminism* 2.
[61] Shildrick, *Embodying the Monster: Encounters with the Vulnerable Self*; Beckett, *Citizenship
and Vulnerability*, 71.

First, it encourages co-operation with others. Our mutual vulnerability requires us to reach out to others to offer and receive help from them. We have to become open to others and our own and other's needs to survive. A recognition of our mutual vulnerability leads to empathy and understanding.[62] It creates intimacy and trust. It compels us to focus on interactive, co-operative solutions to the issues we address. It encourages creativity in finding new ways of overcoming our human limitations and requires a desire to accept others as they are. As Amelia Case puts it: 'Our vulnerability is inextricably tied to our capacity to give of ourselves to others, to treasure and aspire, to commit to endeavors, to care about justice and about our own and other's dignity.'[63] The great achievements of the human race are nearly always the product of co-operation and mutual endeavour. The things we need as individuals, be it healthcare, education or transport, require people to come together recognising their needs and skills and using them to produce social responses to the issues we face.

Second, vulnerability is essential to relationships. In entering a relationship with others this creates an understanding of trust, the assumptions of responsibility and obligations of care. These things create vulnerability: we are in danger of not meeting our obligations; we are at risk of others not meeting theirs to us. Our trust might be misplaced. The opening up of our natures creates a risk we will be taken advantage of;[64] a risk that private information will be used to harm us; and the risk of grief and loss. Yet relationships are good and beneficial. Indeed, they may well be described as one of the basic goods. Relationships, intimacy, care: all of these things in their nature render us vulnerable.[65] Exclusion of the other to achieve invulnerability is an anathema to relationships. Our vulnerability, further, requires us to reach out to others to meet their needs and to have our needs met. These interactions are fulfilling and creative. Our very vulnerability provides us with the seeds for our growth through relationships with others.[66]

Third, the emphasis on vulnerability promotes a particular set of values about the value of 'personhood', about what characteristics generate the high moral status that comes with parenthood. To some commentators it is our rationality and our intellectual capabilities which generate personhood. However, doing so can exclude those with severe cognitive impairments from the status. If our source of value, dignity and humanity is not our intellect but our feelings, relationships, care and love, then separation between children as the vulnerable and the non-vulnerable collapses.

---

[62] E. Feder Kittay, 'The Ethics of Care, Dependence, and Disability' (2011) 44 *Ratio Juris* 49.

[63] A. Carse, 'Vulnerability, Agency and Human Flourishing' in C. Taylor and R. Dell'Oro (eds.) *Health and Human Flourishing* (Georgetown University Press, 2006), 48.

[64] S. Sevenhuijsen, *Too Good to be True?* (IWM Working Paper No. 3/1998).

[65] G. Harris, *Dignity and Vulnerability* (Berkeley University Press, 1997).

[66] Fineman, '"Elderly" as Vulnerable: Rethinking the Nature of Individual and Societal Responsibility', 23.

Fourth, recognising our vulnerability and the vulnerability to others requires us to be open to the world. Our vulnerable selves are dependent, as I have already said, on our mutable bodies and our changing relationships, and inevitability this means they are dynamic and must be open to unpredictable change. As Nussbaum[67] has argued, such relational goods require 'openness towards the world and its possibilities ... a yielding and receptive character of soul that is not compatible with an undue emphasis on self-protection'. And that is good. It means our lives have a journey and alter as our relationships, responsibilities and bodies change. It stops us getting 'into a rut'. As Gilson argues, it is an 'open-ended condition that makes possible learning, love, affection, and self-transformation just as much as it makes possible suffering and harm'.[68] It is true that with this unknown openness to the unbidden can come good and bad things.

As already mentioned, one of the major advantages of the universal vulnerability claim is that it challenges the divisions that can be created between 'them and us'; 'the competent and the not competent'; the 'vulnerable and the non-vulnerable'. It means that in seeking intervention or protection we need to recognise our own fallibility, weakness and vulnerability to influence what is the correct response. Given the stigma that can attach to being labelled 'vulnerable', some people will exaggerate their own abilities. The 'vulnerable' become stigmatised and something to eschew. This will cause people to exaggerate their own understandings and abilities or protect their own interest. Tom Shakespeare has noted that non-disabled people 'project their fear of death, their unease at their physicality and mortality onto disabled people, who represent all these difficult aspects of human existence'. I suspect some of the negative associations with vulnerability can be analysed in the same way. As Fineman puts it[69]:

> The designation of vulnerable (inferior) populations reinforces and valorizes the ideal liberal subject, who is positioned as the polar opposite of the vulnerable population. This liberal subject is thus constructed as invulnerable, or at least differently vulnerable, and represents the desirable and achievable ideals of autonomy, independence, and self-sufficiency.

2.6.5 Vulnerability and Power

Martha Fineman writes:

> [W]ith respect to the assets any one person possesses, it is not multiple identities that intersect to produce compounded inequalities ... but rather systems of

---

[67] M. Nussbaum, *The Fragility of Goodness: Luck and Ethics in Greek Tragedy and Philosophy* (Cambridge University Press, 2001).

[68] E. Gilson, *The Ethics of Vulnerability: A Feminist Analysis of Social Life and Practice* (Routledge, 2013).

[69] Fineman, '"Elderly" as Vulnerable: Rethinking the Nature of Individual and Societal Responsibility', 23, 25.

power and privilege that interact to produce webs of advantages and disadvantages. Thus … a vulnerability analysis provides a means of interrogating the institutional practices that produce the identities and inequalities in the first place.[70]

As that quote indicates, an important part of focussing on vulnerability is that it highlights the importance of how social provision can ameliorate or magnify our vulnerability. That means our focus can shift from calling some people vulnerable to recognising that some people have more resources and more power. A recognition of our mutual vulnerability and the reliance we all have on the provision of help from the state and others must be at the heart of our political and legal response. As Martha Fineman argues:

> When we only study the poor, the rich remain hidden and their advantages remain relatively unexamined, nestled in secure and private spaces, where there is no need for them or the state to justify or explain why they deserve the privilege of state protection. We need to excavate these privileged lives.

As Fineman argues, a universal vulnerability approach highlights the extent to which all of us are supported by social provision but also the way that some people are particularly privileged in terms of state provision. But once that is accepted, the role of the law can shift to restricting and reducing the power of the powerful, rather than seeking to protect the vulnerable from an exercise of power. Those labelled 'vulnerable' are not some pre-existing category but are better seen as having been labelled as such in order to legitimise political ends and to justify current inequalities. And as Jenny Kitzinger suggests, it means we can move from vulnerability to look at oppression. The danger is that use of power not only creates 'particular and deficient vulnerability' but it also justifies it.

Take one example, the position of children. Children are typically portrayed as vulnerable and in need of a range of protections from the state and their parents. In truth, the issue is far more complicated. An appreciation of the common and interlocking vulnerabilities of adults and children can reveal what can otherwise be an unrecognised use of power. Some of children's vulnerability does not rest in the nature of childhood, but the use of power by adults. The use of power not only creates the vulnerability but it thereby creates the justification for its own use. For example, the law's acceptance of corporal punishment is justified in the name of enabling parents to exercise control over children in order to protect children from risk. Yet the practice and acceptance of corporal punishment reveals a diminished acceptance of children's rights and personhood. It creates its own range of vulnerabilities. The vulnerability discourse encourages children to accept obedience and respect their parents and adults. Childhood compliance with adult demands

---

[70] M. Fineman, 'The Vulnerable Subject: Anchoring Equality in the Human Condition' (2008) 20 *Yale Journal of Law & Feminism* 1, 16.

and rules is deeply imbedded in our society's construction of childhood. Ironically, it is this which renders children so vulnerable in the arena of sexual contact.

2.7 Criticisms of the Claim

It is time to consider some of the arguments against universal vulnerability.

Wendy Rogers, Catriona Mackenzie and Susan Dodds have produced some powerful concerns about the claim that everyone is vulnerable[71]:

> The "everyone is vulnerable" approach dulls our responses to particular vulner-abilities, fails to account for context-specific harms, and can lead to discrimin-ation and stereotyping of whole groups as incapable of caring for their own needs or of being self-determining. This finding in turn can then be used to justify unwarranted and unjust paternalistic responses.

This is a serious criticism, but the claim that everyone is vulnerable is different from a claim that everyone is equally vulnerable. A recognition that we are all vulnerable means that there is no stereotyping of groups as incapable of caring for their own needs. Their enhanced vulnerability is a result of the allocation of state resources, not any inherent feature.

A more challenging response is that the claim of universal vulnerability opens the gates to paternalistic intervention. If people are all vulnerable and unable to look after themselves or make decisions for themselves, then the state is entitled to offer protection. The concept of vulnerability is typically used by the state to justify protective coercive measures to avoid the vulner-ability being exploited. Feminists, in particular, might have reasons to be concerned at an approach which seeks to justify state intervention.

I would make two points. First, I would argue that such comments are in danger of underplaying the extent to which the state is already meeting people's needs and intervening in people's lives in a way which is uncontro-versial. Whether it be the provision of sewerage, electricity, transportation or security, the state is already meeting our needs and few would question it doing so. Second, the argument that we are all vulnerable undermines pater-nalism. If vulnerability is seen as weakening the claim that you should be able to make decisions for yourself, so too does it weaken the claim that I am in a good position to make decisions on your behalf. Universal vulnerability might paint a picture of a vulnerable patient, but it also paints a picture of a vulnerable doctor. In acknowledging universal vulnerability, we undermine paternalism not bolster it. The central claim of paternalism, 'I am in a better position than you to make a decision about your life', is lost when universal vulnerability is acknowledged.

---

[71] Rogers, Mackenzie and Dodds, 'Why Bioethics Needs a Concept of Vulnerability', 11, 15.

2.8 Conclusion

This chapter has made the case for and explored the significance of universal vulnerability. It has argued that all humans are in their nature vulnerable. In part, this is due to our relational selves, which make us susceptible to being harmed by others. But it is partly due to our corporal nature and our core needs, which can only be met by provision from others. I have argued that this universal vulnerability is to be welcomed. It requires us to co-operate with others, to find mutual solutions and to be open to change and challenge. Acceptance of universal vulnerability also illuminates the way that the allocation of state resources and the arrangement of public institutions can provide resilience to some people and not others. While therefore under the traditional analysis some people are seen as "vulnerable" and to be blamed for lacking the ability for self-sufficiency, in fact it is the allocation of state resources that provides resilience to some and not others.

The chapter has also explored the impact of universal vulnerability for the law. The law tends to assume that adults have capacity, are autonomous and are able to make decisions for their life which are worthy of respect. The general law's rules apply to such people. There are then special areas of the law which are marked off for those lacking capacity. For example, there are special exceptions to the rules of contract which apply to minors, those under undue influence or those lacking mental capacity. We could, and should, present a rather different legal system, which starts with an acknowledgement of everyone's vulnerability. Law degrees would have the law on mental health, child law, carer law, elder law and undue influence at their heart. This would produce a rather different way of looking at the world. Gone would be the special 'concessions' involved in protecting specially disadvantaged groups such as the disabled or children. Rather, they would be regarded as the norm and the focus would be on the special privileges that are given to the able-bodied or some adults.

Finally, because we are vulnerable, our care of each other is crucial. Currently, care work and caring relationships are seriously undervalued in the law. Recognising our vulnerability requires us to have a law which puts caring relationships at the heart of our legal response. And that will be the subject of the next chapter.

3

Law and the Caring Self

3.1 Introduction

In Chapters 1 and 2 I argued in favour of the ideas of the relational self and universal vulnerability. I argued that the law is currently designed around a norm of an independent, self-sufficient, autonomous man, whereas it should be based on an understanding of the self as vulnerable and relational. In this chapter I argue that it flows from this understanding of the self that caring relationships are essential to human survival and should be of central significance for the law.[1] From our earliest days, we are in caring relationships which are crucial to our physical health, emotional well-being and psychological identity.[2] Caring is hardly some kind of luxury hobby or activity ancillary to other more important activities. It is central to our humanity. Feeding, bathing, changing, comforting, transporting and nurturing are core moral actions.

Sadly, that is not how law seems to see things. Our law reports are replete with cases about money: making, losing and claiming money. They are set in the office, the board room or the casino. Rarely do the nappy changing table, the bed pan or the care home feature prominently. Our law graduates are well trained to advise well-heeled business people on their rights of autonomy, freedom of contract and presumption of innocence. They would be ill equipped to advise the welfare recipient, the exhausted mother of a disabled child or the care home resident with dementia. To these people, the rights of autonomy, freedom of contract and presumption of innocence mean little. The values the law seems to promote and the nature of the self they promote is anathema to them.

Care is side-lined not only in the law but also in public policy and the media. A fine example has been the Brexit referendum and the subsequent coverage of negotiations. The economic impact of Brexit has dominated the discussions. The potential impact on trade, house prices, agriculture, interest rates, traffic jams, currency valuation and the city have dominated the

---

[1] This chapter draws on earlier work, particularly J. Herring, *Caring and the Law* (Hart, 2013).
[2] D. Engster, 'Care in the State of Nature: The Biological and Evolutionary Roots of the Disposition to Care in Human Beings' in D. Engster and M. Hamington (eds.) *Care Ethics and Political Theory* (Oxford University Press, 2015).

coverage. The impact on caring has received very little attention. Our newscasts have plenty to tell us about the pontifications of politicians. But the successful outing with the autistic child or the happy cup of tea with the lonely man with dementia do not make the front page of the newspapers, or, indeed, any page at all.

That said, it might be argued that this is unfair; there has been quite some coverage of the 'care crisis', the social care/health divide and 'bed blocking' in recent years. This is true but the debates are nearly always put in terms of money. The crisis is seen in terms of economic costs, not the quality of care and the fairness of its distribution. Notably, carers advocacy groups often buy into this dialogue, emphasising with startling numbers the amount of money unpaid carers save the government. They realise that the presentation of arguments in financial terms will attract the attention of politicians. As Martha Fineman notes:

> The Dow Jones average is reported daily (even hourly on public radio) as though this reflected our country's health and wealth, an economic indicator substituting for other forms of evaluation of national standing such as the equitableness of the distribution of the wealth the society is producing or the well being of the most vulnerable of our citizens. We seem blinded in a reverie of self satisfaction even as the position of our children and the historically disadvantaged subgroups in society deteriorates both from where they were a few decades ago and relative to the positions of these groups in other industrialized democracies.[3]

As Fineman indicates, our starting point should be the importance, value and need for care, not the 'crisis' caused by care.

Care should not be dismissed as a private activity of no interest to the state. As Maxine Eichner puts it:

> The care that children and other dependents receive from family members is inextricably intertwined with state policies. This care takes place in a matrix of constraints and entitlements that affect family members' ability and opportunity to care for other members. The existence or nonexistence of minimum wage laws, union rights to bargain, and overtime provisions affect parents' ability to meet the financial needs of their children and other dependents. Welfare reform laws requiring recipients to work in order to receive welfare subsidies affect parents' ability to care for those with dependency needs. Family leave laws influence parents' opportunity to stay home with their children. The stability and security of a parent's job affects stress levels in the household, which also affect the quality of parenting. In these circumstances, the family has no "natural" manner of functioning that it can be left to "apart from" the state. Nor does the modern administrative state have a neutral, isolated position it can assume while leaving families autonomously to deal with their own affairs. Instead, the state is always and continually influencing how families conduct their affairs. The issue is not whether state policy will influence families but

---

[3] M. Fineman, 'Contract and Care' (2001) 76 *Chicago-Kent Law Review* 1403, 1436.

whether it will be formulated with this inevitable influence in mind. When it comes to the ways families function, no family is an island.[4]

There is, of course, much to debate about who provides care and how to balance the role of families and the state in the provision of care and support. However, there is clearly an important role for families and friends in providing care in many cases because they will have developed the kind of close relationships which ensure high quality care. At least, the state must provide the broader social and financial support that enables families and friends to care and mitigates the disadvantages that flow from caring. To quote Eichner again:

> Determining that the state and families are both conjunctively responsible for meeting dependency needs does not mean that the state's role should be identical to families'. Rather, each should bear responsibility for the area in which it has greater competence. This means that families should bear responsibility for the day-to-day caring for (or arranging the care for) children and others with dependency needs. Meanwhile, the state should bear the responsibility for structuring institutions in ways that help families meet their caretaking needs, and that support human development. This includes ensuring that families have safe and affordable caretaking options, as well as structuring other societal institutions, such as schools and communities, in ways that foster children's and other dependents' development and well-being. This division of responsibility recognizes the malleability and contingency of institutional structures. It does not artificially separate state action from the realm of families or presume that completely clear boundaries can be drawn between them, but it does assume certain spheres of authority will exist between the two.[5]

One of the significant consequences of the side-lining of care is its impact on gender equality. Care has been seen as 'women's work' and has largely been performed by women. It is seen as a labour of love and this has been used to justify its lack of recognition. Poverty and social exclusion of women have resulted from this downplaying of the significance of women's work. Of course, the position of women in the workplace is changing, but one of the ironies of modern life is that women's increased opportunities in the 'workplace' have only been possible because other women have taken on the role of providing caring services such as child care, cleaning and the like. The children and dependants of the lowest paid workers are the ones who bear the cost of that. The burden of care also exacerbates disadvantages based on race, class and age.[6] In a different society we could see that, as Selma Sevenhuijsen has argued, care is a central aspect of citizenship, where its support is expected of all.

---

[4] Ibid., 1618–1619.

[5] Ibid.

[6] T. Levy (2006) 'The Relational Self and the Right to Give Care' (2006) 28 *New Political Science* 547; S. Moller Okin, *Justice, Gender, and the Family* (Basic Books, 1989); M. Fineman, *The Autonomy Myth: A Theory of Dependency* (New Press, 2004).

There is no doubt that care work is a major aspect of many people's lives. Carers UK,[7] a leading charity promoting the interests of carers, estimates that one in eight of the population, some 6.5 million people, are carers. It is estimated that each year 2 million people take on a caring role. The hours involved can be extensive, with around 1.3 million people caring at least 50 hours a week. The charity claims 'Carers save the economy £132 billion per year, an average of £19,336 per carer.'[8] But this comes at a cost to 'carers', with 72 per cent of carers in the State of Caring Survey saying they had suffered mental ill health as a result of caring; and 61 per cent physical ill health. Of those carers, 24 per cent said they themselves had a disability.

It is common for carers charities to promote statistics of this kind, and they can supply important political leverage. However, they are not unproblematic. It is important to realise that these statistics use a very narrow understanding of care. These statistics do not include, for example, parents caring for children, and are primarily based on those who define themselves as carers. It also presents too sharp a distinction between the 'carer' and 'cared for'. We will return to that issue later in this chapter, but suffice for now to say caring relationships rarely break down into such a straightforward binary model.

3.2 The Definition of Care

We need to define what is meant by care. This has proved controversial and complex. Interestingly, many of the official definitions seek to define a carer rather than care. This is significant, and will be criticised shortly.

The government has recently updated its definition of carer. In 2008, in its document *Carers at the Heart of 21st-Century Families and Communities*, it uses the following definition of a carer:

> A carer spends a significant proportion of their life providing unpaid support to family or potentially friends. This could be caring for a relative, partner or friend who is ill, frail, disabled or has mental health or substance misuse problems.[9]

In 2018, the UK government gave the following definition in its action plan on carers:

> a carer is considered to be anyone who spends time looking after or helping a friend, family member or neighbour who, because of their health and care needs, would find it difficult to cope without this help regardless of age or whether they identify as a carer.[10]

---

[7] Carers UK, *Facts and Figures* (Carers UK, 2018); Carers UK, *State of Caring* (Carers UK, 2018).
[8] Ibid.
[9] HM Government, *Carers at the Heart of 21st-Century Families and Communities* (The Stationery Office, 2008), 18.
[10] Department of Health and Social Care, *Carers Action Plan 2018–2020* (DoHSC, 2018), 4.

There are some notable differences with the more recent definition. First, the 2018 definition seems to apply without any restriction as to time: a few minutes of care would, technically, fall within this definition. By contrast, the 2008 definition required the carer to show they spent a significant proportion of their life caring. Second, the 2018 definition is not limited to those who care for adults, but would seem to include child care within the definition.[11] Third, the 2018 definition is broad in terms of those who receive care. There is no need to show the person is disabled or ill, as required in the 2008 definition, but simply that they will find it difficult to cope without the care. Finally, the 2008 definition only applied to family members and only 'potentially' friends. The 2018 definition clearly covers friends, and indeed neighbours. However, it should be noted it is designed not to apply to 'professional carers'.

Academic definitions tend to be much broader than official ones. Harriet Lefley[12] describes carers as 'individuals whose own happiness is entwined with the well-being of people who are dear to them'. Berenice Fisher and Joan Tronto[13] claim that caring is 'a species activity that includes everything that we do to maintain, continue, and repair our "world" so that we can live in it as well as possible'. These extremely broad definitions would appear to cover a vast range of activities. Indeed, the concept of care under such a definition might be thought to become so vague as to be of little practical use.

Other definitions seek to list the kinds of activities which might be regarded as care:

> washing, feeding, getting in and out of bed, assistance with toileting, giving medication, changing dressings, giving injections or catheterisation, dealing with incontinence, assisting with paperwork and personal business including managing money, negotiation and liaison with "professional" caring agencies and staff, providing transport and undertaking household tasks.[14]

The difficulty with this approach is that it sees care as something that is done by one person to another. As I will suggest shortly, I believe that is mistaken.

It hardly needs to be said that there is no 'correct' definition of care. Much depends on the context within which the term is being used. If one is looking for a definition of a carer for the purposes of the provision of benefits, one might have a very different concept compared to if one was to consider the psychological impact of care. One of the difficulties in producing a definition, at least if it is not to be utterly vague, is that care takes place in

---

[11] The 2008 document makes it clear that although unclear on its face, the definition was not intended to apply to children.

[12] H. Lefley, 'The Impact of Mental Disorders on Families and Carers' in S. Thornicroft (ed.) *Textbook of Community Psychiatry* (Oxford University Press, 2001).

[13] B. Fisher and J. Tronto, 'Towards a Feminist Theory of Caring' in E. Abel and M. Nelson (eds.) *Circles of Care, Work and Identity in Women's Lives* (State University of New York Press, 1990), 40.

[14] M. Barnes, *Caring and Social Justice* (Palgrave, 2006), 6.

so many different contexts and has so many levels that a bright line definition is unhelpful.

Instead of producing a formal definition, I will set out four key 'markers' of
care. I do not suggest that these all need to be present for these to be care, but
the more there are, and the greater the extent, the closer they are to a strong
case of care. I suggest the following four markers of care:[15]

- Meeting needs.
- Respect.
- Responsibility.
- Relationality.

These terms need further explanation. As will become clear, the concepts of
the relational self and universal vulnerability are at the heart of my proposed
definition.

3.2.1 Meeting Needs

At the heart of care is the meeting of the needs of another. Given our universal
vulnerable state, we all have needs that have to be met by others.[16] Needs
should be broadly understood. This is in line with Engster's definition of care
as 'everything we do directly to help individuals to meet their vital biological
needs, develop or maintain their basic capabilities, and avoid or alleviate
unnecessary or unwanted pain and suffering, so that they can survive, develop,
and function in society'.[17]

By emphasising the importance of meeting needs, I emphasise that care is
an activity rather than a feeling.[18] Caring involves the actual giving of care, and
the giving of care effectively. Here it is useful to draw on the distinction drawn
by many care writers being caring *about* and caring *for*.[19] Many people know
someone who claims to care about all manner of things, but does not seem to
put those feelings into practice. That, I would suggest, is not genuine caring.[20]

There has been a lively discussion in the care literature on whether acts
which attempt but fail to meet needs are caring. Joan Tronto has suggested
that 'incompetent' care is not caring. But others, especially those starting out
from virtue ethics, see caring as primarily focused in virtue. On this, I would
refer to the fourth of my markers: relationality. A relationship which is

---

[15] See also Herring, *Caring and the Law*, chapter 2. For an alternative analysis see J. Tronto, *Moral
Boundaries: A Political Argument for an Ethic of Care* (Routledge, 1983) 127–134.

[16] S. Clark Miller, 'Need, Care and Obligation' (2005) 57 *Royal Institute of Philosophy Supplement*
157.

[17] D. Engster, *The Heart of Justice* (Oxford University Press, 2007), 28–29.

[18] A. Barnes, 'Am I a Carer and Do I Care?' (2004) 7 *Medicine, Health Care and Philosophy* 153.

[19] Tronto, *Moral Boundaries: A Political Argument for an Ethic of Care*, 127–134.

[20] K. Lynch, 'Love Labour as a Distinct and Non-Commodifiable Form of Care Labour' (2008) 55
Sociological Review 550.

generally marked by activities which meet the needs of parties is caring. The odd mistake does not negate the caring nature of that relationship. Indeed, an occasional 'failure' can be amusing and productive to the relationship where no serious harm is done. However, a caring relationship which is marked by consistent failures to adequately meet the needs of the other is not marked by care.

There is a further reason why it is important to emphasise that caring is a practical activity and not just an emotional feeling: the fact that care work is bodily work.[21] As Julia Twigg[22] has emphasised, much care involves negotiating nakedness, touch, dirt, disgust and intimacy. This is significant for two reasons. First, as already discussed in Chapter 1, the bodily nature of care work challenges the standard presentation of bodies as bounded and self-contained. The 'foulness' of the one body enters and interacts with her body. Second, this helps explain why care is undervalued. It is 'dirty work'. Twigg notes the high respect given to doctors whose bodily work is limited to diagnoses, or mediated through machines, or performed in sterile environments, meaning that dirtiness is avoided. Emphasising the activity in care work makes it clear we are not talking about high-minded emotions but hard work. Third, Clare Ungerson suggests that its bodily nature explains why care work has been seen as women's work. She argues that women are seen as appropriate dealers with bodily waste, reflecting assumptions that women's bodies are polluted. As Julia Twigg puts it, 'women's work is here constructed out of the rejected and unacknowledged aspects of men's lives'.[23]

The link between care and vulnerability is emphasised by the importance of meeting needs. It is because we are vulnerable that we have needs that must be met by caring. But it is through caring that vulnerability is generated. As Susan Dodds writes:

> Human vulnerability arises from our embodiment, which exposes us to the risk of suffering harm or injury or of failing to flourish or develop our capacities in ways that may be minor or devastating ... Dependence is one form of vulnerability. Dependence is vulnerability that requires the support of a specific person (or people) – that is, care. To be dependent is to be in circumstances in which one must rely on the care of other individuals to access, provide or secure (one or more of) one's needs, and promote and support the development of one's autonomy or agency.[24]

---

[21] J. Twigg, C. Wolkowitz, R. Cohen and S. Nettleton, 'Conceptualising Body Work in Health and Social Care' (2011) 33 *Sociology of Health and Illness* 171; C. Stacey, 'Finding Dignity in Dirty Work: The Constraints and Rewards of Law-Wage Home Care Labour' (2005) 27 *Sociology of Health & Illness* 831.

[22] J. Twigg, 'Carework as a Form of Bodywork' (2000) 20 *Ageing and Society* 389.

[23] Ibid.

[24] S. Dodds, 'Dependence, Care and Vulnerability' in C. MacKenzie, W. Rogers and S. Dodds (eds.) *Vulnerability: New Essays in Ethics and Feminist Philosophy* (Oxford University Press, 2014), 182–183.

3.2.2 Respect

Respect is the second marker of care. This is about treating the other as a fellow human being, with whom one is in relationships, not an object to be dealt with. It means being alert to the needs of the other and responding to those needs in a way that respects the person's wishes, feelings and interests. Robin Dillon[25] captures this with the word attention, and argues:

> The term 'care' denotes here an epistemic attitude, understood as a moral ideal of attention: a commitment to attend, with intensely focused perception to all aspects of the irreducible particularity of individual human persons in their concrete contexts.[26]

The concept of respect requires treating the other as a person with their own particular character, beliefs and interests. Care which treats people in categories ('an old man with dementia', 'a wheel chair user' etc.) is failing to respect their individuality. This means that care must involve empathy.[27] Virginia Held[28] mentions seven potential values of care: attentiveness, empathy, mutual concern, sensitivity, responsiveness, taking responsibility and trustworthiness. These are all tied up in with treating the other person with respect.[29]

It follows from the respect aspect that care involves listening to the other and seeking consent, or at least assent. It means treating their views and feelings as worthy of respect and not the object of power.[30] It means respecting the person's dignity: ensuring intimate aspects of care are done in private and showing respect for what the person can do themselves.[31] It involves an awareness of how the other is experiencing the 'care'. This involves interacting and engaging with them, finding forms of communication, even where speech is not possible.[32]

3.2.3 Responsibility

Caring which is only done when it is convenient is not the highest quality care. A caring relationship brings with it responsibilities to the other. Virginia Held, for example, writes that 'the central focus of the ethics of care is on [...] meeting the needs of the particular others for whom we take responsibility'.[33] In part, this is because if one person enters a caring relationship with someone, others may not then offer care for that person. They may assume that any

---

[25] R. Dillon, 'Respect and Care' (1992) 22 *Canadian Journal of Philosophy* 105.
[26] Ibid., 128.
[27] L. Blum, *Moral Perception and Particularity* (Cambridge University Press, 1994), 30–61.
[28] V. Held, *The Ethics of Care* (Oxford University Press, 2006).
[29] T. Randall, 'Values in Good Caring Relations' (2018) 4 *Feminist Philosophy Quarterly* https://doi.org/10.5206/fpq/2018.3.5781.
[30] V. Dalmiya, 'Why Should a Knower Care?' (2002) 17 *Hypatia* 34.
[31] C. Foster, *Human Dignity in Bioethics and the Law* (Hart, 2011).
[32] Engster, *The Heart of Justice*, 55.
[33] Held, *The Ethics of Care*, 10.

needs are met within that relationship. The parties in the relationship may not seek care from others, relying on each other to meet their needs. This is particularly likely to happen because a person's capacity to offer care is limited and inevitably can only be focused on a finite number of people.

Responsibilities arise simply because the needs of the other generate obligations on those around them. As Stephanie Collins explains, 'dependency relationships generate responsibilities'.[34] This responsibility can extend to avoiding harms that might arise. As Daniel Engster[35] explains:

> Good caregivers generally do more than just attend and respond to the needs of individuals as they arise. They work at a step before needs or harms manifest themselves – anticipating individuals' vulnerability to unmet needs and harms so that real threats to their well-being never arise. Good caregivers stock the pantry with food, if possible, to ensure that real hunger never afflicts their loved ones. They repair leaky roofs before the rain comes in. They steer loved ones clear of danger so that even the threat of harm remains a distant possibility.

Of course, it may be that there are good reasons why a person cannot meet their responsibilities at a particular moment in time. In particular, there may be competing caring responsibilities, including care to the self, which may conflict with their duties to other. But care ethicists tend to accept that the obligations to those we are caring for or who are dependent on us for care are stronger than obligations to other people.

3.2.4 Relationality

A final, and very important, aspect of care is that it is relational. This is why I am rather wary of talking about a 'carer' and a 'cared for' person. In fact, care is rarely, if ever, uni-directional. All parties should be open to receiving care and support.[36] Rosie Harding, Ruth Fletcher and Chris Beasley[37] refer to 'cycles of care' to capture the idea that people move between and among differing roles in caring relationships over time and space.

One of the problems with the standard separation between carer and cared for is that it presents the recipient of care in a passive way and a source of problems. Peter Beresford has captured the concerns over the idea of care well:

> The reality seems to be that while care might be regarded by many of us as a good idea in principle and something that some people might need at some time, few of us identify with it for ourselves and actually want to be "cared for"

---

[34] S. Collins, *The Core of Care Ethics* (Palgrave, 2015).

[35] D. Engster, 'Care Ethics, Dependency, and Vulnerability' (2019) 13 *Ethics and Social Welfare* 100.

[36] Dalmiya, 'Why Should a Knower Care?', 34.

[37] R. Harding, R. Fletcher and C. Beasley, 'ReValuing Care' in R. Harding, R. Fletcher and C. Beasley (eds.) *Revaluing Care in Theory, Law and Practice* (Routledge, 2018), 1.

in this sense. There is a strong reluctance to see ourselves or to be in this position, because it implies dependence. Care is a concept that is primarily associated with children. Models for adult caring have tended to be borrowed from childcare and grow out of the unequal relationships associated with looking after children. This has been the basis for many people's assumptions and understanding of such care.[38]

So, it is crucial that caring is seen as a relational activity. As Carol Gilligan writes, 'The ideal of care is thus an activity of relationships, of seeing and responding to need, taking care of the world by sustaining the web of connection so that no one is left alone.'[39] This acknowledges the complex ways in which the interests, bodies and identities of the parties to a caring relationship become entwined. The relational view of care would emphasise interdependence over dependency; and mutual vulnerability over the frailty of one person. The relational approach is likely to see care in the context of the relationship between two people in which each is contributing care to the other: be that in terms of psychological, emotional or physical sense.

Studies of care suggest that qualities of reciprocal dependence underlie much of what is termed 'care'. Rather than being a unidirectional activity in which an active care-giver does something to a passive and dependent recipient, these accounts suggest that care is best understood as the product or outcome of the relationship between two or more people.[40] There is also the danger of seeing the 'cared for' as being a problem which the 'carer' is seeking to remedy. This is in danger of regarding dependency as a bad thing, with the aim of care to achieve independence for the person needing care. Michael Fine and Caroline Glendinning write of dependency:

> This has proved a complex concept. It has been seen by some politicians as a sign of moral weakness: 'the dependency culture'. By some sociologists it has been seen as a social construction of groups to permit paternalistic interventions; for others it is what justifies intervention. It is interesting that independence is assumed to be an automatic good. It is linked to autonomy and that must be a good thing.[41]

Yet, as argued in Chapter 2, dependency is an essential aspect of the human condition.

A good example of what I have in mind is the L'Arche community, in which those with a range of abilities live.[42] A study by Pamela Cushing and Tanya Lewis found many stories of mutually beneficial relationships in these

---

[38] P. Beresford, *What Future for Care?* (Joseph Rowntree Foundation, 2008).

[39] C. Gilligan, *In a Different Voice* (Harvard University Press, 1982), 73.

[40] M. Fine and C. Glendinning, 'Dependence, Independence or Inter-Dependence? Revisiting the Concepts of Care and Dependency' (2005) 25 *Ageing and Society* 601, 619.

[41] Ibid.

[42] M. Spezio, G. Peterson and R. Roberts, 'Humility as Openness to Others: Interactive Humility in the Context of l'Arche' (2019) 48 *Journal of Moral Education* 27.

communities.[43] All members of the community were open to learning from and growing with each other. To the community, it is not a case of a set of 'carers' looking after 'those in need' but a community learning from, and helping, another. To that community and to all good caring, the relationships are multi-directional. Those who might be labelled 'normal' gain as much from the community and give as much to it as those who would not be labelled 'normal'. Indeed, it is only through abandoning the division between 'carer' and 'cared for' that the community thrives. What is revealing is that the power imbalances are recognised within the community but are acknowledged and negotiated by the members. This provides a dramatic opposition to the normally negative portrayal of those with intellectual abilities. The authors comment: 'In a healthy environment they can also reveal myriad, idiosyncratic gifts and talents that family or caregivers without intellectual disabilities can appreciate, foster, and learn from as they share their lives with them.'[44]

That is surely not news to those who live with, or are, people with learning or other disabilities. The 'mutuality of care' that was found in the L'Arche communities can be found in all caring relationships.[45] This shows the benefit of moving to a relational understanding of care in which care is an interrelationship and where the 'dependent' person is not seen as an object which receives care but a party to a relationship, giving and taking. Indeed, studies of those in caring relationships show that these are often dynamic relationships with the precise quality of the relationship changing over time.[46] A similar point can be made of the parent–child relationship as Virginia Held argues:

> A mother taking care of a small child for whom she is responsible does not pit her own interests against those of the child, aiming to maximize her interests in competition with the child's, or altruistically her child's at her own expense. Although taking care of children is full of conflict, parents aim at the relation between themselves and their children being loving, trusting, and considerate. They aim at the well-being of their children along with themselves, at what would be best for them *together*, at their mutual interests, rather than at individual gain.[47]

This relational aspect is also important because it puts the activities within their context, a context which provides those acts with meaning.[48]

[43] P. Cushing and T. Lewis, 'Negotiating Mutuality and Agency in Care-Giving Relationships with Women with Intellectual Disabilities' (2002) 17 *Hypatia* 173.
[44] Ibid.
[45] J. Pols, B. Althoff and E. Bransen 'The Limits of Autonomy: Ideals in Care for People with Learning Disabilities' (2017) 36 *Medical Anthropology* 772.
[46] L. Skar and M. Tamm, 'My Assistant and I: Disabled Children's and Adolescents' Roles and Relationships to their Assistants' (2001) 16 *Disability and Society* 917.
[47] V. Held, 'Care and Justice Still' in D. Engster and M. Hamington (eds.) *Care Ethics and Political Theory* (Oxford University Press, 2015), 12.
[48] M. Daly and J. Lewis, 'The Concept of Social Care and the Analysis of Contemporary Welfare' (2000) 51 *British Journal of Sociology* 281.

The provision of care only makes sense and can be properly understood when placed in the context of the parties' relationships.[49] An act of caring for the parties can have a meaning well beyond the here and now. It may reflect a long-standing commitment or a mutual responsibility. The act may have overtones recalling aspects of the relationship many years ago. Consider the following comment from a woman about using her husband, Andy, as a 'carer':

> I prefer to have Andy's help as a caregiver as little as possible, simply because if your husband becomes your caregiver, then he isn't your husband any more. The relationship is blurred there. If I still want to be a person unto myself, then I don't want to include him in some parts of care, like a bowel treatment or a shower day.[50]

This quotation captures the fact that activities of care can take on different meanings, depending on the relationship between the parties. Here, because of their relationship, the most caring thing was for Andy not to undertake these tasks.

As Eva Feder Kittay argues:

> There appear to be universal aspects of the meaning and experience of caring. In a paradigmatic sense, all caregiving involves a direct, intimate relationship between two or more people. All caregiving occurs in a psychological and social context that has shaped, and shapes the experiences of the participants in the caring practice. All caring, therefore, is at once intensely personal and inextricably social, symbolic, and meaningful. It is both deeply emotional and a rational, pragmatic, and practical endeavor. It is a practice that comprises certain fundamental moral virtues and human goods.[51]

A final point is to acknowledge that one of the most basic human needs is the need to care for others. We have profound relational needs that require reciprocity and mutuality. We don't just want our own needs met but the needs of those we are engaging and relating to. So being a 'care recipient' fails to meet that person's fundamental need to be caring.[52]

3.3 Care Ethics

The moral significance of care has often been ignored in mainstream ethical analysis. As a challenge to that there is now a substantial and rich literature on

---

[49] S. Schwarzenbach, 'On Civil Friendship' (1996) 107 *Ethics* 97, 102.

[50] K. England and I. Dyck, 'Managing the Body Work of Home Care' (2011) 33 *Sociology of Health & Illness* 206.

[51] E. Feder Kittay, 'Dependency, Difference and the Global Ethic of Longterm Care' (2005) 13 *Journal of Political Philosophy* 433.

[52] M. Winance, A. Damamme and E. Fillion, 'Thinking the Aid and Care Relationship from the Standpoint of Disability: Stakes and Ambiguities' (2015) 9 *European Journal of Disability Research* 163.

ethics of care.[53] It is not possible to do more than provide a very brief overview here. At its core is the claim that caring should be the most highly valued activity in society. A central role of any state is to ensure the essential needs of its citizens are met, and care is required to meet those needs. Caring is often invisible in public policy and ethics, when it should be at the heart of it.

Joan Tronto[54] explains that ethics of care is:

> a set of moral sensibilities, issues and practices that arise from taking seriously the fact that care is a central aspect of human existence . . . a species activity that includes everything that we do to maintain, continue and repair our 'world' so that we can live in it as well as possible. That world includes our bodies, ourselves and our environment, all of which we seek to interweave in a complex, life-sustaining web.

As this quotation indicates, ethics of care cannot be reduced to simply the ethics of personal relations as some have suggested.[55] Its application can have a profound impact on political thought, international relations, environmental law[56] and core concepts of legal rights and responsibilities.[57]

The central themes of ethics of care are set out in the following subsections.

3.3.1 Care Is Part of Being Human

We all have needs, and caring for others in meeting these needs and having our needs met by the care of others is a universal experience. Wendy Holloway[58] argues that 'care is the psychological equivalent to our need to breathe unpolluted air'. There will be few, if any, stages during anyone's life when they are not in caring relationships. As Eva Feder Kittay, Bruce Gennings and Angela Wassuna[59] put it:

[53] C. Gilligan, 'Moral Orientation and Moral Development' in E. Feder Kittay and D. Meyers (eds.) *Women and Moral Theory* (Rowman and Littlefield, 1987), 19; J. Tronto, *Moral Boundaries* (Routledge, 1993); S. Sevenhuijsen, *Citizenship and the Ethics of Care* (Routledge, 1998); R. Groenhout, *Connected Lives: Human Nature and an Ethics of Care* (Rowman and Littlefield, 2004); Held, *The Ethics of Care*; D. Engster, *The Heart of Justice: Care Ethics and Political Theory* (Oxford University Press, 2007); J Bridgeman, *Parental Responsibility, Young Children and Healthcare Law* (Cambridge University Press, 2009); Herring, *Caring and the Law*; M. Barnes, T. Brannelly, L. Ward and N. Ward (eds.) *Ethics of Care: Critical Advances in International Perspective* (Policy Press, 2015); Collins, *The Core of Care Ethics*; R. Harding, *Duties to Care* (Cambridge University Press, 2017); R. Harding, R. Feltcher and C. Beasley (eds.) *Revaluing Care in Theory, Law and Policy* (Routledge, 2016).

[54] Tronto, *Moral Boundaries*, 12.

[55] J. Rachels, *The Elements of Moral Philosophy* (McGraw-Hill Education, 7th ed., 2012).

[56] H. Olofsdotter Stensöta, 'Public Ethics of Care: A General Public Ethics' (2015) 9 *Ethics and Social Welfare* 183.

[57] Held, *The Ethics of Care*; Engster, *The Heart of Justice. Care Ethics and Political Theory*.

[58] W. Holloway, 'Introducing the Capacity to Care' in W. Holloway (ed.) *The Capacity to Care: Gender and Ethical Subjectivity* (Routledge, 2006), 2.

[59] E. Feder Kittay, B. Jennings and A. Wassuna, 'Dependency, Difference and the Global Ethic of Longterm Care' (2005) 13 *Journal of Political Philosophy* 433.

People do not spring up from the soil like mushrooms. People produce people. People need to be cared for and nurtured throughout their lives by other people, at some times more urgently and more completely than at other times.

Not only is care essential, but it should be accepted as a moral good. Care should be treasured and valued as a good part of life. As Robin West[60] explains:

Caregiving labour (and its fruits) is the central adventure of a lifetime; it is what gives life its point, provides it with meaning, and returns to those who give it some measure of security and emotional sustenance. For even more of us, whether or not we like it and regardless of how we regard it, caregiving labour, for children and the aged, is the work we will do that creates the relationships, families, and communities within which our lives are made pleasurable and connected to something larger than ourselves.

Care is the outworking of that most core moral value: love. It involves achieving a primary good: meeting the needs of others.[8] It follows that the promotion of caring relationships is the primary aim of an approach based on care ethics.

3.3.2 Emotions Are Ethically Significant

The law has traditionally been rather sceptical of emotions. It has preferred the idea of law to be governed by rationale and rule following, rather than turning on the whims of emotions. Emotions cannot be assessed by empirical evidence and cannot be trusted. As a result, emotions are largely ignored, or even treated with suspicion. Kant believed that reason and 'considered judgement' were needed to make morally good decisions and that decisions motivated by feelings lacked moral worth.[61] Such an approach means that the love which is part of caring, and the grief, disappointment, frustration, anger and despair which are all part of life find no place.[62] Ethics of care, by contrast, regards emotions as offering important moral insights. For care work, values such as trust, empathy, compassion and sensitivity are key. A decision made without empathy will not be able to meet another's need. If a legal intervention undermines such emotional values the intervention will be ineffective.

3.3.3 Intermingled Interests

Ethics of care is based on the belief that people are relational. People understand themselves in terms of their relationships. They do not seek to promote

---

[60] R. West, 'The Right to Care' in E. Feder Kittay and E. Feder (eds.) *The Subject of Care: Feminist Perspectives on Dependency* (Rowman & Littlefield, 2002), 89.

[61] V. Held, 'The Ethics of Care as Normative Guidance: Comment on Gilligan' (2014) 45 *Journal of Social Philosophy* 107.

[62] J. Herring, 'Compassion, Ethic of Care and Legal Rights' (2017) 13 *International Journal of Law in Context* 158.

only their own interests, not because they are 'selfless', but because their interests are tied up with the interests of others. They cannot seek to promote their own interests with no attention paid to others. If good things happen to those who they are in a positive relationship with then that is good for them.[63]

Care ethicists tend, therefore, to support the concept of the relational self discussed in Chapter 1.[64] In relationships of caring and dependency, interests become intermingled. We do not break down into 'me' and 'you'. As Virginia Held[65] puts it:

> Care should not be understood as self-sacrifice. Egoism versus altruism is the wrong way to interpret the issues. Yes, the interests of care giver and care receiver will sometimes conflict, but for the most part we do not pit our own interests against those of others in this context. We want what will be good for both or all of us together. We want our children and others we care for to do well along with ourselves, and for the relations between us to be good ones. If we are the recipients of care we want our care givers to do well along with us.

3.3.4 The Importance of Responsibilities

Ethics of care emphasise the importance of responsibilities within caring relationships.[66] Indeed, many care ethicists claim that responsibilities should be the primary ethical tool, with rights playing a subordinate role. The classic liberal perspective is that one is 'born free' and that any responsibilities one takes must be in some sense voluntarily assumed. However, for the ethics of care approach, with its starting point being that people are relational, then the supposition is that there will be responsibilities for others. We are born into relationships which carry responsibilities with them. So, the central legal or ethical question on a given issue should not be 'do I have a right to do X?'; the question should be 'what is my proper obligation within the context of this relationship?'[67] Under this vision, rights primarily exist to enable people to carry out their responsibilities.[68] And the role of the law should primarily be to encourage and enable people to fulfil their responsibilities to each other, rather than enforce their rights.

A good example of this is the debate over who should be responsible for a new-born child. While it is generally accepted that the responsibility should fall on parents, it is difficult to explain this in terms of choice. Gillian Douglas makes the best argument in favour of a choice-based approach:

---

[63] J. Downie and J. Llewellyn, *Being Relational* (UBC Press, 2011).
[64] C. Foster and J. Herring, *Identify, Personhood and the Law* (Springer, 2017).
[65] V. Held, 'Care and Human Rights' in R. Cruft, M. Liao and M. Renzo (eds.) *Philosophical Foundations of Human Rights* (Oxford University Press, 2015).
[66] Collins, *The Core of Care Ethics*.
[67] Held, *The Ethics of Care*.
[68] Herring, 'Compassion, Ethic of Care and Legal Rights', 158.

Willingly engaging in behavior that runs the risk of creating a child, or failing to terminate a pregnancy that will result in the birth of a child, who will inevitably be vulnerable and dependent, seems a valid moral basis for imposing the priori obligation to "take care of" that child . . . on the child's progenitors.[69]

Neither engaging in sex nor refusing to have an abortion appear to constitute acceptance of an obligation to take care of a child. More persuasive is the simple fact that the child has needs and there is an obligation on those best placed to provide the necessary care. John Eekelaar[70] explains why parents are best placed to do so:

It coincides with the wishes and instincts of most parents and will usually be well performed; it is linked to a bonding process which can be of great importance for the child's sense of identity; it allows the costs of childrearing to accrue incrementally, and marginally, to the costs of an adult household, and is therefore economically sufficient.

Care ethics, with its explanation that responsibilities emerge from our mutual vulnerability and basic needs, is far more effective than the traditional liberal choice paradigm in explaining the most basic obligation for parents to care for children.

3.3.5 The Importance of Non-Abstraction

One of the key aspects of care ethics is that an ethical analysis must start with the context and concrete reality of the particular situations and the individuals and their relationships and characteristics. It rejects the approach of many mainstream ethical approaches which seek to develop general rules that apply across all cases. Ethics of care argues that what might work for one group of people in one situation will not work in another. What will be defined as caring will depend on the particular individuals and the obligations they have. What will meet a person's needs cannot be generalised. To determine what a person needs cannot be resolved by a single person: they need to have a dialogue with the others about it and work together on the solution. That is why we cannot give an answer in advance to a particular dilemma. It is not, and should not simply be, a matter of our analysis.

3.3.6 Gender and an Ethics of Care

Carol Gilligan[71] is the leading pioneer of ethics of care thinking. In her 1980s writing she developed her approach as a response to the writing of

---

[69] G. Douglas, *Obligation and Commitment in Family Law* (Hart, 2019), 20.

[70] J. Eekelaar, 'Are Parents Morally Obliged to Care for Their Children?' (1991) 11 *Oxford Journal of Legal Studies* 340.

[71] C. Gilligan, *In a Different Voice: Psychological Theory and Women's Development* (Harvard University Press, 1982).

Lawrence Kohlberg, who had argued that universalised and principled thinking was the highest and most sophisticated moral analysis. Kohlberg found that a greater percentage of boys in his samples scored higher than girls. Gilligan's response to this was that the girls were speaking in a 'different voice', ethics of care as opposed to ethics of justice. Although she has sometimes been interpreted as suggesting that the ethics of care reflects a feminine voice, it seems her writing does not support the view that by that she means that women are more likely to adopt it than men. Certainly, nowadays few ethics of care supporters claim it represents a particularly female way of ethical analysis. For example, Nel Noddings's influential book *Caring* was subtitled *A Feminine Approach to Ethics and Moral Education* in its 1984 edition, but subtitled *A Relational Approach to Ethics and Moral Education* in its 2013 edition.

Care ethics has attracted considerable support among feminists, although it has supporters who do not explicitly adopt a feminist approach.[72] Its support among feminists can in part be explained by the fact that women undertake a significantly greater proportion of care work compared to men and the political, social and ethic neglect of this work results in disadvantages for women. Martha Fineman states, 'In the pattern of long-standing tradition, caretaking continues to be delegated to women – assigned as the responsibility of the person occupying the gendered role of wife, or mother, or grandmother, or daughter, or daughter-in-law or sister.'[73]

Before moving to explore the significance of care ethics, it is necessary to discuss an important critique of it: from disability studies.

3.4 The Disability Critique of Care Ethics

Ethics of care has received a strong challenge from some disability theorists.[74] To understand the nature of the challenge it is helpful to recall the hotly debated issue of the nature of disability, touched on in Chapter 1. There, it was explained that there are two contrasting models of disability: the individual model and the social model.[75] Under the individual model a disability is a difference in a person's body or mind that causes them to have impaired functioning, when compared to a 'normal person'. Under this model the cause of any disadvantage flowing from disability is the limited functional or psychological loss the individual is thought to suffer from. Under the social model, by contrast, the problems flowing from disability are society's failure

---

[72] M. Slote, *The Ethics of Care and Empathy* (Routledge, 2007).

[73] Fineman, *The Autonomy Myth*, 37.

[74] F. Williams, 'The Presence of Feminism in the Future of Welfare' (2002) 31 *Economy and Society* 502.

[75] T. Shakespeare, *Disability Rights and Wrongs* (Routledge, 2006).

to provide the necessary services to ensure no difficulties flow from the difference in function or psychology. Some commentators argue that we can combine the two theories to explain that some disadvantages are a result of a physical impairment but others result from a failure to make social provision. Myrian Winance[76] suggests we can:

> separate the deficiency (an individual biological characteristic) from the disability (a social reality, a position of exclusion defined in relation to the balance of power between people) ... Disability is a social difference piled on top of a natural specificity.

This debate between the social and individual models of disability is complex and has become intense. This chapter is not the place to explore all the issues properly.

The disability critique claims that the standard presentation of care plays into the individual model of disability. Presenting care as the meeting of needs appears to locate the 'problem' in the body of the disabled person, whose needs are met by the carer. In particular, it assumes a norm for bodies; disabled bodies depart from this norm, requiring care from an 'able bodied person' which can bring them back to the norm.

This becomes all the more problematic given that much writing on care, and particularly the organisations promoting the interests of carers, highlight the burdens and disadvantages that care work brings. This impliedly paints the disabled person as the cause of carers' disadvantage. Further, the ethics of care literature can overlook the dark side of care. The ethics of care literature certainly acknowledges that there can be abuse within caring relationships. Jenny Morris[77] has also argued that care itself is a form of oppression against disabled people:

> The only way to empower disabled people is to throw off the ideology of caring which is a form of oppression and an expression of prejudice. Empowerment means choice and control; it means that someone has the power to exert choice and therefore maximise control in their lives (always recognising that there are limits to how much control any of us have over what happens in our lives). Care – in the second half of the twentieth century – has come to mean not caring about someone but caring for in the sense of taking responsibility for. People who are said to need caring for are assumed to be unable to exert choice and control. One cannot, therefore, have care and empowerment, for it is the ideology and the practice of caring which has led to the perception of disabled people as powerless.

---

[76] M. Winance, 'Rethinking Disability: Lessons from the Past, Questions for the Future' (2016) 10 *European Journal of Disability Research* 99, 107.

[77] J. Morris, 'Care or Empowerment: A Disability Rights Perspective' (1997) 31 *Social Policy & Administration* 54, 64.

To similar effect, Richard Woods[78] contends:

> Disabled people have never demanded or asked for care! We have sought independent living, which means being able to achieve maximum independence and control over our own lives. The concept of care seems to many disabled people a tool through which others are able to dominate and manage our lives.

What these quotes capture is the way that 'caring for another' can readily amount to an exercise of power. The 'carer' identifies the need of the 'cared for' and then decides how to meet it. The carer is the active person and the 'cared for' is passive. Zygmunt Bauman[79] warns that 'the impulse to care for the other, when taken to its extreme, leads to the annihilation of the autonomy of the other, to domination and oppression'. There are horrific examples of this, as Christine Kelly[80] writes:

> In the name of 'caring for' individuals or society at large, disabled people have been subjected to multiple forms of oppression, including forced sterilization, painful and ineffective physical 'therapies', physical and emotional abuse, and of course, institutionalization.

Many writing from a disability study perspective have argued that we need to shift away from the notion of care, and towards attendant services. The shift in terminology from carer to attendant or assistant is that it makes it clear that the disabled person is the one who directs the services. Rather than being the passive recipient of care, they control, direct and utilise the service to achieve independence. This understanding it is said promotes empowerment, choice and control.

It must be a cause of some embarrassment to the ethics of care literature that most attention has been on those 'giving care'. Much is written in the care literature on the social isolation of carers; the personal and economic disadvantages of carers; and the lack of recognition that carers are given in society. This is all welcome and important, but in making such points those 'receiving' the care, and the disadvantages they face, have also been ignored. Further, there is the possibility that the abuse of care gets overlooked in the care literature.

However, I do not think the disability critique requires an abandonment of ethics of care. It does show that care needs to be used when discussing it. As mentioned earlier, I think it is crucial to see care as relational. That we cannot break down those involved into carers and cared for. This fails to capture the dynamic of a caring relationship. We are all givers and receivers of care. What we do is not understood as an 'activity' but a part of a fluid and complex relationship. The relationship gives what is done meaning and value. Our

---

[78] T. Shakespeare, *Help* (Venture Press, 2001).

[79] Z. Bauman, *Postmodern Ethics* (Blackwell, 1993), 11.

[80] C. Kelly, 'Making "Care" Accessible: Personal Assistance for Disabled People and the Politics of Language' (2011) 31 *Critical Social Policy* 562, 564.

universal and mutual vulnerability means we are all dependant on others for the care.

I would argue care ethics also provides arguments to be wary of adopting the personal assistant model to replace the concept of care. A core idea within the personal assistant model is that the disabled person directs what is done. Judy Heumann,[81] one of the founders of the Independent Living Movement, wrote: 'To us, independence does not mean doing things physically alone. It means being able to make independent decisions. It is a mind process not contingent upon a normal body.'

However, such an approach assumes an ability to make decisions and direct the services. It can only be plausible for some people with disability, perhaps the most articulate and vocal. For the profoundly disabled and those with intellectual challenges the responsibility of directing their care may be an impossibility or a burden.

Further, this approach adopts the language of individualist autonomy. It overlooks the essentially relational nature of autonomy, as discussed in Chapter 1. Most people, when making decisions about care, discuss the issues with their family members, carers and friends.[82] A dialogue about the best way to arrange care is empowering.[83] This language of making caring decisions jointly ensures that care is not provided uni-directionally and ensures the disabled person is not left to make the decision in an isolated environment.

In good caring relationships, the parties do not treat each other as objects but recognise each other as a fellow human being. The person providing services should not be seen simply as an 'assistant' who follows the direction of the disabled person. They should work together to find solutions to the issues they both face. This is important because good caring involves the parties recognising that each of them is a unique individual. This requires empathy and anticipation. Joan Tronto,[84] for example, has been clear that a central part of care is responsiveness: consideration of the position of others as they see it and responding in the way they want. It is not the doing of the job (as the term personal assistant might suggest) but working together at a task. Obviously, care provided with no thought to the response of the person receiving it is in danger of objectifying the person receiving the care. The relational model of care highlights how good care is a two-way interaction.

The personal assistant model oversimplifies the nature of caring relationships. In the UK, 27 per cent of carers were found in one study to be

---

[81] Cited in S. Stoddard, 'Independent Living: Concepts and Programs' (1978) 3 *American Rehabilitation* 2.

[82] C. Glendinning, W. Mitchell and J. Brooks, 'Ambiguity in Practice? Carers' Roles in Personalised Social Care in England' (2016) 19 *Sexualities* 959.

[83] S. Keyes, S. Webber and K. Beveridge, 'Empowerment through Care' (2015) 9 *European Journal of Disabilities Research* 236.

[84] Tronto, *Moral Boundaries*, 15.

themselves recipients of benefits on account of their disability.[85] As this shows, it is often impossible to separate the person needing care and the person receiving care. Kelly Fritsch[86] has provided a powerful practical example of how in caring relationships individual identities become merged. In her sensitive analysis of the use of carers or attendants to facilitate and enable sexual encounters for disabled people she shows how the line between bodies in these cases is complex. The carer and the cared for

> experience a leaking of their identities, a mingling of their sexualities, and multiple intimate slippages of selves as the attendant participates in the daily work of feeding, bathing, shopping, facilitating sex, and numerous other activities. In the interaction between a disabled person and an attendant, both bodies extend into one another, displacing the limits of their assumedly contained sovereign selves ... The emphasis, then, is placed not on what you can do for me but rather what we can create together.

Caring relationships are therefore far more complex than the carer/care for, disabled person/personal assistant models will allow. As Twigg[87] writes, care is better seen as a co-production: 'It is in the dynamics of the care encounter that the nature of what is produced is defined; production and consumption collapse into one another. [...] users and workers are co-producers of care.'

It might be claimed that this is idealised in cases where a person has a profound disability. But that is not the experience of those caring for such people. Eva Feder Kittay's daughter Sesha has cerebral palsy and has profound physical and intellectual impairment. However, Feder Kittay[88] writes that Sesha possesses:

> the most important faculties of all. The capacities for love and for happiness. These allow those of us who care for her, who love her, who have been entrusted with her well-being to form deep and abiding attachments to her. Sesha's coin and currency is love. That is what she wishes to receive and that is what she reciprocates in spades.

So, I believe that as long as care ethics emphasises the importance of care as a relationship, rather than care as a practice, it avoids the danger of enhancing inappropriate models of disability.

3.5 Care Ethics and the Law

While an ethic of care might be attractive to a philosopher, sociologist or professional seeking ethical guidance, is it helpful for lawyers? The argument

---

[85] NHS Information Centre, *Survey of Carers in Households* (NHS, 2015).

[86] K. Fritsch, 'Intimate Assemblages: Disability, Intercorporeality, and the Labour of Attendant Care' (2011) 1 *Critical Disabilities Discourse* 2.

[87] Twigg, 'Carework as a Form of Bodywork', 389, 392.

[88] E. Feder Kittay, 'Not My Way Sesha Your Way' in C. Mui and J. Murphy (eds.) *Gender Struggles: Practical Approaches to Contemporary Feminism* (Rowman & Littlefield, 2002), 100.

that it might not would go as follows. Law operates when people are in disagreement. Spouses only need lawyers when their relationship breaks down. People only go to court when their relational tools cannot provide a solution. Is not an approach based on promoting caring relations particularly inappropriate in a legal system which is trying to resolve disputes between people whose relationship has broken down?

This kind of concern has even been recognised by Virginia Held,[89] who suggests the analogy of friends engaged in a competitive game:

> When they play tennis, each tires above all to win, limited only by what the fair rules of the game require. If this approach were generalized to the whole of their relation, they would no longer be genuine friends, though it is suitable for limited interactions. Analogously, persons should be tied together as caring members of the same society, yet can agree to treat their limited legal interactions in ways that give priority to justice. When justice should then prevail in certain contexts, it need not oppose or cancel the care in which legal systems should be built.[90]

This seems to suggest that while an ethic of care can operate when relationships are working well, there needs to be a more abstract 'ethic of justice' to provide for rules to apply when the couple cannot agree.

I do not agree with Held's analysis on this issue. Law can have an influence far beyond the cases that come to court. To take a trivial example, the law on illegal parking impacts on a far larger range of people than simply those who receive parking fines. To take a more serious issue, the law on who can marry sends powerful messages to society about what kinds of relationships are approved of and why. Hence the intense debate over same-sex marriage. Legal regulations and the messages from them force or nudge people in various ways. They provide generalised guidance as to how people arrange their interactions. Court cases are but a small part of how the law operates. Law can therefore be used powerfully to encourage people to act in a way which will promote caring relationships.

One example would be contract law. It is rare that people come to court following a breach of contract. But it is, in part, a testament to the effectiveness of contract law. Contract law provides a mechanism for people to enter contractual relationships and to give weight to the obligations created as a result. A legal, political and social system structured around an ethic of care would hope to see few cases reaching court. However, it would still have a powerful influence on how people behave.

Law can also operate to control or require state intervention to enable (or indeed discourage) caring relationships. The response of the state to caring relationships through financial and social support can have a significant

---

[89] V. Held, 'Can the Ethics of Care Handle Violence?' (2010) 4 *Ethics and Social Welfare* 115.
[90] Ibid., 115, 117.

impact on them. We can design our state support mechanisms to encourage or discourage care; to reward or ignore it. We shall be returning to this issue shortly.

A final point is that it is wrong to assume that all people coming to court have relationships that have come to an end. Many cases involve people in ongoing relationships, such as family cases involving children and separated parents. Even if that is not so, the legal remedies that are sought in many cases are designed to move people on from where they are to find new caring relationships.

3.6 State Support of Care

Traditionally, the state's primary role was to regulate the public areas of life: commercial dealings; crime and disorder on the street; protection of property; and the like. Behind the closed curtains of the house or private institution, the Government was not to peep. Hence care work was seen as not appropriate for state intervention, in part because it was seen as insufficiently important but also because it was an improper interference in family life. The *pater familias*, the 'father figure', was the person who controlled that area and the state should not undermine his proper role by seeking to interfere in his dominion.[91]

Of course, this public–private divide has been much debated and few commentators would support the straightforward presentation of it just given.[92] Even if the divide is recognised, the notion of non-intervention in the private sphere is highly problematic.[93] The precise way the state arranges welfare, tax and educational policies can all encourage or discourage certain 'private' caring practices. It is impossible for the state to take a neutral stance towards forms of caring.

It is clear now that the provision of care should be an issue of considerable public concern.[94] As Martha Fineman[95] argues 'Caretakers should have the . . . right to have their society preserving labor supported and facilitated. Provision of the means for their task should be considered the responsibility of the collective society.' The state response to it, however, must be considered alongside a range of other developments in society.

[91] S. Fredman, *Women and the Law* (Oxford University Press, 1998).
[92] See e.g. S. Okin, *Justice Gender and the Family* (Basic Books, 1991); R. Gavison, 'Feminism and the Public Private Distinction' (1992) 45 *Stanford Law* 1.
[93] F. Olsen, 'Feminist Critiques of the Public/Private Distinction' (1993) 10 *Constitutional Commentary* 319.
[94] M. Fine, *A Caring Society? Care and the Dilemmas of Human Service in the 21st Century* (Palgrave, 2007); C. Glendinning and D. Bell, *Rethinking Social Care and Support: What Can England Learn from the Experiences of Other Countries?* (Joseph Rowntree, 2008).
[95] Fineman, *The Autonomy Myth*, 49.

First, there has been a move away from state-provided care. Most prominent is the move towards 'community care'.[96] In part, this move is motivated by the recognition of the unsatisfactory nature of institutional care, with concerns about abuse in large-scale institutional settings, still very much present today. It is also motivated by a desire to promote the well-being of those needing care. A more cynical view will see community care as an attempt to shift the financial burden of care from the state to family members. To the cynics, the state was abandoning vulnerable people in the community, rather than ensuring their care.[97] There are a sufficient number of reports of horrific abuse of those in the community to raise concerns.[98]

A second issue has been the rise of feminism and a widespread acceptance, even among those who do not buy into the whole feminist agenda, that we should remove sources of disadvantage for women. The lack of pay or recognition for much care is now generally recognised as a significant source of disadvantage for women.[99]

A third issue has been the move to increase economic productivity among all members of society. In recent years governments have attacked 'the dependency culture'. No one is entitled to rely on state support. Everyone is expected to at least attempt to become economically self-sufficient. Former Prime Minister David Cameron explained:

> We've got to recognise that in the end, the only thing that really beats poverty, long-term, is work. We cannot emphasise this enough. Compassion isn't measured out in benefit cheques – it's in the chances you give people . . . the chance to get a job, to get on, to get that sense of achievement that only comes from doing a hard day's work for a proper day's pay.[100]

This thinking has led to attempts to encourage parents, the disabled and those with caring responsibilities to all be involved in economic work, if possible. Interestingly, in the context of parents, that has meant the state has been willing to assist in the cost of child care in order to enable parents to work.[101] Of course, promoting employment as the way out of poverty for disadvantaged groups can be seen as a way for the Government to avoid its responsibilities in seeking to tackle social inequality.

Fourth, within political debates the concept of social exclusion has become a major one.[102] The EU Employment and Social Affairs Directorate defines social exclusion as 'The development of capacity and opportunity to

---

[96] Daly and Lewis, 'The Concept of Social Care and the Analysis of Contemporary Welfare', 51.
[97] Ibid.
[98] Mencap, *Pair Jailed for Murder of Vulnerable Man* (Mencap, 2010).
[99] Daly and Lewis, 'The Concept of Social Care and the Analysis of Contemporary Welfare', 51.
[100] D. Cameron, Speech at Bluewater, Kent, 25 June 2012, www.telegraph.co.uk/news/politics/david-cameron/9354163/David-Camerons-welfare-speech-in-full.html [accessed 1 February 2019].
[101] Daly and Lewis, 'The Concept of Social Care and the Analysis of Contemporary Welfare', 51.
[102] L. Kessler, 'Getting Class' (2008) 56 *Buffalo Law Review* 91.

play a full role, not only in economic terms, but also in social, psycho-logical and political terms.'[103] The term captures the idea that groups of people may not only suffer poverty but also lack the opportunity to access social, psychological and political benefits. Caring can certainly bring with it social exclusion.

Fifth, the major political focus on 'austerity' and 'deficit cutting' clearly impacts on responses to care, but not in a straightforward way. In so far as support for carers can help people whose care might otherwise fall fully on the state, or prevent carers giving up on care, expenditure on support for care may be seen as a long-term gain. Yet for local authorities seeking to cut budgets, the care budget is a natural target. In the longer term, the increasing role of women in paid work and changing demographics mean the larger economic issues surrounding care are going to be of increasing significance.[104]

Into this maelstrom of changing attitudes and forces is the simple point that caring is required to meet the basic needs of people and someone must be involved in the caring. And caring often carries costs. That cost must be borne by someone. Currently, that largely falls on individuals within those relationships. But if people stop caring, through choice or economic need, that burden would fall on the state. If the state, through a relatively low level of payment, can ensure carers keep caring and/or that people are not deterred from caring, then the payments can be said to make much economic sense.[105] By supplying sufficient economic and support services to maintain care levels, the Government would in fact be saving significant sums of money.[106]

The argument is not just that carers are saving the Government money, but rather that carers are undertaking a job on behalf of society that is a core obligation of a decent society. If so, it is only fair that their work be recognised. Martha Fineman argues that there is a social duty to compensate carers as a result of their social contribution:

> If infants or ill persons are not cared for, nurtured, nourished, and perhaps loved, they will perish. We can say, therefore, that they owe an individual debt to their individual caretakers. But the obligation is not theirs alone – nor is their obligation confined only to their own caretakers. A sense of social justice demands a broader sense of obligation. Without aggregate caretaking, there could be no society, so we might say that it is caretaking labour that produces and reproduces society. Caretaking labour provides the citizens, the workers, the voters, the consumers, the students, and others who populate society and its

[103] EU Employment and Social Affairs Directorate, *Social Exclusion* (European Union, 2012).
[104] Daly and Lewis, 'The Concept of Social Care and the Analysis of Contemporary Welfare', 51.
[105] L. Lloyd, 'Call Us Carers: Limitations and Risks in Campaigning for Recognition and Exclusivity' (2006) 26 *Critical Social Policy* 945.
[106] S. Himmelweit and H. Land, *Reducing Gender Inequalities to Create a Sustainable Care* (Joseph Rowntree Foundation, 2008).

institutions. The uncompensated labour of caretakers is an unrecognized subsidy, not only to individuals who directly receive it, but more significantly, to the entire society.[107]

Further, the state clearly has an interest in promoting gender equality.[108] As we saw in Chapter 2, the majority of care work is undertaken by women. In particular, the economic costs of care are largely borne by women. The state, therefore, has an interest in ensuring that the costs of care are fairly shared. As Susan Himmelweit and Hilary Land argue:

> The level of public expenditure on care is therefore a gender issue, since women have greater care needs than men and fewer resources to meet them. Inadequate funding also affects women in the paid care workforce and, when paid care is not forthcoming, as those more likely to end up providing unpaid care. Thus, inadequate spending on care is effectively a transfer of resources (unpaid labour) from women to relieve taxpayers, disproportionately men, of their responsibilities to provide for the most vulnerable citizens.[109]

Many of the claims made so far can be brought together in a central moral claim that caring itself should be seen as a central value and practice for any state. Selma Sevenhuijsen argues: 'It is argued that care should be seen as a democratic practice, and that democratic citizenship supposes that everybody would be guaranteed equal access to the giving and receiving of care.'[110]

Seeing caring as a central aspect of citizenship and an essential part of a democracy is very helpful. Sevenhuijsen goes on to explain how this radically changes the approach the state takes to responsibilities:

> An ethics of care implies a radically different argument on the relationship between morality and politics, and thus about responsibility and obligation. Because it starts from a relational ontology, it focuses primarily on the question of what politics could mean for the safeguarding of responsibility and relationship in human interactions. A relational approach would start from the idea that policy-making needs elaborated insights into the way individuals frame their responsibilities in the context of actual social practices and how they handle the moral dilemmas that go with the conflicting responsibilities of care for self, others, and the relationship between them.[111]

The fact, however, that care is valuable to the state does not mean that the state necessarily needs to support it. There are plenty of activities that the state does

---

[107] M. Fineman, 'Cracking the Foundational Myths: Independence, Autonomy and Self-Sufficiency' (2000) 8 *American University Journal of Gender, Social Policy and Law* 12.

[108] M. Case, 'Feminist Fundamentalism at the Intersection of Government and Familial Responsibility for Children' in C. Lind, H. Keating and J. Bridgeman (eds.) *Taking Responsibility, Law and the Changing Family* (Ashgate, 2011).

[109] Himmelweit and Land, *Reducing Gender Inequalities to Create a Sustainable Care*.

[110] S. Sevenhuijsen, 'Caring in the Third Way: The Relation between Obligation, Responsibility and Care in *Third Way* Discourse' (2000) 20 *Critical Social Policy* 5.

[111] Ibid., 18.

not support despite their social value. Susan Himmelweit gives some powerful reasons why the state should not simply leave care alone:

> Without intervention people may be less willing and able to fulfil caring norms, which may thereby be eroded. Those who assume caring responsibilities despite such pressures will pay a higher price for doing so and may have less influence on policy than those conforming more to increasingly less caring dominant norms. Not to adopt a generous strategy for caring now will shift power away from those who continue to care, erode caring norms, and make it more difficult to adopt a more caring strategy in the future. Without such a strategy, standards and availability of care will fall with high cost to society as a whole and fall particularly heavily on those who continue to care.[112]

One of the great benefits of this approach is that it moves away from the idea that care work is some kind of optional extra that especially good people undertake. Rather, it sees care as a central aspect of citizenship. It is not performing care work that is seen as surprising. If care work is a taken for granted responsibility for citizens then all aspects of society need to be reworked around that responsibility to ensure it can be done.

So support by the state for care can be justified in terms of economics, justice and gender discrimination. Looking at it another way, as Joan Tronto argues, the distribution of care is an exercise of power:

> Relatively more powerful people in society have a lot at stake in seeing that their caring needs are met under conditions that are beneficial to them, even if this means that the caring needs of those who provide them with services are neglected. More powerful people can fob caregiving work on to others: men to women, upper to lower class, free men to slaves. Care work itself is often demanding and inflexible, and not all of it is productive. People who do such work recognize its intrinsic value, but it does not fit well in a society that values innovation and accumulation of wealth.[113]

The distribution of care work and the costs associated with it are of fundamental importance to society, yet they receive inadequate attention. Care ethics shows it should be a major political and ethical issue.

3.7 Conclusion

In the first three chapters I have made an argument that we should understand ourselves as profoundly relational: that we are all vulnerable and need to be in caring relationships that meet our needs. How is law and our society to respond. Elsewhere I have imagined two societies. The first is a society that reflects the values promoted in this book:

---

[112] S. Himmelweit, *Can We Afford (not) to Care: Prospects and Policy* (Open University, 2005). See also D. Bubeck, *Care, Gender and Justice* (Oxford University Press, 1995), 243–244.

[113] J. Tronto, 'The Value of Care', *Boston Review*, 6 February 2002.

Imagine a society where care is central. Where its primary purpose is to care for those who are dependent on others to meet their needs. Where all activities are assessed on what they contribute to the care of others. Economic productivity would be valued in so far as it produces what is needed to support care and in so far as it is consistent with care. Those with needs would be recognised for all they contribute and would not be seen as an expensive burden. Employees would be expected to combine their employment with meeting their caring responsibilities. Workplaces would expect workers to have caring responsibilities and so have flexible hours of work and leave, and would encourage working from home where possible. The work of women and men would be valued equally. It would be a society with a low GDP compared with others no doubt. But one where older people were left with a decent standard of life; disabled people were empowered through caring relationships to live the lives they wish; and where children spend more time with people caring for them, than with characters on computer games.[114]

The second is a society which you might think describes our current position:

Imagine a society in which the generation of wealth is the primary goal. Where success is measured solely by income. Children are left uncared for by parents obsessed with generating more income. Older people are left in squalid conditions, provided with the minimum level of care by the lowest paid workers. Those who could not face leaving their parents or children in these dire situations and undertook care themselves are left in poverty and social exclusion. Exhaustion, loneliness and hardship are the order of the day for these carers, even if cheered by the rewards of the caring itself. Women who undertake the majority of care and make up the larger portion of older people suffer significantly more than men. The ever increasing number of older people is seen as a nightmare scenario, a route to catastrophe, rather than a cause for celebration. Disabled people are viewed as a burden and inconvenience. A society in which the highest court in the land accepts that someone would have to wear incontinence pads and spend the night soaked in urine and excreta because it is too expensive to provide a night time carer.[115] Any suggestion that her human rights were breached are brushed aside because doing so was justified by the difficulties in funding care.[116]

This chapter has sought to emphasise that we need to move towards that first model of society: that puts care at its heart. We need to use care ethics to provide insights into the legal and ethical challenges that we face. That is valuable too in the next topic we will examine: abuse within intimate relationships.

---

[114] Herring, *Caring and the Law*, 319.
[115] *R(Macdonald)* v. *Kensington and Chelsea* [2011] UKSC 33.
[116] Herring, *Caring and the Law*, 319–320.

4

Law and the Abused Self

4.1 Introduction

In this chapter I will explore the law's response to abuse.[1] I will argue that the gravity of intimate relationship abuse can only be appreciated once the relational understanding of the self is adopted. For a long time, domestic abuse was regarded as not as serious as abuse in the street. "Only a domestic" was a common term in policing.[2] Much work among feminist writers has been done to ensure that domestic violence is taken as seriously as other assaults. In this chapter I will argue that we need to broaden our understanding of domestic abuse and use the terminology of intimate abuse. This will capture the idea that we are looking at relational abuse. Once understood in this way, the true gravity of intimate abuse can be understood. Before exploring the significance of relational abuse I will start by setting out some of the statistics. These tend to be gathered under the more standard terminology of domestic abuse.

4.2 Statistics

The statistics indicate that for many families domestic violence is a commonplace part of life. The World Health Organization reports:[3]

- ... about 1 in 3 (35%) women worldwide have experienced either physical and/or sexual intimate partner violence or non-partner sexual violence in their lifetime.
- Most of this violence is intimate partner violence. Worldwide, almost one third (30%) of women who have been in a relationship report that they have experienced some form of physical and/or sexual violence by their intimate partner in their lifetime.

---

[1] I draw on J. Herring, 'The Serious Wrong of Domestic Abuse and the Loss of Control Defence' in A. Reed and M. Bohlander (eds.) *Loss of Control and Diminished Responsibility* (Ashgate, 2011), 65.

[2] Staffordshire's Women's Aid, *Myths and Stereotypes* (Staffordshire's Women's Aid, 2018).

[3] WHO, *Violence against Women* (WHO, 2017).

- Globally, as many as 38% of murders of women are committed by a male intimate partner.

The United Nations[4] cite the figure of 35 per cent of women having experienced physical and/or sexual intimate partner violence or sexual violence. However, they note that some individual countries have up to 70 per cent of women suffering physical and/or sexual abuse from a partner. It has been estimated that worldwide half of all women who were killed were killed by intimate partners or family relatives.[5] The studies quoted so far related to physical and/or sexual violence. If psychological abuse is included, clearly a higher figure will be found. A study of twenty-eight EU member states[6] found that 43 per cent of women had experienced psychological violence at the hands of an intimate partner. The survey of women in the EU found that:

- One in three women (33 %) has experienced physical and/or sexual violence since she was 15 years old.
- Some 8 % of women have experienced physical and/or sexual violence in the 12 months before the survey interview.
- Out of all women who have a (current or previous) partner, 22 % have experienced physical and/or sexual violence by a partner since the age of 15.[7]

In the UK, it is estimated that 31 per cent of women and 18 per cent of men have experienced some form of domestic abuse since the age of sixteen. These figures were equivalent to an estimated 5 million female victims of domestic abuse and 2.9 million male victims between the ages of sixteen and fifty-nine.[8] An incident of killing, stabbing or beating takes place on average every six minutes in a home in Britain.[9] A recent survey of disadvantaged youth found over half of girls reported being the victim of physical violence from their partners.[10] There is a strong link between suffering domestic abuse and suicide, with 24 per cent of one refuge's clients feeling suicidal and over 3 per cent attempting suicide.[11]

It seems sadly true that, as Anthony Giddens has claimed,

> The home is, in fact, the most dangerous place in modern society. In statistical terms, a person of any age or of either sex is far more likely to be subject to physical attack in the home than on the street at night.[12]

---

[4] UN Women, *Facts and Figures: Ending Violence against Women* (United Nations, 2017).

[5] Ibid.

[6] European Union Agency for Fundamental Rights, *Violence against Women: An EU-wide Survey* (European Union, 2014), 71.

[7] Ibid.

[8] A. Dar, *Domestic Violence Statistics* (House of Commons Library, 2013).

[9] Ibid.

[10] M. Wood, C. Barter and D. Berridge, *'Standing on My Own Two Feet': Disadvantaged Teenagers, Intimate Partner Violence and Coercive Control* (NSPCC, 2011).

[11] R. Aitken and V. Munro, *Domestic Abuse and Suicide* (Refuge and Warwick Law School, 2018).

[12] A. Giddens, *A Sociology* (Polity Press, 1989).

4.3 Defining Intimate Abuse

The definition of abuse within the context of domestic relationships has proved controversial. The language used has varied from the old-fashioned 'wife beating' to the more contemporary 'domestic abuse'. As mentioned in the introduction to this chapter, I will advocate for the terminology of intimate abuse to make it clear we are discussing abuse between those in an intimate relationship, and that is not restricted to those living together. To give a background for my argument, I will summarise some of the main definitions of domestic abuse that have been used in the literature.

4.3.1 International Definitions

The WHO uses the term 'intimate partner violence' rather than domestic abuse. It defines this as:

> Behaviour by an intimate partner that causes physical, sexual or psychological harm, including acts of physical aggression, sexual coercion, psychological abuse and controlling behaviours.[13]

This definition focuses on the effect of the behaviour. By contrast, Article 3 of the Istanbul Convention defines domestic violence in this way:[14]

> all acts of physical, sexual, psychological or economic violence that occur within the family or domestic unit or between former or current spouses or partners, whether or not the perpetrator shares or has shared the same residence with the victim.

The Council of Europe uses a more extended definition of violence:[15]

> Domestic violence is one of the most serious and pervasive forms of violence against women. It exists in all Council of Europe member states and occurs at all levels of society. Domestic violence is most often perpetrated by men against former or current intimate partners, although it is recognised that violence is also perpetrated by women and occurs in same-sex relationships.

> Violence is used to exert power and control over another individual. Domestic violence typically comprises abusive and coercive behaviour such as physical, psychological or sexual abuse. A common pattern of domestic violence often starts with intimidation, humiliation and threatening behaviour, including threats of self-inflicted pain. Violence is reinforced by establishing control over another person's life through isolation, manipulation and by placing limits on personal choices and freedoms. A typical pattern of violence may also involve economic abuse by denying financial independence and controlling economic

---

[13] World Health Organization, *Responding to Intimate Partner Violence and Sexual Violence against Women: WHO Clinical and Policy Guidelines* (World Health Organization, 2013).
[14] Council of Europe, *Convention on Preventing and Combating Violence against Women and Domestic Violence* (The Istanbul Convention) (Council of Europe, 2011), 11.V.2011.
[15] Council of Europe, *Stop Domestic Violence* (Council of Europe, 2017), 2.

decisions. Violent behaviour of this sort can never be considered a series of unconnected events as actual physical violence is often the end result of months or years of intimidation and control.

Domestic violence needs to be understood in a wider social context which permits the perpetrators to assume the right to use violence as a means of exercising dominance and control. As it is mainly perpetrated against women because they are women, it constitutes a form of gender-based violence. If not addressed adequately, it constitutes a violation of women's human rights.

This definition puts it in an explicitly broader context. It is in line with the view that domestic violence must be understood in the context of violence against women. The European Commission generally prefers to use the language of violence against women.[16] It defines this as:

violence directed against a person because of that person's gender (including gender identity/expression) or as violence that affects persons of a particular gender disproportionately. Women and girls, of all ages and backgrounds, are most affected by gender-based violence. It can be physical, sexual and/or psychological, and includes:

- Violence in close relationships;
- Sexual violence (including rape, sexual assault and harassment or stalking);
- Slavery;
- Harmful practices, such as forced marriages, female genital mutilation (FGM) and so-called 'honour' crimes;
- Cyberviolence and harassment using new technologies.

4.3.2 UK Governmental Definitions

The definition of domestic violence used by the UK government has varied over time.

In the Legal Aid, Sentencing and Punishment of Offenders Act 2012, the following definition of domestic violence is used for the purposes of that statute:

domestic violence means any incident, or pattern of incidents, of controlling, coercive or threatening behaviour, violence or abuse (whether psychological, physical, sexual, financial or emotional) between individuals who are associated with each other.[17]

Recently, the government has produced the Domestic Abuse Bill 2019, which defines domestic abuse in this way in clause one:

---

[16] Council of Europe, Convention on Preventing and Combating Violence against Women and Domestic Violence.

[17] Legal Aid, Sentencing and Punishment of Offenders Act 2012, Sch 1, para 12(9).

(2) Behaviour by a person ("A") towards another person ("B") is "domestic abuse" if –
  (a) A and B are each aged 16 or over and are personally connected, and
  (b) the behaviour is abusive.

(3) Behaviour is "abusive" if it consists of any of the following –
  (a) physical or sexual abuse;
  (b) violent or threatening behaviour;
  (c) controlling or coercive behaviour;
  (d) economic abuse (see subsection (4));
  (e) psychological, emotional or other abuse.

(4) "Economic abuse" means any behaviour that has a substantial adverse effect on B's ability to –
  (a) acquire, use or maintain money or other property, or
  (b) obtain goods or services.

(5) For the purposes of this Act A's behaviour may be behaviour "towards" B despite the fact that it consists of conduct directed at another person (for example, B's child).

  . . .

2 Definition of "personally connected"
(1) Two people are "personally connected" if any of the following applies –
  (a) they are, or have been, married to each other;
  (b) they are, or have been, civil partners of each other;
  (c) they have agreed to marry one another (whether or not the agreement has been terminated);
  (d) they have entered into a civil partnership agreement (whether or not the agreement has been terminated);
  (e) they are, or have been, in an intimate personal relationship with each other;
  (f) there is a child in relation to whom they each have a parental relationship (see subsection (2));
  (g) they are relatives.

(2) For the purposes of subsection (1)(f) a person has a parental relationship in relation to a child if –
  (a) the person is a parent of the child, or
  (b) the person has, or has had, parental responsibility for the child.

(3) In this section –
  "child" means a person under the age of 18 years;
  "civil partnership agreement" has the meaning given by section 73 of the Civil Partnership Act 2004;
  "parental responsibility" has the same meaning as in the Children Act 1989;
  "relative" has the meaning given by section 63(1) of the Family Law Act 1996

4.3.3 Discussions of Domestic Violence Definitions

As will be clear, there is no consistent view over the definition of domestic abuse. A consideration of these certainly reveals some key questions for anyone seeking to produce a definition:

1. Should domestic abuse be limited to physical attacks or should it include non-physical abuse, such as emotional or financial abuse?[18]
2. To what extent should domestic abuse be understood as a single incident or to what extent a relationship of abuse?
3. Should domestic abuse be limited to cases where people live together in marriage or marriage-like relationships?
4. Should domestic abuse be understood in a gendered way or is gender not particularly relevant to domestic abuse?

We will explore these questions as the chapter develops.

4.4 Developing a Definition

I am not convinced that a definition of domestic abuse is helpful per se. The phenomenon is complex and involves the interaction of a range of factors. Drawing a sharp line between what is and is not domestic abuse is likely to create artificial distinctions. The kind of approach that is most helpful to producing a clearer understanding is the seminal work of Michelle Madden Dempsey on the definition of domestic abuse.[19] She developed a sophisticated analysis which draws on the intersection of three concepts:

- violence;
- domesticity; and
- patriarchy.

She separates out thirteen different ways in which these concepts could intersect (violence and domesticity, but no patriarchy; violence and patriarchy, but no domesticity and so forth). She argues that it is only at the intersection of the three concepts that we have 'domestic violence in the strong sense': '[A] violent act occurring in a domestic context, which tends to sustain or perpetuate patriarchy and is, all things considered, unjustified.'[20] Other intersections of the concepts can amount to domestic violence, but only in the weak sense. For example:

---

[18] *Yemshaw* v. *London Borough of Hounslow* [2011] UKSC 3, discussed in R. Ekins, 'Updating the Meaning of Violence' (2013) 129 *Law Quarterly Review* 17.

[19] M. Madden Dempsey, *Prosecuting Domestic Violence* (Oxford University Press, 2009).

[20] Ibid., 209.

[A] violent act occurring in a domestic context, which does not tend to sustain or perpetuate patriarchy but is, all things considered, unjustified. I will refer to this concept as 'domestic violence in its weak sense'.[21]

It is important to note here that she is not claiming that violence in the home which does not sustain or perpetuate patriarchy is not domestic violence, but that it is only so in a 'weaker sense'. She explains the significance of this distinction in later writing:

when a prosecutor is faced with two sets of cases that are otherwise identical in all salient respects (that is, other things being equal), there is an important value to be realized in targeting cases of domestic violence in its strong sense for aggressive prosecution and, in comparison, declining to target cases of domestic violence in its weak sense for equally aggressive prosecution.[22]

This is not, therefore, an argument that cases outside the 'strong sense' of domestic abuse are not domestic abuse or that they should not be taken seriously or have resources devoted to them. It is rather a claim that there is a particular wrong in strong domestic violence cases (namely the sustenance and perpetuation of patriarchy) that is not present in other cases.

Slightly amending the kind of approach Madden Dempsey uses, I would advocate using the intersection of these three categories:

- A controlling relationship
- Intimacy
- Structural inequality.

So, I use the concept of a controlling relationship in place of Madden Dempsey's terminology of violence; intimacy of relationship in place of domesticity; and structural inequality in place of patriarchy.[23]

I use these three concepts as the features of intimate abuse in a similar way to Madden Dempsey: not as requirements that must be met to fall within the definition, but rather as indicators of intimate abuse.

As well as slightly changing the terminology that Madden Dempsey uses, I will not use her distinction between strong and weak senses of domestic violence. She developed that in the context of police prosecution policies and it may be rather crude as a device for more general analysis.

In developing and explaining these concepts, I have very much had in mind the wrongs which are particular to intimate abuse. This approach is based on the argument that an act of domestic abuse can be understood as a wrong for

---

[21] Ibid., 211. Other combinations do not amount to domestic violence in any sense: e.g. an act which is violent but outside the domestic context.

[22] M. Madden Dempsey, 'Response to Commentators' (2014) 8 *Criminal Law and Philosophy* 557, 559.

[23] In fact, a careful reading of Madden Dempsey's writing suggests she would not be unsympathetic to this change in terminology.

reasons unconnected with its relational or broader context. Hitting someone is a wrong for reasons connected with rights to bodily integrity. Here I will focus on four particular wrongs that make acts within the context of intimate pattern abuse particularly wrong. All of these are best understood within the context of the relational self. So in seeking to start with the particular wrongs of intimate abuse, this enables us to find a definition of the concept and develop some strategies to combat it.

4.4.1 Intimate Abuse as 'Coercive Control'

The law typically assesses the harms done to a victim in terms of the physical injury that is caused by the defendant.[24] We teach criminal law students to consider whether the injury caused is a battery, actual bodily harm, wounding or grievous bodily harm. This will require them to consider to what extent the injuries impacted on the body of the victim, for example, whether there was a breaking of the skin. Yet, the assessment of the severity of the harm by focusing on the extent of bodily impact at a particular moment in time is a narrow construction of harm. This abstracting of the injury avoids an assessment of the severity of the attack in the overall context of the relationship between the parties and the life of the victim and of the broader social context within which the act is done.

It is crucial to understand intimate abuse as a relational wrong. It must be seen, therefore, as a pattern of behaviour, rather than a single incident. At its heart, intimate abuse is about controlling the other person and this can be done through a range of behaviours, including, but not limited to, physical attacks. The result is to produce a relationship where one party has control over another. Evan Stark, a leading commentator on coercive control, defines it as:

> a course of calculated, malevolent conduct deployed almost exclusively by men to dominate individual women by interweaving repeated physical abuse with three equally important tactics: intimidation, isolation and control.[25]

He goes on to explain:

> most abused women have been subjected to a pattern of sexual mastery that includes tactics to isolate, degrade, exploit, and control them as well as to frighten them or hurt them physically . . . These tactics include forms of constraint and the monitoring and/or regulation of commonplace activities of daily living, particularly those associated with women's default roles as mothers, homemakers, and sexual partners, and run the gamut from their access to money, food, and transport to how they dress, clean, cook, or perform sexually.[26]

---

[24] See Chapter 7 for further discussion.
[25] E. Stark, *Coercive Control* (Oxford University Press, 2007).
[26] Ibid.

The coercive control model of domestic violence is, then, different from the common image of domestic abuse involving a man hitting his partner. It claims the nature of the wrong cannot be captured by a description of a particular act, but must be understood in its relational context, specifically in terms of whether it is a relationship marked by coercion and control.

The fact that an incident of violence has taken place may be of limited use unless it is put in the context of the relationship between the parties. Michael Johnson[27] distinguishes three kinds of cases in which a violent incident has taken place: patriarchal terrorism, 'situational couple violence' or 'mutual violence'. Patriarchal terrorism is, he explains, 'violence enacted in the service of taking general control over one's partner'. By contrast, in the situational couple violence or mutual violence case, there is violence but there is no attempt to control the relationship. Rather, there is an incident of violence that arises in a moment of conflict during an intimate relationship which is not generally marked with inequality. Situational couple violence is the term he uses to refer to a single incident of violence that is explained solely by a particular context (e.g. a moment of high stress), and does not reveal a relationship that is otherwise marked by inequality. Mutual violence he describes as where the couple are equally violent to each other. These latter two categories include lashing out in self-defence, anger or frustration, rather than an attempt to exercise control. As this distinction shows, it is not whether or not there is violence which matters, so much as whether there is a pattern of coercive control. As psychologist Mary Ann Dutton explains:

> Abusive behaviour does not occur as a series of discrete events. Although a set of discrete abusive incidents can typically be identified within an abusive relationship, an understanding of the dynamic of power and control within an intimate relationship goes beyond these discrete incidents. To negate the impact of the time period between discrete episodes of serious violence – a time period during which the woman may never know when the next incident will occur, and may continue to live with on-going psychological abuse – is to fail to recognize what some battered woman experience as a continuing "state of siege."[28]

The abuser may use a broad range of tools to control their partner. The tactics used may vary and depend on what will be most effective to gain control over the victim. Evan Stark and Marianne Hester[29] note that:

> Control tactics endorsed by women in international surveys range from the constraints partners place on their time, spending, socializing, dieting, or other

---

[27] M. Johnson, 'Apples and Oranges in Child Custody Disputes: Intimate Terrorism vs. Situational Couple Violence' (2005) 2 *Journal of Child Custody* 43.

[28] M. Dutton, 'Understanding Women's Response to Domestic Violence' (2003) 21 *Hofstra Law Review* 1191, 1204.

[29] E. Stark and M. Hester, 'Coercive Control: Update and Review' (2019) 25 *Violence against Women* 81.

facets of everyday living to the psychological or "gaslight games" used to "make me feel crazy."

An important tactic to add to that list is the use of disputes over child contact, and behaviour during child contact as a tool to continue control even after the relationship has broken down.[30]

A central aspect of coercive control can be to undermine the self-worth of the victim by emotional abuse; isolation from friends; controlling access to employment.[31] This facilitates control over the victim. Mary Ann Dutton and Lisa Goodman list nine areas of life which can be subject to control: 'personal activities/appearance', 'support/social life/family', 'household', 'work/economic/resources', 'health', 'intimate relationship' 'legal', 'immigration' and 'children'.[32] In one study of men arrested for domestic violence, 38 per cent admitted preventing partners freely coming and going in their daily routine and 59 per cent had denied partners access to money or resources.[33] In another study, in a third of cases involving domestic violence the man had sought to prevent the woman from working and in half taken steps to ensure she remained at home looking after children.[34] Bridget Harris and Delanie Woodlock[35] record the use of technology and social media to control victims and propose the phrase 'digital coercive control'. Delanie Woodlock explains that the use of this can create a 'sense of the perpetrator's omnipresence'.[36]

A powerful example of the extent of domestic violence can be found in this case:

> Mark restricts Vanessa's access to money and employment. At home, Mark keeps all household supplies and toiletries under lock and key. If Vanessa or her three children need anything they must prove it is necessary; and only then will he unlock a cabinet and provide them with it. This includes tooth paste. Tampons. Laundry detergent. At dinner, Mark tells the children to ignore their mother because Vanessa is too stupid to be able to understand their conversations. Instead, Mark tells them she is there simply to make the food and serve it.

---

[30] B. Hayes, 'Indirect Abuse Involving Children during the Separation Process' (2017) 32 *Journal of Interpersonal Violence* 2975; J. Callaghan, J. Alexander, J. Sixmith and L. Fellini, 'Beyond "Witnessing": Children's Experiences of Coercive Control in Domestic Violence and Abuse' (2018) 33 *Journal of Interpersonal Violence* 1581.

[31] O. Rachmilovitz, 'Bringing Down the Bedroom Walls: Emphasizing Substance Over Form in Personalized Abuse' (2007) 14 *William & Mary Journal of Women & Law* 495.

[32] M. Dutton and L. Goodman, *Development and Validation of a Coercive Control Measure for Intimate Partner Violence* (US Department of Justice, 2006).

[33] E. Buzawa, G. Hotaling, A. Klein and J. Byrne, *Response to Domestic Violence in a Pro-Active Court Setting: Final Report Submitted to the National Institute of Justice* (University of Massachusetts–Lowell, 1999).

[34] Stark, Coercive Control.

[35] B. Harris and D. Woodlock, 'Digital Coercive Control: Insights from two Landmark Domestic Violence Studies' (2019) *British Journal of Criminology* forthcoming.

[36] D. Woodlock, 'The Abuse of Technology in Domestic Violence and Stalking' (2017) 23 *Violence against Women* 584.

Privately, Mark often tells Vanessa that if they ever separated, the children would never choose to live with her because they do not respect her.[37]

A key aspect of this control is restricting access to external sources of help or independence. Reports of domestic abuse often note the abuse is heightened when women seek to find employment or undertake study outside the home.[38] One striking report notes a woman whose husband attempted to burn three years of research in an attempt to prevent her completing her university course.[39]

Another important aspect of control is to devalue the victim. If the abuser can persuade the victim she is useless, this will discourage any attempts to find affection or help outside the relationship. One woman reports:

> He always found something wrong with what I did, even if I did what he asked. No matter what it was. It was never the way he wanted it. I was either too fat, didn't cook the food right ... I think he wanted to hurt me. To hurt me in the sense ... to make me feel like I was a nothing.[40]

One of the difficulties with determining coercive control is that it often starts with a period of grooming which can appear like intense courtship. One survivor explained to Cassandra Wiener,[41] 'I would say that the first three months were like being in a complete bubble.

> We were inseparable ... he would talk about his values of needing absolute loyalty, absolute transparency ... having any sense of space or privacy or independence was kind of seen as not acceptable.' This can make appreciating that one is the victim of domestic abuse complex.

This 'gaslighting'[42] can play an important part of coercive control. It has been defined as 'a form of persistent manipulation and brainwashing that causes the victim to doubt her or himself, and ultimately lose her or his own sense of perception, identity, and self-worth'.[43] In its most serious forms the victim can lose sight of what is or is not acceptable behaviour and, worse, come to blame herself for the behaviour of the abuser.

These points are important in understanding why it is that some victims fail to recognise domestic abuse for what it is. As Victor Tadros argues, 'domestic abuse is not just that the defendant denies the victim options, but also that he

---

[37] M. Johnson, 'Redefining Harm, Reimagining Remedies and Reclaiming Domestic Violence Law' (2009) *U.C. Davis Law Review* 1107.

[38] L. Kelly, *Surviving Sexual Violence* (Polity Press, 1988), 129.

[39] Ibid.

[40] D. Tuerkheimer, 'Recognizing and Remedying the Harm of Battering' (2004) *Journal of Criminal Law and Criminology* 959.

[41] C. Wiener, 'Seeing What Is Invisible in Plain Sight: Policing Coercive Control' (2017) 56 *The Howard Journal* 500.

[42] The term comes from the 1944 film *Gaslight*, in which a husband tries to convince his wife that she is insane and that she cannot perceive reality.

[43] P. Ni, 'Seven Stages of Gaslighting in a Relationship' (2017) *Psychology Today* 30 April 2017.

denies her the freedom to recognize and exploit the options that she has'.[44]
Paula Nicolson quotes from Connie:

> At the time I didn't really know, I didn't recognise it for what it was because
> I mean it was things like not speaking to you, like nudging you and bumping
> into you and at one point he pulled my hair and pushed me over, things like
> that. I just thought that was sort of life a bit over zealous but I didn't really
> recognise it from the start off.[45]

Another common feature of intimate abuse concerns a loss of freedom. As we
have seen, the coercive control model explains domestic abuse as coercive
control and one where every aspect of a person's life is controlled.[46] This is not
just temporary interference but controls a person's choices over time.[47]
A typical crime such as an assault may momentarily impede the victim and
may have impacts on the body of the victim for some time afterwards, but
these are limited and not the complete control and taking over of the victim
which takes place in the case of intimate abuse.[48] This is why kidnapping and
torture are used as the closest analogies from traditional crimes.[49] The study of
women who kill their abusive partners summarises the research well:

> Women who killed their abusers were more likely to have experienced frequent
> attacks, severe injuries, sexual abuse, and death threats against themselves or
> others. They were caught in a web of abuse that seemed to be out of control.
> Seventy-six percent of Browne's homicide group reported having been raped,
> 40% often. Sixty-two percent reported being forced or urged to engage in other
> sexual acts that they found abusive or unnatural, one-fifth saying this was a
> frequent occurrence. For many of these women, the most severe incidents took
> place when they threatened or tried to leave their partner. Another major factor
> that distinguished the homicide group from women who had not killed their
> abusive partners is that many of them had either attempted or seriously con-
> sidered suicide. These women felt that they could no longer survive in this
> relationship and that leaving safely was also impossible.

The emotional abuse in coercive control often involves 'put downs' in
gendered terms that concern criticisms of the mothering, housework and

---

[44] V. Tadros, 'The Distinctiveness of Domestic Abuse: A Freedom Based Account' (2005) 65
Louisiana Law Review 989.

[45] P. Nicolson, *Domestic Violence and Psychology* (Routledge, 2010), 35.

[46] A. Burke, 'Domestic Violence as a Crime of Pattern and Intent: An Alternative
Reconceptualization' (2007) *George Washington Law Review* 552.

[47] V. Bettinson and C. Bishop, 'Is the Creation of a Discrete Offence of Coercive Control
Necessary to Combat Domestic Violence?' (2015) 66 *Northern Ireland Law Quarterly* 179.

[48] J. Belknap, A. Chu and A. DePrince, 'The Roles of Phones and Computers in Threatening and
Abusing Women Victims of Male Intimate Partner Abuse' (2012) 19 *Duke Journal of Gender
Law & Policy*, 373.

[49] C. Wright, 'Torture at Home: Borrowing from the Torture Convention to Define Domestic
Violence' (2013) 24 *Hastings Women's Law Journal* 457.

appearance of the woman.[50] One survivor told Cassandra Wiener[51] that it involves:

> controlling your entire life, how you eat how you sleep, what you wear. When you answer your phone, everything to how you look, your hair, how you cook you know, just literally your life is consumed by control.

Another explained:

> one of the reasons that they blame themselves is that they feel then like they have a degree of control, like they can prevent it from happening again. So it's like I was raped because I did X, so if I don't do X again, then I won't get raped. Which means that I can now have control over my life so that I don't get raped. The reality is that's not why she got raped. She got raped because he's a perpetrator. Part of blaming yourself is about giving yourself back a degree of control.

As these points demonstrate, it can be difficult to explain to an outside authority the nature of the abuse. The examples that might be used can sound trivial: he bumps into me; he does not like the way I make his sandwich; he thinks I am fat. All of these might be readily dismissed as 'a normal relationship' or even paranoia, but in combination they can operate as a controlling relationship.

Before leaving this factor it is worth noting the arguments against the view that coercive control should be seen as at the heart of intimate abuse. Helen Reece has argued against the weight placed on coercive control, expressing a concern that it 'represents a remarkable downplaying of the physical'.[52] It is true that traditionally the criminal law, and indeed the law generally, has regarded physical attacks as more serious than an emotional or psychological one.[53] In part, this a matter of proof. Whether a person has been cut or bruised can be determined easily. However, the lines between emotional abuse and 'nagging' or 'uncouth' behaviour may be harder to define. However, we think it is appropriate to downplay the distinction between physical and emotional harms. The line between physical and mental health is increasingly hard to draw. Indeed, the impact of many physical crimes can be found in terms of the emotional, psychological or social impact, rather than the physical injuries per se. Rape is a particularly strong example of this.

To summarise, the importance of understanding intimate abuse as a form of coercive control is threefold. First, it moves beyond simply examining the

---

[50] Ibid.

[51] Ibid.

[52] H. Reece, 'Feminist Anti-violence Discourse as Regulation', in E. Jackson et al. (eds.) *Regulating Autonomy: Sex, Reproduction and Families* (Hart Publishing, 2009), 46.

[53] M. Burton, 'Commentary: *R v Dhaliwal*', in R. Hunter, C. McGlynn and E. Rackley (eds.) *Feminist Judgements* (Hart Publishing, 2010), 258.

individual incident in isolation but considers the overall impact of the series of acts together.[54] It also shows that conduct which can appear trivial changes its character once appreciated as part of a pattern of controlling behaviour. Second, the control can be managed through acts which do not involve violence. It is the level of control which is more significant than the level of violence in this model. Third, it reflects the motivation for intimate abuse: as a means of exercising control over a partner.[55] The violence or abusive conduct is not used in its own right but as a means to an end: intimidation, isolation and control.[56] Intimate violence should not, therefore, be readily dismissed as merely the symptoms of a failing relationship or an 'anger management problem'.[57]

4.4.2 Intimate Abuse as a Breach of Trust of an Intimate Relationship

Intimate relationship abuse involves a serious breach of trust. John Eekelaar has argued that trust is at the heart of the intimacy, and that enables love and autonomy to develop.[58] It is in being able to be completely honest and vulnerable with someone that relationships can deepen, an understanding of self can grow and sense can be made of life. But all of that depends on trust. In a case of intimate violence, the abuse has misused the private sphere as a tool against the victim. There are four points to emphasise.

First, an intimate relationship involves 'thick interpersonal trust',[59] which is distinct from how we might simply trust an acquaintance. An intimate relationship involves the disclosing of parts of ourselves (both physical and emotional) that we wish to keep free from another. The kind of openness necessary for intimacy is so extensive that there are particularly strong bonds of trust. The trust involves not only imposing an obligation not to misuse information acquired during the relationship (something the law is generally ready to protect) but also that the relationship is not used to take advantage of the other person. Notably, the law is more ready to protect confidential information disclosed in a personal relationship than to control the misuse of the relationship to exercise power or control over the other party. Marilyn Friedman writes:[60]

> Intimate partner abuse denies to the abused person, in her very home life and her intimate bodily existence, the safety and security she needs to try to live her

---

[54] Burke, 'Domestic Violence as a Crime of Pattern and Intent', 552.

[55] N. Jacobson and J. Gottman, *When Men Batter Women: New Insights into Ending Abusive Relationships* (Simon & Schuster, 2007).

[56] Stark, Coercive Control, 5.

[57] Bettinson and C. Bishop, 'Is the Creation of a Discrete Offence of Coercive Control Necessary to Combat Domestic Violence?' 179.

[58] J. Eekelaar, *Family Law and Personal Life* (Oxford University Press, 2017), 4–47.

[59] D. Khodyakov, 'Trust as a Process: A Three Dimensional Approach' (2007) 41 *Sociology* 116.

[60] M. Friedman, *Autonomy, Gender, Politics* (Oxford University Press, 2003), 368.

life as she thinks she ought to do. Instead of being able to live according to her values and commitments, an abused woman is reduced to seeking bare survival and security ... An abused woman tends to develop a heightened awareness of what her partner wants and needs as she tries to accommodate his wishes and whims, all this as a way to minimize his violent reactions.6 Such focused attention on what another person wants distracts someone from the task of understanding herself or being guided by her own self-defining concerns.7 Her goals are survival and security, which are not, as such, autonomy-conferring goals. And her means of pursuing those goals involve mere deferential or heteronomous reactions to the abuser's actual or anticipated desires or moods.

Second, the abuse of trust within an intimate relationship causes a special harm. Intimate relationships are central to our identity and sense of self.[61] Within our intimate relationships we can be truly ourselves, free of pretence. Through them, we can explore and discover ourselves. Domestic abuse strikes at the very conception of the self for the victim. As Evan Stark[62] puts it: 'he changes who and what she is'. He explains:

> In the romantic vernacular, love and intimacy compensate women for their devaluation in the wider world. Personal life does something more. It provides the state where women practice their basic rights, garner the support needed to resist devaluation, experiment with sexual identities, and imagine themselves through various life projects. Coercive control subverts this process, brining discrimination home by reducing the discretion in everyday routines to near zero, freezing feeling and identity in time and space, the process victims experience as entrapment. Extended across the range of activities that define women as person, this foreshortening of subjective development compounds the particular liberty harms caused by coercive control.[63]

As it is through our relationships we form our identities as to who we are and try and make sense of the world, domestic abuse turns what should be a tool for self-affirmation and self-identification into a tool for alienation and self-betrayal. The victim almost becomes used as a tool against herself.[64] It is not surprising therefore that domestic violence causes a wide range of mental health problems for victims, ranging through anxiety, depression, posttraumatic stress, substance abuse and suicidal tendencies.[65] A REFUGE report on the impact of domestic abuse[66] concludes 'there can be a persistent negative

---

[61] Rachmilovitz, 'Bringing Down the Bedroom Walls: Emphasizing Substance Over Form in Personalized Abuse', 495.

[62] Stark, Coercive Control, 262.

[63] Ibid., 363.

[64] L. Arnault, 'Cruelty, Horror, and the Will to Redemption' (2003) 18 *Hypatia* 155.

[65] E. Williamson, *Domestic Violence and Health* (University of Chicago Press, 2000); C. Itzen , A. Taket and S. Barter-Godfrey, *Domestic and Sexual Violence and Abuse* (Routledge, 2010), 61; X. Arriaga and N. Capezza, 'Targets of Partner Violence: The Importance of Understanding Coping Trajectories' (2005) 20 *Journal of Interpersonal Violence* 89.

[66] Cited in V. Munro and S. Shah, 'R v Dhaliwal' in Rosemary Hunter, Clare McGlynn and Erika Rackley, *Feminist Judgments* (Hart, 2011), at para 10.

changes to thoughts, feelings and behaviours, including a lack of trust in people, social isolation, self-medication using alcohol or drugs, a distorted appraisal of the abuse and one's reality, resulting guilt, self-blame, crippling low self-esteem and helplessness about the future.' In domestic abuse, the intimacy that should make us whole is used to destroy us.

Third, there is more to domestic abuse than simply depriving the victim of the benefits of an intimate life. Domestic abuse can involve the use of information gathered during the relationship so that the abuse can be personalised.[67] In *Attorney-General's Reference (No 90 of 2009)*,[68] where a sentence of ten years was increased to eighteen in a case of marital rape, the Court of Appeal explained that the defendant had used his knowledge of the victim's phobias and dislikes to aggravate the attack.

One reason for preferring intimacy to cohabitation or domesticity is that a key aspect of intimate abuse is the difficulties the victim has escaping from the abuse. It is the isolation of the victim from outside support or self-help, trapping the victim into a cycle of abuse, which is a hallmark of domestic abuse. This might typically occur in cases where the couple are living together. However, it is not limited to those relationships. Cases of elder abuse can, for example, arise where one person becomes dependent upon another person for their care, even though they are not living together. Similarly, there have been several cases in England in recent years of vulnerable adults with learning difficulties being 'befriended' and coming to have a strong emotional attachment to someone who then sexually or financially abuses them.[69] It is therefore clear that coercive control is not restricted to cases of couples living together; it is the closeness of the relationship, rather than its geography, which is key. Indeed, we can see with the increasing number of couples living apart together that the days of cohabitation equating to commitment or dependency are long past.

4.4.3 Intimate Abuse and Structural Inequality

Feminist commentators have long argued that domestic abuse sustains or perpetuates patriarchy and thus creates a very particular kind of wrong.[70] I will argue here it is more helpful to use the term structural inequalities to make it clear that intimate abuse is not simply a matter of gender inequality but also raises issues around race, sexuality, class and disability and the interactions

---

[67] Stark, Coercive Control, 376.

[68] [2009] EWCA Crim 2610. For further discussion of marital rape see J. Herring, 'No More Having and Holding: The Abolition of the Marital Rape Exemption' in S. Gilmore, J. Herring and R. Probert (eds.) *Landmarks in Family Law* (Hart, 2011), 225.

[69] *R v Howe* [2014] EWCA Crim 114.

[70] N. Lombard and N. Whiting "What's in a Name? The Scottish Government, Feminism and the Gendered Framing of Domestic Abuse' in N. Lombard (ed.) *Routledge Handbook of Gender and Violence* (Routledge, 2018), 28.

between these and gender. Of course, a rich and nuanced understanding of the concept of patriarchy can encompass these,[71] but it can also be misunderstood to mean that patriarchy is only a matter of gender. I accept that gender and intersections with gender are particularly relevant in an understanding of intimate abuse, but the importance of other factors should be considered.

I will start by exploring how gender inequality is sustained or perpetuated by intimate abuse and how intimate abuse is sustained or perpetuated by gender inequality. I will start by describing in outline the concept of structural inequality. As already indicated, the best known example is patriarchy. Michelle Madden Dempsey defines patriarchy in this way: 'a collection of social forms which constitute a structural inequality, whereby men hold systematic social power in society more generally'.[72] Patriarchy is a range of forces which restricts the ability of women to access valuable resources and exercise their options. This can be through active misogyny (hatred of women) but also through a failure to value the work or characteristics of women. It can be expressed in a range of ways: from sex discrimination where barriers are put in place; to social resources which favour men over women; to sexual harassment in the street which discourages women from accessing public spaces; to a devaluing of care which is predominantly performed by women. It involves denying women access to resources they need to live valuable lives. These same points can be made in relation to race, class, ethnicity, disability and other social forms. Structural inequality refers to the multiple and intersecting forces that restrict people's access to economic, material and public resources on account of their characteristics.

The argument in this chapter is that patriarchy and other structural inequalities support and are supported by intimate abuse. As already indicated, most work in supporting this claim has been done in the context of gender and I will start by expanding this claim in that context.

At a simplistic level, intimate abuse seems obviously gendered. As Andy Myhill in a detailed analysis of the statistics concludes 'coercive control is highly gendered and is significantly more damaging to its primarily female victims than is situational violence'.[73] But the relationship between patriarchy and intimate abuse is more complex than this. As the United Nations Special Rapporteur on Violence against Women puts it: 'violence is not an isolated incident targeting vulnerable women but a systematically used tool of patriarchal control to ensure that "women stay in their place."'[74] It does this in several ways.

---

[71] S. Walby, *Theorizing Patriarchy* (Oxford University Press, 1990).

[72] Madden Dempsey, Prosecuting Domestic Violence, chapter 7.

[73] A. Myhill, 'Measuring Coercive Control: What Can We Learn From National Population Surveys?' (2015) 21 *Violence against Women* 355.

[74] Y. Ertürk, 'Violence against Women: From Victimization to Empowerment'. Paper presented at the ESCAP forum 'Where's the Power in Women's Empowerment?' Bangkok, Thailand, 4 August 2008.

First, intimate abuse reinforces the messages sent more broadly by patriarchy that women should be subservient to men and are inferior to them. The Convention on the Elimination of All Forms of Discrimination against Women, General Recommendation 19, states that domestic abuse is based on 'traditional attitudes by which women are regarded as subordinate to men'. Gender stereotypes typically underpin domestic abuse. Consider, for example, this incident in the American case, *State* v. *Norman*:[75]

> John Norman asked Judy Norman to make him a sandwich; when Judy brought it to him, he threw it on the floor and told her to make him another. Judy made him a second sandwich and brought it to him; John again threw it on the floor, telling her to put something on her hands because he did not want her to touch the bread. Judy made a third sandwich using a paper towel to handle the bread. John took the third sandwich and smeared it in Judy's face.

As explored in the section on coercive control, intimate abuse often focuses on reinforcing a 'traditional role' for women (e.g. having absurd standards for cooking or household; constantly complaining about appearance) and having lower status than men (e.g. demeaning the value of her work).[76] Charlotte Bishop and Vanessa Bettinson[77] explain that intimate abuse involves 'the micro-regulation of everyday activities already typically associated with women in their roles as homemakers, parents and sexual partners, such as how the victim dresses, cooks, cleans, looks after children and performs sexually'. This kind of control echoes similar messages found in advertising, street harassment and the media about the place of women.

Second, intimate abuse reinforces the practical barriers that exist to restrict women's access to the labour market and reinforces traditional roles for women. Evan Stark reports how domestic abuse may intensify when women seek to gain independence, by, for example, finding employment.[78]

Third, intimate abuse is often used to deny access to an autonomous life, by restricting movement, association with friends and economic independence. Evan Stark comments on the role of control in domestic abuse: 'Perpetrators commonly spy on or stalk partners even when they are living together and control their access to and means of transportation, monitor them at work, and use beepers, cell phones, or human proxies to monitor their activities.'[79] These combine with other patriarchal forces restricting access to public spaces. Mary Ann Dutton and Lisa Goodman, examining the experiences of victims of

---

[75] *State of North Carolina* v. *Norman* 366 SE 2d 586, 588 (NC App 1988).
[76] Stark, Coercive Control.
[77] C. Bishop and V. Bettinson, 'Evidencing Domestic Violence, Including Behaviour That Falls Under the New Offence of Controlling or Coercive Behaviour' (2018) 22 *International Journal of Evidence and Proof* 3.
[78] Ibid.
[79] E. Stark, 'Commentary on Johnson's "Conflict and Control: Gender Symmetry and Asymmetry in Domestic Violence"' (2006) 12 *Violence against Women* 1019.

domestic abuse, have explored the forms of coercion and see these as covering nine areas of control: 'personal activities/appearance', 'support/social life/ family', 'household', 'work/economic/resources', 'health', 'intimate relationship', 'legal', 'immigration' and 'children'.[80]

So far, I have been looking at how intimate abuse sustains patriarchy. But it is important to also appreciate how intimate abuse is sustained by and supported by patriarchy. Ruth Gavison[81] explains: 'When women are battered at home, it is not because each particular victim has triggered an unfortunate "individual" tragedy ... Social structures are involved, social structures which are not simply "natural". They are person-made, and they benefit males.' The refusal to link gender and domestic violence reinforces the notion that domestic abuse is simply a private matter; that family life should be a privileged sphere in which the state does not intervene. Domestic abuse is not just supported by patriarchy's conceptions of the private. Michelle Madden Dempsey explains:

> the patriarchal character of individual relationships cannot subsist without those relationships being situated within a broader patriarchal social structure. Patriarchy is, by its nature, a social structure – and thus any particular instance of patriarchy takes its substance and meaning from that social context.[82]

Elizabeth Frazer and Kimberly Hutchings[83] refer to 'the gendered social structures and discourses through which such violence may be rendered meaningful and legitimate, or even invisible, to perpetrators and victims alike'.

These arguments have focussed on gender and explain why intimate abuse has a particular significance for women, but that is not the only lens through which intimate abuse can be viewed. There is, of course, intimate abuse which takes places outside the context of heterosexual relationships. Indeed, some have criticised the focus on intimate abuse as violence against women because it excludes the experience of others. Julie Goldscheid writes:[84]

> Heterosexual, gay, trans men and trans women are subjected to sexual assault as well as intimate partner violence at rates that are difficult to quantify, though no doubt are higher than commonly recognized. The woman-specific frame erases the experiences of these survivors and excludes them from services as well as from legal and other forms of redress.

I do not think this is an argument against using gender as a significant aspect of intimate abuse but highlights the significance of other structural inequalities

---

[80] Dutton and Goodman, *Development and Validation of a Coercive Control Measure for Intimate Partner Violence*, 3.

[81] R. Gavison, 'Feminism and the Public/Private Distinction' (1992) 45 *Stanford Law Review* 1, 3.

[82] M. Madden Dempsey, 'Towards a Feminist State' (2007) 70 *Modern Law Review* 908, 909.

[83] E. Frazer and K. Hutchings, 'Violence and Vulnerability' in A. Garry, S. Khadar and A. Stone (eds.), *The Routledge Companion to Feminist Philosophy* (Routledge, 2017).

[84] J. Goldscheid, *Gender Neutrality and the "Violence Against Women" Frame* (City University of New York Academic Works, 2014).

that can be reflected in intimate abuse. Part of patriarchy is the promotion of heteronormativity and that can certainly play a role in same-sex violence.[85] And even among same-sex couples we can see a difference between gay and lesbian couples, indicating that gender norms may be playing a role.[86] Clearly, this issue requires more research and analysis, but I accept that in so far as the Violence against Women approach may indicate that only violence against women reinforces patriarchy, that may be inaccurate. That is why I use structural inequality in my outline.

A real danger with simply focussing on gender is that it homogenises women as a category. This is the powerful intersectionality.[87] Julie Gold-schied[88] complains that relying on gender alone has the problem that:

> This single axis of focus obscures the complexities of survivors' experiences and fails to take into account the variability in survivors' experiences of abuse based on structural factors other than gender, such as race, immigration status, class, and gender identity.

Responding to such challenges, there is now a growing body of literature promoting intersectionality.[89] Traditional feminist approaches assumed one could write about the experiences of 'women', but in reality this presented the voice of powerful women, typically said to be white, middle-class women, and silenced the other voices of non-mainstream women.[90] So, the argument goes, it makes no sense to talk about VAW because there is no unifying feature of womanhood that we can identify. The experience and impact of domestic abuse on women depends on so much more than their sex; it depends on race, class, religion, poverty, sexuality,[91] disability[92] and so forth.

Lena Gunnarsson[93] writes,

> there are no discrete racial, gender and class parts at the level of concrete identity; nevertheless, the structures of race, gender and class have distinct existences insofar as they exercise their causal force on our lives in ways relatively independent from each other.

---

[85] Madden Dempsey, Prosecuting Domestic Violence, chapter 7.

[86] C. Donovan and M. Hester, *Domestic Violence and Sexuality* (Policy Press, 2006).

[87] K. Crenshaw, 'Mapping the Margins: Intersectionality, Identity Politics, and Violence against Women of Color' (1991) 43 *Stanford Law Review* 1241.

[88] Goldscheid, *Gender Neutrality and the "Violence Against Women" Frame.*

[89] A. Gruber, 'Neofeminism' (2013) 50 *Houston Law Review* 1325.

[90] S. Choudhry, 'Towards a Transformative Conceptualisation of Violence Against Women: A Critical Frame Analysis of Council of Europe Discourse on Violence against Women' (2016) 79 *Modern Law Review* 406.

[91] R. Barnes and C. Donovan, 'Domestic Violence in Lesbian, Gay, Bisexual and/or Transgender Relationships' in N. Lombard (ed.) *Routledge Handbook of Gender and Violence* (Routledge, 2018), 162.

[92] J. Breckenridge, 'The Relationships between Disability and Domestic Abuse' in N. Lombard (ed.) *Routledge Handbook of Gender and Violence* (Routledge, 2018).

[93] L. Gunnarsson, 'A Defence of the Category "Women"' (2012) 11 *Feminist Theory* 23.

For law, political interaction and policy engagement categories must inevitably be used. The nature of bureaucracy requires categorisation. The danger of abandoning categories such as gender in the face of the intersectional challenge is that it can lead to failure to challenge structures.[94] Iris Marion Young[95] explains that we need tools for 'understanding how and why certain patterns in the allocation of tasks or status recognition remain persistent in ways that limit the options of many women and of most people whose sexual and intimate choices deviate from heterosexual norms'. Without the use of concepts such as patriarchy we lose these.[96]

As a form of structural inequality, patriarchy is neither episodic nor discrete, but is in its nature systematic. As Marilyn Frye has observed, the systematic nature of patriarchal structural inequality denies valuable options to women much as the intertwined wires of a birdcage deny flight[97]:

> The cage makes the bird entirely unfree to fly. If one studies the causes of this imprisonment by looking at one wire at a time, however, it appears puzzling. How does a wire only a couple of centimetres wide prevent a bird's flight? One wire at a time, we can neither describe nor explain the inhibition of the bird's flight. Only a large number of wires arranged in a specific way and connected to one another to enclose the bird and reinforce one another's rigidity can explain why the bird is unable to fly freely.

While I am making the case that it is proper to see patriarchy as having a particularly significant role in intimate abuse, other forms of structural inequality can be highly significant too. The points just made can be applied in relation to, for example, race, disability and age. To take the example of age, elder abuse reinforces and relies upon ageist attitudes. They are seen as doddery and confused, with limited awareness of what is going on. This makes it easy to downplay the impact of crimes upon them. Indeed, much abuse in the home is (inaccurately) put down to 'carer stress'. Ageism as a cause of abuse can be most apparent in maltreatment in care homes. Research has demonstrated that abusive behaviour in a nursing home is often normalised and can easily come to be regarded as 'standard treatment'. Thus the use of force against uncooperative older people is accepted as necessary for the 'smooth running' of the home. Older people in some residential settings are seen as a waste of space, incapable of feeling. The routines and bureaucracy of the nursing home sometimes seem to count for more than the interests of the individual residents. Even where there are not such overly hostile attitudes, many older people in residential

---

[94] J. Conaghan, 'Intersectionality and the Feminist Project in Law' in J. Conaghan and D. Cooper (eds.) *Law, Power and the Politics of Subjectivity: Intersectionality and Beyond* (Routledge, 2008), 21.

[95] I. Young, 'Lived Body vs Gender: Reflections on Social Structure and Subjectivity' (2002) 15 *Ratio* 410.

[96] L. Gunnarsson, 'A Defence of the Category "Women"' (2012) 11 *Feminist Theory* 23.

[97] M. Frye, *Oppression: The Politics of Reality* (Crossing Press, 1993), 54.

settings are seen as needing 'looking after' and infantilised in a way which perpetuates and enables the abuse itself. For example, 'baby talk' or overtly insulting terms are demeaning. Often, abusive behaviour is not even recognised as such and is dismissed as 'what she wants' or 'she doesn't mind because she doesn't really know what's going on'. Even very serious incidents of abuse tend to be seen as 'one offs' rather than reflecting broader attitudes towards older people. At worst it may be labelled 'bad practice'. But their treatment is often but a reflection of broader ageist attitudes within society and the social structures that set the social position of care homes.

4.5 Intimate Abuse and Children

An issue of particular recent concern is the impact of intimate violence on children.[98] There is widespread acceptance that children raised in a household where there is domestic violence suffer in many ways, as compared to households where there is not.[99] This includes psychological disturbance and often a feeling that they are to blame for the violence.[100] The impact of domestic violence on the mother may itself harm the child.[101] Indeed, one study of children who had suffered abuse showed that 39 per cent of them had come from families in which there was domestic violence.[102] Marianne Hester found that children were present in 55 per cent of cases of domestic violence.[103] Ten per cent of children who witnessed domestic violence witnessed their mother being sexually assaulted.[104]

There is ample evidence that intimate violence harms children.[105] This is so not only where the child has witnessed the incidents directly, but even where the child is living in the same house as the behaviour. Children raised in families characterised by domestic violence are 30–60 per cent more likely to suffer child abuse themselves.[106] The impact on children includes behavioural,

---

[98] M. Hester, *Who Does What to Whom? Gender and Domestic Violence Perpetrators* (Northern Rock, 2009).

[99] A. Mullender, *Tackling Domestic Violence: Providing Support for Children Who Have Witnessed Domestic Violence* (Home Office, 2005).

[100] Barnado's, *Bitter Legacy* (Barnado's, 2004).

[101] L. Harne and J. Radford, *Tackling Domestic Violence: Theories, Policies and Practice* (Open University Press, 2008).

[102] E. Farmer and S. Pollock, *Sexually Abused and Abusing Children in Substitute Care* (Wiley, 1998).

[103] M. Hester, *Who Does What to Whom? Gender and Domestic Violence Perpetrators* (Northern Rock, 2009).

[104] A. Mullender, *Tackling Domestic Violence: Providing Support for Children Who Have Witnessed Domestic Violence* (Home Office, 2005).

[105] The research is summarised in J. Kelly and M. Johnson, 'Differentiation among Types of Intimate Partner Violence' (2008) 46 *Family Court Review* 467 and Royal College of Psychiatrists, *Domestic Violence: Its Effect on Children* (RCP, 2010).

[106] C. Itzen, A. Taket and S. Barter-Godfrey, *Domestic and Sexual Violence and Abuse* (Routledge, 2010), 4.

cognitive and emotional problems, leading to depression, anxiety, truancy and low educational achievement. It also can lead to interpersonal problems and poor social skills. There are higher rates of sibling violence in cases of domestic violence. In one Scandinavian study, half of the girls who had grown up in violent households were subject to physical violence by their boyfriends, yet nearly all maintained that relationship.[107] The evidence shows that children are harmed by living with coercive control even if there is no violence.[108]

The law generally recognises that crimes against children involve a greater wrong than crimes against others.[109] This recognises the particular obligation that adults owe to children, particularly those who are playing a parental role. It also recognises that children often lack the physical, emotional and social capabilities to respond to harmful incidents. All of these points emphasise the wrongfulness of intimate violence where children are involved.

All of this means that in cases where children are present in the house the intimate violence can correctly be regarded as a form of child abuse.[110] It provides additional reasons why the state should take intimate abuse seriously. It also indicates why the issue is not simply a private matter or one that only involves the interest of the adults involved.

4.6 Developing a Legal Response

I believe that the deeper relational understanding of intimate abuse can assist us in fashioning an effective response to it. There is not space to set out in detail how the law should respond to domestic abuse,[111] but I will highlight a few key points.

First, it should be clear that the wrong done through intimate abuse is a very serious wrong and it is the state, through its support of patriarchy and other structural inequalities, that has enabled this. The state therefore has positive obligations to protect those suffering intimate abuse: to prevent that abuse; to offer resources for those escaping the abuse; and effective remedies where it is occurring. This could be framed, as Shazia Choudhry and I have argued, in

---

[107] K. Weinehall, "'Take My Father Away from Home'": Children Growing Up in the Proximity of Violence' in M. Eriksoon, M. Hester and S. Keskinen (eds.) *Tackling Men's Violence in Families: Nordic Issues and Dilemmas* (University of Chicago Press, 2005).

[108] E. Katz, 'Beyond the Physical Incident Model: How Children Living with Domestic Violence are Harmed By and Resist Regimes of Coercive Control' (2016) 25 *Child Abuse Review* 46.

[109] See e.g. the particular offences protecting children under the Sexual Offences Act 2003.

[110] T. Herrenkohl, C. Sousa, E. Tajima, R. Herrenkohl and C. Moylan, 'Intersection of Child Abuse and Children's Exposure to Domestic Violence' (2008) 9 *Trauma Violence Abuse* 84; P. Romito, *A Deafening Silence: Hidden Violence against Women and Children* (Polity, 2008).

[111] S. Choudhry and J. Herring, *European Human Rights and Family Law* (Hart, 2010), ch 9; J. Herring, 'The Istanbul Convention: Is Domestic Abuse Violence against Women?' in G. Douglas, M. Murch and V. Stephens (eds.) *International and National Perspectives on Child and Family Law* (Intersentia, 2018).

terms of the Human Rights Act 1998.[112] Indeed, the European Court of Human Rights has become increasingly willing to impose positive obligations on the state to take reasonable steps to protect people from intimate abuse.[113] I will not go into the details of those arguments here. These are reflected too in the Istanbul Convention.[114] Article 12, para. 1, of the Istanbul Convention acknowledges the broader measures that are needed:

> Parties shall take the necessary measures to promote changes in the social and cultural patterns of behaviour of women and men with a view to eradicating prejudices, customs, traditions and all other practices which are based on the idea of the inferiority of women or on stereotyped roles for women and men.

The Convention goes on to require awareness-raising campaigns or programmes,[115] education,[116] general support services,[117] shelters[118] and telegraph helplines[119] to combat domestic violence. All of these are essential, in addition to the legal measures, if there is to be a resolute response to domestic violence.

Second, legal interventions should be aimed at the understanding of intimate abuse explained in this chapter and training for relevant professionals is required so this understanding is appreciated. In particular, as this chapter has shown, intimate abuse can occur without their being physical injuries. The victim may be unaware they are being subjected to this behaviour. Further, what might appear to be minor issues can, in combination, produce a profound effect on the victim.

Third, the discussion in this chapter demonstrates that removing the abuser from the house will not be an adequate solution. As Nicola Sharp-Jeffs, Liz Kelly and Renate Klein[120] explain, in their sample:

> Removing themselves from the immediate control of an abusive man was ... only the first step. Over 90 per cent experienced post-separation abuse, which interfered with both being and feeling safe. The limited effectiveness of criminal and civil law enforcement required women to undertake a huge amount of "safety work." ... The prevalence of perpetrator manipulation of statutory

---

[112] Choudhry and Herring, *European Human Rights and Family Law*), ch 9.

[113] Ibid.

[114] J. Herring, 'The Istanbul Convention: Is Domestic Abuse Violence against Women?' in G. Douglas, M. Murch and V. Stephens (eds.) *International and National Perspectives on Child and Family Law* (Intersentia, 2018), 124.

[115] Article 13.

[116] Article 14.

[117] Article 22.

[118] Article 23.

[119] Article 24.

[120] N. Sharp-Jeffs, L. Kelly and R. Klein, 'Long Journeys Toward Freedom: The Relationship between Coercive Control and Space for Action: Measurement and Emerging Evidence' (2018) 24 *Violence against Women* 163, 176.

agencies post-separation also revealed the importance of factoring ongoing support needs into responses to domestic violence.

This highlights the limits of the standard domestic violence legal interventions. The provision of refuges, state funding housing, pro-active policing and expert advice and support also have an important role.

4.7 Conclusion

This chapter has explored the nature of intimate abuse, particularly from the viewpoint of the relational self, as argued for in this book. It has been argued that seeing domestic abuse through this lens highlights the wrongs that are involved in domestic abuse: by highlighting the coercive control nature of the issue; the breach of trust involved in domestic abuse; the harm to children and others by the abuse; and the relationship between intimate abuse and structural inequalities. These reinforce the case for seeing abuse within intimate relationships as a major wrong to the victim and being a major wrong to social endeavours to promote inequality.

5

Medical Law and the Relational Self

5.1 Introduction

This chapter will explore the significance of using a relational understanding of the self to medical law. Many of the themes in the first three chapters will re-emerge and we will be able to apply them to concrete applications. Clearly, it is not possible to cover all the potential ramifications of the understanding of the relational self in the medical context. In this chapter I will focus on four issues:

- The nature of the body
- The nature of mental capacity
- The nature of best interests
- The nature of personhood.

5.2 Bodies and Body Ownership

One of the great debates in medical law and ethics at the moment surrounds the question of whether you own your own bodily material, particularly once it is separated from the body.[1] There is consensus that the current law is unsatisfactory and there is considerable support for the view that we should recognise ownership rights in bodily material.[2] Supporters argue that such an approach will ensure the person has control over their bodily material and that there is an effective legal regime governing control of the material.

In this section I will start by very briefly setting out the current law and the difficulties with it. I will then explore the appeal of the use of property. Finally, I will bring in an analysis based on the relational self to promote what I believe to be a better approach[3]

---

[1] I. Goold, K. Greasley, J. Herring and L. Skene (eds.) *Persons, Parts and Property* (Hart, 2014).
[2] Ibid.
[3] This chapter draws on and develops previous writing of mine, particularly J. Herring, 'Why We Need a Statute for Bodily Material' in I. Goold, K. Greasley, J. Herring and L. Skene (eds.) *Persons, Parts and Property* (Hart, 2014), 186.

5.2.1 The Traditional Common Law Approach: *Res Nullius*

For centuries, the common law took the view that the body and body parts were *res nullius*.[4] They could not be owned or subject to property rights. That fitted in with Christian theology, which taught that people were created by God and it was presumptuous of anyone to claim they owned what belonged to God. It also was compatible with the predominant philosophical approaches to property which claimed that property claims emanated from labour. As a person could not claim to have produced their body as a result of their labour they could not claim to own it. But, perhaps most significantly, there was simply no need for the body to be regarded as property. The power to buy and sell bodies might appeal to slave masters or grave robbers, but no decent person would have need for property rights. The law's response to the body was, therefore, limited to criminal offences prohibiting assaults, batteries and the like; and a limited number of offences dealing with the interference in proper burial.

Times change. Now the theological concerns play little role in legal thought. The argument that bodies are not produced by labour seems outdated in this age of gym membership, cosmetic surgery, steroid use, body adornment etc. But most significantly, there are perfectly good reasons why a person might want a property interest, or something like it, in their body. They may wish a hospital to store their gametes for use in assisted reproduction; to retain an organ or other human material for transplant or treatment; researchers may wish to store human material for research. The idea that people should be permitted to buy and sell parts of their bodies has some highly respectable advocates.[5] The *res nullius* approach no longer seems fit for purpose.

The current law on the legal status on bodies is confused. The safest thing that can be said is that there are some respects in which the body can be treated as property, and other respects in which it cannot. The starting point is the traditional common law rule that the human body is *res nullius*: it cannot be property.[6] Despite the widespread acceptance by lawyers of this principle, in fact, explicit authority for it is limited.[7] Nevertheless, the law is generally understood to start with the *res nullius* principle and then to acknowledge that there are exceptions to it: circumstances in which the body is recognised as property. The best known is the 'work and skill' exception. In *Kelly*,[8] the Court of Appeal held that:

---

[4] See J. Wall, *Being and Owning: The Body, Bodily Material and the Law* (Oxford University Press, 2016) for a detailed discussion of the law.
[5] E.g. R. Hardcastle, *Law and the Human Body* (Hart, 2007).
[6] *Doodeward* v. *Spence* (1908) 6 C.L.R. 906.
[7] See Wall, *Being and Owning: The Body, Bodily Material and the Law*.
[8] [1998] 3 All E.R. 714, 749.

> ... parts of a corpse are capable of being property ... if they have acquired different attributes by virtue of the application of skill, such as dissection or preservation techniques, for exhibition or teaching purposes.

The case law leaves undecided what precisely must be done to a part of a body in order for it to acquire the nature of property. The exercise of skill in dissection or preservation appears to be sufficient. Although there has been little explicit discussion, presumably the person who applied the skill to the bodily material becomes its owner. The problems with that approach were revealed in *Yearworth* v. *North Bristol NHS Trust.*[9] Some men were undergoing treatment which carried a risk of infertility and hence asked a hospital to store sperm for them. The hospital negligently destroyed the sperm. The court acknowledged that it was far from straightforward what legal claim the men had. They accepted that the 'no property' rule was outdated and needed to be re-examined:

> In this jurisdiction developments in medical science now require a re-analysis of the common law's treatment of and approach to the issue of ownership of parts or products of a living human body, whether for present purposes (viz. an action in negligence) or otherwise.[10]

The work and skill exception did not operate well in this context. If anyone had applied work and skill to the sperm it was the hospital, and yet that seemed an inappropriate conclusion. The court declined to undertake a thorough review of the law and preferred to list a number of particular features of the case, which indicated the sperm was the property of the men which had been bailed to the hospital, enabling a claim in bailment to be brought.

5.2.2 The Case for Property

As already mentioned, there is considerable agreement that the law needs to be reformed. One popular proposal, and the case law seems to be moving in that direction, is to determine that bodily material can be property. To understand the appeal of this proposal it is necessary to say a little more about the nature of property.

Ownership rights are about giving someone control over an item.[11] You can decide whether to destroy your pencil, put it in a draw, use it up or sell it to another. If someone takes your pencil without your permission then the

---

[9] [2009] EWCA Civ 37.

[10] At [33].

[11] When a person owns a piece of property, that usually denotes a number of rights or entitlements, e.g. the right to use or enjoy the property; the right to exclude others from using the property; the right to sell or transfer the property to someone else. Full blooded ownership involves possession of all of these rights. But a lesser form of ownership may involve only some of them. It would, therefore, be permissible to declare that bodily materials were property, but they could not be sold in commercial dealings.

criminal law of theft and civil law of conversion can be used to punish the taker and order the return of your property. There is no ready mechanism in law to give a person a stronger set of rights over an object than is available through property. Larissa Katz[12] has captured the nature of property interests well. She writes:

> property law doctrines ... carve out a position of authority for owners that is neither derived from nor subordinate to any other's. These and other rules create the institutional structure that permits the owner to function as the supreme agenda setter for the resource.

Supporters of the property approach justifiably claim that determining someone owns a bodily part or product gives them legal powers to control what happens to the property, deal with it as they wish and exclude others from it.[13] Seen in this way it is not surprising that the property approach has attracted significant support among academic commentators. It appears to chime with the principles of bodily integrity and autonomy which play such a central role in the law. The idea that anyone else, apart from ourselves, should have powers to control what happens to our bodily material sounds highly dangerous.

A particular advantage of the property approach is that it gives rights to the thing itself (*in rem*), meaning that the owner has rights against the whole world. For example, if a hospital holds some sperm for a man and that sample is taken by an intruder, only a right *in rem* will provide the man with a remedy against the intruder. Broadly speaking, other legal claims based in contract or tort, for example, are rights claimed against individuals (*in personam*) and only available against an individual who is linked to the claimant (in this example, the hospital) and would be limited to financial compensation.

Property, therefore, appears to offer a convenient solution to some of the problems with the current law. It would confirm that we own and are in control of our bodies, bodily material and products and that others cannot touch or remove body parts or deal with separated bodily material without our permission. It can give legal protection to patients who ask a hospital to store material on their behalf (such as the sperm in *Yearworth*). It protects the rights of researchers who have been given material by patients to exclude others from interfering with the material.

However, the property regime gives the generator of the bodily material primary control over what happens to it. That means the societal interests in bodily material or the claims of other people are downplayed. Of course, that is precisely the appeal of the property approach to many of its advocates. They regard the person who generates the material (normally the person from

[12] L. Katz, 'Exclusion and Exclusivity in Property Law' (2008) 58 *University of Toronto Law Journal* 275, 277.
[13] I. Goold, 'Property or Not Property? The Spectrum of Approaches to Regulating the Use of Human Bodily Material' (2013) 21 *Journal of Law and Medicine* 299.

whose body it originated) as having the strongest claim to it. It is precisely for that reason I would argue against its use.

5.2.3 The Case for a Relational Understanding

The property regime for bodies presents a very particular model of what our bodies our like. It imagines the body as a thing that is controlled, bounded and secured. Something that can be transferred to others and have others excluded from it. It is notable that, for example, wild animals are not regarded as property. That is because they cannot be retained and caged in.[14] I believe these features are shared with human bodies. Our bodies are constantly changing, impacted upon by the environment and outside forces and utterly dependent on others for survival. Our bodies are profoundly leaky.[15] Cells in our bodies are constantly dying and falling off and new cells are being created. By the time we die there is little of us that is biologically the same as when we were born. Whenever people are in proximity, bodily material can be passed through the air. As Kenneth Gergen[16] writes:

> [T]he idea of the skin as a container seems inappropriate. The metaphor of a sieve might be more relevant, with material moving in both directions. On the one hand we could say that nothing that passes through me is distinctly mine (my body); all that I call "my body" belongs to the larger world out of which it is but a transient conglomerate.

Our bodies are not made up solely of material we create. Our bodies contain bacteria, fungi and protozoa which are not human but biological organisms in their own right. We depend on these for our well-being.[17] We are less us than we like to think!

Our bodies are deeply connected with other bodies. This is powerfully shown in genetics. As Isabel Karpin[18] puts it:

> The individual in the age of the gene is fundamentally connected and vulnerable. The individual in the age of the gene always contains a trace of the other; not-one but not-two.

As argued in Chapter 3, in relationships of care, which are at the heart of our everyday lives, the bodies of carer and cared for are interdependent. For example, not only is a child dependent on their carer but the carer becomes

---

[14] Theft Act 1968, s. 4(4).

[15] M. Shildrick, *Leaky Bodies and Boundaries. Feminism, Postmodernism and (Bio)Ethics* (Routledge, 1997).

[16] K. Gergen, *Relational Being* (Oxford University Press, 2011), 23.

[17] J. Herring and P-L. Chau, 'Interconnected, Inhabited and Insecure: Why Bodies Should Not Be Property' (2014) 40 *Journal of Medical Ethics* 39.

[18] I. Karpin, 'Genetics and the Legal Conception of Self' in M. Shildrick and R. Mykitiuk (eds.) *Ethics of the Body* (MIT Press, 2005), 210, 211.

dependent on the child. If the child suffers an infectious childhood illness and is required to remain indoors, in effect this quarantine is imposed on the body of the carer too. If the child will not sleep, nor, in reality, will the parent. This is true not just in child–parent relationships but in any close relationship involving caring. In far broader ways, we are all dependent on others to meet our most basic needs: the supplying of food, warmth and shelter.

So, the image of the body presented in the property model as controlled by us, created by us and self-contained is a false one. Bodies are dependent on each other; they are deeply interconnected with other organisms and with the environment; and are in constant flux.

As will be clear from the first two chapters of the book, the issues at stake in the debates over the nature of bodies reflect the debates over the selves. The property model ties in neatly with the individualistic understanding of the body. For the relational theorist, vulnerability and dependency are central, essential, defining aspects of humanity. The division between the body of one and the body of another makes no sense in relationships of intimacy or our psychological conception of the self. All of this clashes sharply with the claims of one person seeking ownership of their bodies with the corresponding rights to exclude others. Such an approach finds a very different understanding of the role of the law from that found in the individualised conception of the self. It sees the purpose of the law as being to help maintain good relationships. Rather than keeping people apart, it is to enable caring relationships to thrive.[19]

The statement 'my body is mine' is over-simplistic. Our bodies are the product of multiple interactions with other bodies and the environment and are dependent on other bodies. We cannot claim to be entitled to own and control our bodies. We must accept there are important and legitimate interests of communities, society and those in relationship with us. These interests are not easily captured by a common law property regime. I am not saying property is not a subtle enough legal tool to be able to capture any societal, relational or communal values. My claim is that property law is particularly well honed to protect individual interests and to prioritise those interests. It is not naturally designed to protect communal interests.[20] The standard property regime is designed to protect individuals' interests from invasion from others or claims based on the social good. Although there is scope for an individual's property to be taken from them for the good of society, for example, through compulsory purchase, it normally requires an extremely strong justification based on the social good.

[19] E. Feder Kittay, 'The Body as the Place of Care' in D. Landes and A. Azucena Cruz-Pierre (eds.) *Exploring the Work of Edward S. Casey* (Bloomsbury Publishing, 2013), 205; J. Herring *Caring and the Law* (Hart, 2013).

[20] See J. Harris, *Property and Justice* (Oxford University Press, 1996) for an imagination of a property regime which is much more attuned to communal interests. It is a very different regime from the one we have.

A relational understanding shows us that relational, social and communal interests in bodies need to be recognised. The social and communal interests include those in body parts as organs that can save the lives of others; of material that can be used for crucial medical research for the benefit of all; of material that can be used for the education of future medical practitioners; and for information that is essential for the boring, but important, task of audit. Elsewhere,[21] I have argued at length in favour of a statutory regime to govern interests in human material, which can respect societal and relational claims over bodily material and I will not repeat all of the arguments here. A statutory approach enables us to differentiate between different parts of the body and different contexts of the removal of bodily parts. It might well, for example, have different regulation in relation to gametes than it does to toe nail clippings. By contrast, under the property approach, toenail clippings and gametes fall under the same property regime. A statutory approach enables us to find a balance between individual, communal and relational interest which will differ depending on the different contexts that arise and the nature of the bodily material. It will permit the law to find remedies that recognise the real nature on the wrong done, rather than treat all cases as limited to property law remedies. In short, the statutory approach offers a much more nuanced approach to the issues raised by bodily material than a property approach.

The point just made is a straightforward one. We have different interests in different body parts. The value to us of our dandruff is very different to the values we have in reproductive material. Why is that?

We can have three primary kinds of value in our bodily material. For example, in some material there are instrumental values. There is bodily material which can be used to produce good ends: it is useful for our treatment, or the treatment of others, or is useful for research, or useful for reproduction. However, other bodily material will have no use. Dried skin or waste products are rarely of interest. Indeed, not only do we have no use for them, we positively do not want to have control of them. We do not want the responsibility that flows from property interests. These responsibilities might include being responsible for disposing of the material and requiring others to obtain our consent before dealing with it.

Second, there can be expressive interests. Some body parts and material represent us in a special way and cause us to identify with them. Perhaps the best-known example is parenthood, where many biological parents feel a strong attachment to their children as a result of the biological connection. Another example is the unease people feel about face transplants, as compared with other types of transplants. This is in part due to the identifying nature of the face, unlike, say, a kidney that does not normally have expressive value. So, there are some parts of our bodies with which we particularly identify and

---

[21] Herring, 'Why We Need a Statute for Bodily Material'.

other material to which we feel no connection. We feel no connection with the hair that falls from our head as we walk down the street, but might feel legitimate concerns with what happens to our corpse on death.

Third, there are informational values. Our bodily material can tell us about ourselves. It can reveal biological origins or play a role in a criminal trial as evidence of where a person was at a particular time.

From this we can see that the values we have will differ enormously in terms of our instrumental, informational and expressive interests. There are particular body parts which, in particular circumstances, can have instrumental and/or expressive value. But for most of the time we have no interests in, for example, a cyst removed in an operation, our waste products, the bead of sweat which falls from our forehead or the flake of dandruff left on a table. Indeed, as suggested earlier, giving us property interests in this material can be potentially burdensome. In fact, I suggest, the occasions in which the average person has values in separated bodily material might arise a few times, at most, in their lifetime. We do not need, do not want, any responsibility or rights over the vast amount of bodily material that emerges from our bodies pretty much constantly.

The creation of such a statute may appear a Herculean task, but The Human Tissue Act 2004 and the Human Fertilisation and Embryology Act 1990 in the United Kingdom are statutes offering sophisticated regulation of bodily material. Neither statute is based on an explicitly property model. Yet they certainly provide real solutions in the areas they cover. What can be seen in both statutes is a recognition and balancing of competing claims over the bodily material. Indeed, these statutes have covered some of the most controversial areas involving bodily material. So, completing the task of finding a statutory regime for all human tissue and material is not as daunting as may at first appear.

I will now explore three leading cases and demonstrate the advantages of the statutory approach over a property approach.

5.2.4 Resolving Cases

In this section I will explore three cases which have arisen concerning bodily material and argue that treating the body as property would not, in fact, have produced a satisfactory solution.

5.2.4.1 *Yearworth* v. *North Bristol NHS Trust*

This case,[22] as already mentioned, involved some men who had sperm stored frozen at a hospital as they were about to undergo medical treatment which carried a risk of infertility. The plan was that the sperm could be used in

---

[22] [2009] EWCA Civ 37.

assisted reproduction if the men were indeed rendered infertile. Due to the hospital's negligence, the sperm was defrosted and rendered useless. The solution found by the court, which would be supported by supporters of the property approach, is that the sperm was the property of the men; they had bailed it to the hospital. In breach of the terms of the bailment, the hospital had rendered the sperm useless and so damages could be awarded.

However, that, I suggest, is not a satisfactory approach to take. A property approach would see damage to the sperm in this case as the same as the damage when a nurse throws away a urine sample without checking with the patient first? Categorising what happened in *Yearworth* as a case about property damage completely fails to capture the nature of the wrong that has taken place. Unless we place the harm within the context of the men's plans and hopes for a family, for the precious child–parent relationship which was to come, unless we see it in the context of the special trust between a patient and a hospital committed to care for things beyond value, unless we see it in the context of the hopes and plans of the partners of the men, we cannot really understand the nature of what has happened. The property approach fails to properly capture the wrong in issue.

5.2.4.2 *A, B and Others* v. *Leeds Teaching Hospital*

This case[23] emerged from the organ retention scandal, where it was discovered that hospitals had retained material removed from children during operations without the consent of parents. As there was no property in bodily material the parents were not able to seek any remedy from the hospital.

That case is commonly presented as a case demonstrating the failures of the law to recognise bodily material as property. However, that is not convincing. Describing the children's bodies and organs as 'property' fails to accurately describe the interests the parents have in this case.[24] The wrong here is not analogous to someone who has stolen from their deceased child's purse. The wrong here is a relational one. In caring for their sick child, the parent's emotional and psychological wellbeing has become deeply connected to the child's body. Mavis Maclean sat on the panel hearing the inquiry at the Bristol Royal Infirmary and reported that the parents did not talk of 'parental rights to the body of their child as property' but instead spoke of interference in their responsibilities as parents.

> The only immediate form of care which a parent can offer their child after death is to arrange the funeral. When this event is based on lack of information about the physical state of the child, this final act of care may for some families seem to be somehow be devalued and damaged.[25]

---

[23] [2004] EWHC 644 (QB).

[24] It may be argued that it is more important if the rights protect the interest than that they describe them. However, the language used is important when borderline cases arise.

[25] M. Maclean, 'Letting Go. Retention of Human Material after Post Mortem' in S. Day Sclater, M. Richards and A. Bainham (eds.) *Body Lore and Laws* (Hart Publishing, 2001), 81.

The loss for the parents was described in terms of failing to complete the final duty of a parent (to ensure a proper burial of their child), rather than a property loss. A right of interference in respect for family life, for example, seems to capture far more effectively the loss in question. Further, the kind of remedies that a property wrong offers, typically financial compensation, seem inappropriate here. What the parents needed was a return of the remains, psychological support, an apology and assistance with arranging for suitable disposal of the remains, rather than money to compensate for damaged property.

5.2.4.3 *Evans* v. *UK*

This case[26] involved a couple who had donated their gametes to produce stored embryos, but then disagreed on how they should be used. Property rights supporters would have us resolve this case in terms of whether the embryo was the property and who owned it. That seems to rely on the arcane rules of property ownership to resolve a case which raised complex issues over rights to reproduction, efficiency and consistency in state regulation of assisted reproduction, interests of the embryo, gender discrimination and so on. While, I accept that people can reasonably disagree on the outcome of the case, surely considering the case in terms of property offers little insight. The property approach would draw no distinction between the facts of this case and one where an artwork had been created using the hair of two people. Yet, surely the issues raised are very different.

5.2.5 Conclusion on Body Parts

This section has argued against the use of a property model to govern the legal response to bodies and bodily material. It is true that the property model presents a reassuring model of the body: our bodies are self-sufficient, secure and bounded. It claims we should have rights to control our bodies, exclude others and be independent. This is comforting, maybe, but false. The truth is our bodies are constantly changing, dependent on others for survival and subject to environmental factors.

This chapter has argued for rejoicing in the fact that our bodies are leaky, interconnected, and interdependent in biological, social and psychological senses. Our true sense of self and identity is not found in our bounded, owned body, but in the breaking, mixing and interaction of our bodies with others and with the wider environment. These important features of our fleshy nature are lost in a property account.

I have argued in favour of a statutory approach which can acknowledge that bodies are the site of conflicting individual, communal, relational and social

---

[26] *Evans* v. *UK* (2006) 43 EHRR 21.

concerns and interests. Our bodies are not simply our own, for us to profit from as individuals. They exist within, and are supported by, a broad relational framework. Our legal response must recognise that.

5.3 Capacity

The relational self model also has much to teach us about the concept of mental capacity, which plays such a major role in medical law.

A central aspect of the Mental Capacity Act 2005 (MCA)'s approach to capacity is that it is 'issue specific'. So the question is always whether a person (P) has capacity to decide a particular question. Someone may have the capacity to decide some issues, but not others. For example, P may be able to decide whether they would like a cup of hot chocolate or not but lack the capacity to be able to execute a will. In other words, P should not be dismissed as 'simply incompetent'. Except in the most extreme cases, there are likely to be at least some issues which P is able to decide for themselves. The thinking behind this stance is that we should maximise the opportunity for people to make decisions for themselves.

Section 2(1) MCA states:

> [A] person lacks capacity in relation to a matter if at the material time he is unable to make a decision for himself in relation to the matter because of an impairment of, or a disturbance in the functioning of, the mind or brain.

There are, therefore, two elements to the capacity test.[27] First, under the 'diagnostic test' it must be found that P has an impairment or a disturbance in the functioning of the brain. Under the 'functional test' it must be determined whether as a result of the disturbance P is unable to make the decision. Importantly, it must be shown that the inability to make the decision results from the impairment.[28] So, if P has a mental disorder, but it is their recalcitrance that is preventing them making a decision, they will not lack capacity for the purposes of the Act. This is a very important aspect of the test. It means that a person with a mental disorder is not automatically treated as lacking capacity. If the disorder has not impaired their decision-making ability, they will retain capacity. It also means that even if a person is unable to make a decision, but not as a result of a mental impairment, then they will not lack capacity under the MCA. For example, a person who is hopelessly in love and unable to weigh issues up in the balance will still retain capacity! Similarly, a person who has unusual religious beliefs and so understands the world in a very different way from everyone else will not as a result lack capacity.

People lack capacity if they are unable to make a decision for themselves. Section 3(1) explains:

---

[27] *A Local Authority* v. *TZ* [2013] EWHC 2322 (COP).
[28] *PC* v. *York* [2013] EWCA 478.

[A] person is unable to make a decision for himself if he is unable –

(a) to understand the information relevant to the decision,
(b) to retain that information,
(c) to use or weigh that information as part of the process of making the decision, or
(d) to communicate his decision (whether by talking, using sign language or any other means.

Once a patient is found to have capacity, their refusal to accept treatment must be respected, unless the case falls into one of the exceptional circumstances. If the patient lacks capacity then their refusal can be overridden if it is determined the treatment will promote their best interests. Clearly, there is much more to be said about this concept, and material on that can be found in the standard accounts of medical law.[29]

Much of my criticism of the current law will be based on its justification in terms of autonomy, and so before getting to the specifics of my concerns I will outline the links between autonomy and capacity.

5.3.1 Autonomy and Capacity

In this section I will seek to explore the gaps between the definition of capacity in the MCA and the nature of autonomy. In other words, I will be arguing that the MCA's definition of capacity results in some people being found to have capacity, even though in fact they are not autonomous.

There are two terrible things that can go wrong in an assessment of capacity. First, you could be assessed to lack capacity when you do not. Others will make decisions on your behalf and set aside your own wishes based on what they think is in your best interests. You lose control over your life. You are no longer in charge of your destiny. But second, you could be assessed to have capacity when you do not have it. You could suffer harms and injuries and you would be told that this was your choice, even though in fact it was not what you were choosing at all. I will argue that current law is guilty of making both of these errors. I will highlight six circumstances in which the law's use of capacity fails to properly correlate with a proper understanding of the principle of respect for autonomy.

It is worth remembering why the test for capacity is seen as important. Underpinning the law on capacity is an attachment to the principle of autonomy. We discussed this in Chapter 1, but it is commonly tied to the idea that people should be able to 'write their own story' and determine how they would like their life to go.[30] Supporters of autonomy will argue that however much others might believe that P's decision is harmful or immoral

---

[29] E.g. J. Herring, *Medical Law and Ethics* (Oxford University Press, 2018).
[30] I. Berlin, *Four Essays on Liberty* (Clarendon Press, 1961), 131.

and that an alternative course of action would be better for them, P's right to autonomy allows them to decide for themselves how they wish to live their life. The idea of someone else coming along and telling you what to do with your life, and how to live, is repellent to most people. As Ronald Dworkin explains:

> autonomy makes each of us responsible for shaping his own life according to some coherent and distinctive sense of character, conviction, and interest. It allows us to lead our own lives rather than being led along them, so that each of us can be, to the extent a scheme of rights can make this possible, what he has made himself. This view of autonomy focuses not on individual decisions one by one, but the place of each decision in a more general program or picture of life the agent is creating and constructing, a conception of character and achievement that must be allowed its own distinctive integrity.[31]

However, it flows from this that autonomy supports respecting decisions which reflect a decision we have reached based on our values and which will help us be the author of our lives. In legal terms, this is commonly put in terms of a person having capacity to make the decision. It is not protective of autonomy to respect a decision which is made by a person who lacks capacity. For example, if P is diagnosed with a terrible illness and a doctor recommends a certain medication and P does not believe they are ill and so refuses the treatment, it is far from clear that respecting P's decision to decline medication is respecting her autonomy. She believes she is not ill and will live happily as a result of her decision. But all the evidence is that she is unwell and if we follow her wishes she will die. That is not where she wants to be. Respecting her decision is not making her the author of her life. Indeed, arguably, giving her the medication, so that she is better, will be closer to putting her in the position she would like to be. This is why capacity is so important. It tells us whether a person's decision is their own and whether respecting it will be allowing a person to 'shape their lives' or not. I believe that a relational perspective greatly enriches an understanding of capacity and leads us to question the extent to which autonomy should be a paramount principle in medical law. I will develop a few points.

5.3.2 Individualised Assessment of Capacity

The first point is that assessment of capacity tends to be carried out on a highly individualistic basis. Typically, the person is sat down in front of a medical professional and asked a series of questions. Their answers are used to make determination of mental capacity. People are assessed and treated in isolation, and not seen as relational people, in mutually inter-dependant relationships.

---

[31] R. Dworkin, 'Autonomy and the Demented Self' (1986) 64 *The Milbank Quarterly* 4, at 5.

The focus is on whether the individual *on their own* can understand the relevant information, weigh it up and make a decision.[32]

This reflects a very particular understanding of what it means to have capacity to make a decision. It seems to be based on the archetype of the philosopher sitting alone in his study carefully and rationally thinking through his decision. But that is not how most people make decisions. Most think it through with others and rely on their insights. The friends chatting through a topic with a cup of tea might be the archetype of decision making, rather than the philosopher alone in his study.[33] Even if you are more of a loner, nowadays you will consult with others via the internet! One reason why consultation nearly always takes place is that important decisions are made in a relational context, looking at the burdens that may flow from the decisions and how they impact on the different responsibilities the parties have, but also within the context of the history of the relationship. In many couples and families, there is a recognition that one or other parties has expertise and a decision is delegated. For example, I know nothing at all about cars, but my partner is very knowledgeable about them. If there are car decisions to be made I follow my partner's advice. As Anita Ho argues:

> We are socially-embedded beings, such that autonomy often incorporates intrinsically relational or social content, and it is thus impossible to assess patient autonomy without critically evaluating how or whether the interconnected social, political, and health-care structural frameworks often foreclose certain opportunities or pre-determine how individuals approach various health-care situations.[34]

A relational approach would, therefore, support an assessment of capacity of an individual located within their network of family, friends and care-givers.[35] Can P, situated within their relational context, with the support and assistance of those around them, make this decision? This is not as bizarre a suggestion as it might seem to some. Professionals have become used to the idea of supported decision making when dealing with people who have learning difficulties or other impairments.[36] I am simply suggesting we apply this to all. Jennifer Nedelsky captures the approach well:

[32] N. Stoljar, 'Informed Consent and Relational Conceptions of Autonomy' (2011) 36 *Journal of Medicine and Philosophy* 375; T. Breden and J. Vollmann, 'The Cognitive Based Approach of Capacity Assessment in Psychiatry: A Philosophical Critique of the MacCAT-T' (2004) 12 *Health Care Analysis* 273.

[33] R. Gilbar, 'Family Involvement, Independence, and Patient Autonomy in Practice' (2011) *Medical Law Review* 192.

[34] A. Ho, 'The Individualist Model of Autonomy and the Challenge of Disability' (2008) 5 *Journal of Bioethical Inquiry* 193.

[35] H. Mun Chan, 'Sharing Death and Dying: Advance Directives Autonomy and the Family' (2004) 18 *Bioethics* 87.

[36] J. Craigie, M. Bach, S. Gurbai, A. Kanter, S. Kim, O. Lewis and G. Morgan 'Legal Capacity, Mental Capacity and Supported Decision-Making' (2019) 62 *International Journal of Law and Psychiatry* 160.

I see autonomy as the core of a capacity to engage in the ongoing, interactive creation of our selves – our relational selves, our selves that are constituted, yet not determined, by the web of nested relations within which we live ... As we act (usually partially) autonomously, we are always in interaction with the relationships (intimate and socialstructural) that enable our autonomy. Relations are then constitutive of autonomy rather than conditions for it.[37]

Of course, considering a person's relational context might, in some cases, mean that a person is found to lack capacity, rather than have it.[38] *A Local Authority* v. *Mr and Mrs A*[39] shows that well. Mrs A was held to be so dominated by her husband that she was unable to make a decision for herself as to contraceptive treatment. For her, the Court held, capacity was to be found not in removing her from the relationship, but rather enabling the decision to be made with others (her social worker support team) that would better help her make her own mind up.[40]

5.3.3 The Presumption of Capacity

The second issue around capacity which can be helpfully examined through a relational lens is the presumption in favour of capacity.[41] Section 1(2) of the MCA makes it clear that the law presumes that a person (P) is competent unless there is evidence that they are not.[42] If the case comes to court, the burden is on the person who treated P as lacking capacity to demonstrate that P indeed lacked capacity on the balance of probabilities.[43] Understandably, when the court is determining whether P has capacity the views of the medical experts carry 'very considerable importance'.[44] In this section I will challenge this assumption.[45]

In order to consider the legitimacy of the presumption it is helpful to explore the two primary reasons why lawyers use presumptions. The first is for evidential reasons based on statistical observation. The second is a matter of principle. So, the first presumption may simply be that if there is a

---

[37] J. Nedelsky, *Law's Relations* (Oxford University Press, 2012), 45–46

[38] Ibid.

[39] [2010] EWHC 1549 (Fam).

[40] S. Moorman, 'Older Adults' Preferences for Independent or Delegated End-of-Life Medical Decision Making' (2011) 23 *Journal of Ageing and Health* 135.

[41] R. Berghams, D. Dickenson, and R. Ter Meulen, "Mental Capacity: In Search of Alternative Perspectives" (2004) 12 *Health Care Analysis* 251.

[42] *R* v. *Sullivan* [1984] AC 156, 170–171.

[43] *R (N)* v. *Dr M, A NHS Trust* [2002] EWHC 1911. Section 5 of the MCA offers a legal protection to those who treat a patient based on a reasonable but incorrect assessment that they lack capacity.

[44] *A NHS Trust* v. *Dr A* [2013] EWHC 2442 (COP).

[45] J. Herring, 'Peter Skegg and the Question No-One Asks: Why Presume Capacity?' in J. Wall and M. Henaghan (eds.), *Law, Ethics, and Medicine: Essays in Honour of Peter Skegg* (Thomson, 2017), 41.

correlation whereby if fact A is shown to be true then B is very likely to be true, the court can presume from proof of fact A that fact B is true. For example, the law presumes a father named on a birth certificate is the father of the child, because most (but not all!) named men are indeed the father. Presumptions based on principle are rather different; they are designed to protect a legal policy which should be followed, save where there is clear evidence otherwise.[46] A good example is the presumption of innocence. This is probably not based on statistical evidence. It is (presumably!) not true that the clear majority of people charged with criminal offences are innocent. Nevertheless we presume they are because we think the conviction of the innocent is such a serious outcome, liable to cause the defendant such harm that we should only do this if we are certain, or as certain as we can be about the guilt.

So, looking at the presumption of capacity, this might be seen as a statistical claim or one based on legal principle.

Let us first consider whether it is statistically true that people have capacity to make decisions for themselves. I very much doubt anywhere close to a clear majority of people have mental capacity to make decisions, certainly decisions in a medical context. As Welie and Welie suggest:[47]

> the autonomous patient – or, more precisely, the patient who invokes his right to respect his autonomy in order to exert his freedom and personal responsibility – is the exception rather than the rule. The incompetent patient is the rule, the starting point – or, more precisely, the patient in the care of whom concerns about autonomy (in the libertarian sense of that term) do not even arise. ... The question, then, is not when does a patient become incompetent, but what makes him competent such that his call for respect of his autonomy must be granted, notwithstanding risk to well-being, health or life.

I have developed this argument elsewhere,[48] but will summarise it briefly here. To have capacity a person (P) must understand the key facts relevant to the decision. P cannot be taken to have made a decision unless she understands her current position, the treatment that is being offered and the potential consequences of the treatment. It seems unlikely that we could presume that a patient will know the information concerned. Consider, for example, the question of consent to delivery of a baby. Cobb J has held:[49]

In considering the mode of the delivery of the baby, I suggest that a prospective mother would need to be able to understand, retain and weigh the information relevant to:

---

[46] J. Salmond, *Jurisprudence or the Theory of the Law* (Stevens and Haynes, 1902), 590.

[47] J. Welie and S. Welie, 'Is Incompetence the Exception or the Rule?' (2001) 4 *Medicine, Health Care and Philosophy* 125, 125.

[48] Herring, 'Peter Skegg and the Question No-One Asks: Why Presume Capacity?'.

[49] *The Mental Health Trust* v. *DD* [2014] EWCOP 11, [65].

(i) Ante-natal care and monitoring, including blood tests to check for anaemia and diabetes; urine tests to check for infections; the benefits of discussion with health services about delivery options;

(ii) Ante-natal monitoring of the foetus; the value of an ultra-sound imaging;

(iii) Mode of delivery of the baby, including vaginal delivery, and caesarean section;

(iv) Natural and/or induced labour;

(v) Anaesthesia and pain relief;

(vi) The place of delivery – e.g. at home or in a hospital – and the risks and benefits of each option;

(vii) The risk of complications, arising from conditions relevant to the mother or the baby;

(viii) Post-natal care of mother and baby.

It is hard to believe that a very high percentage of the population could be taken to know this information.

To be autonomous a person must not only understand the information: they must be able to use it. Jennifer Drobac and Oliver Goodenough, in their analysis of the psychology of decision making, list the following requirements for rational use of information:[50]

(i) parties with stable, well ordered preferences,

(ii) choices that are fully voluntary and unconstrained;

(iii) relatively equal, and ideally complete, information;

(iv) relatively equal bargaining power and experience;

(v) sufficient cognitive capacity to evaluate the transaction and to exercise voluntary control over the conflicting factors and emotions involved;

(vi) the absence of monopoly power or other distortions of the market;

(vii) the presence of good faith and absence of fraud in both parties; and

(viii) a level of consequence for a mistake that is not disastrous to the party.

The authors, after examining the latest neuroscience and psychology, suggest that few people have capacity.[51] They are not alone in their analysis. Neil Levy refers to a wide range of psychological studies which reveal 'fallibilities of human reasoning' (including 'myopia for the future', 'motivated reasoning' and 'biases' in 'assessing probabilities ... exacerbated ... under cognitive load').[52] He concludes that 'Human beings are, under a variety of conditions, systematically bad reasoners, and many of their reasoning faults can be

---

[50] J. Drobac and O. Goodenough, 'Exposing the Myth of Consent' (2015) 12 *Indiana Health Law Review* 1.

[51] Ibid.

[52] N. Levy, 'Forced to Be Free? Increasing Patient Autonomy by Constraining It' (2014) 40 *Journal of Medical Ethics* 293.

expected to affect the kind of judgements that they make when they are called upon to give informed consent.' To similar effect, Sarah Conly writes:[53]

> As has by now been discussed convincingly and exhaustively (notably by Nobel Prize-winning Daniel Kahneman and Amos Tversky), we suffer from common, apparently ineradicable tendencies to "cognitive bias," which means that in many common situations, our decision-making goes askew. These biases are many and varied, but they have in common that they interfere with our appreciation of even quite simple facts, and lead us to choose ineffective means to our ends.

Not only must a person be able to think rationally; if a person it to be able to act autonomously, it is necessary for a person to have values and relate the information to their goals.[54] Catriona Makenzie and Wendy Rogers argue that to be able to exercise autonomy people need to be the following:[55]

> self-determining: being "able to determine one's own beliefs, values, goals and wants, and to make choices regarding matters of practical import to one's life free from undue interference. The obverse of self-determination is determination by other persons, or by external forces or constraints."[56]

> Self-governing: "being be able to make choices and enact decisions that express, or are consistent with, one's values, beliefs and commitments. Whereas the threats to self-determination are typically external, the threats to self-governance are typically internal, and often involve volitional or cognitive failings. Weakness of will and failures of self-control are common volitional failings that interfere with self-governance."[57]

> Having authenticity: "a person's decisions, values, beliefs and commitments must be her 'own' in some relevant sense; that is, she must identify herself with them and they must cohere with her 'practical identity', her sense of who she is and what matters to her. Actions or decisions that a person feels were foisted on her, which do not cohere with her sense of herself, or from which she feels alienated, are not autonomous."[58]

I would certainly question how many people are in a position to do all of these things, particularly in the case of patients refusing strongly recommended treatment. A good number of cases where patients are refusing treatment are those where a patient is affected by a fear or disorder where there is a question mark over the extent to which their decisions are genuinely their own. Of course, there are plenty of those refusing who do have capacity. My point is simply that we are well short of the kind of percentages which would justify a statistical presumption.

---

[53] S. Conly 'Against Paternalism' (2014) 40 *Journal of Medical Ethics* 349.
[54] See, for further discussion, J. Herring and J. Wall, 'Autonomy, Capacity and Vulnerable Adults: Filling the Gaps in the Mental Capacity Act' (2016) *Legal Studies* 698.
[55] C. Mackenzie and W. Rogers, 'Autonomy, Vulnerability and Capacity: A Philosophical Appraisal of the Mental Capacity Act' (2013) 9 *International Journal of the Law in Context* 37.
[56] Ibid.
[57] Ibid.
[58] Ibid.

My conclusion is, then, that any argument that states we can properly assume that the large majority of people have capacity to make an autonomous decision is unfounded. It cannot form the basis of a presumption of capacity.

But what about justifying the presumption as a presumption of principle? It might be suggested that the presumption of capacity is based on the principle of respect for human rights. For example, Berghams, Dickenson and Ter Meulen suggest the presumption expresses 'respect for autonomy and dignity rights'.[59] Eric Vogelstein writes:[60]

> A competent patient has a strong prima facie right, based on the moral value of her autonomy or self-determination, to determine her own medical treatment (or lack thereof); an incompetent patient lacks that strong prima facie right.

The presumption of capacity on this understanding plays its role in maximising the number of people able to exercise their right to make their own decisions. As Michael Gunn puts it 'Respect for autonomy is the guiding principle in health care law. It is, therefore, essential that a test for capacity sets a standard which allows as many people as possible to take their own treatment decisions.'[61] The argument is, therefore, that just as the presumption of innocence is designed to support the view that we would rather the guilty go free than the innocent be acquitted, so the presumption is based on a claim that we would rather find a person without capacity to be capacitous, than treat a patient as lacking capacity who in fact has capacity. However, that, unlike the presumption of innocence, is highly questionable. Where an innocent person is found guilty they suffer nothing but harm, serious harm, and it is right we should avoid this at all costs (including acquitting the guilty). Where a person is found to lack capacity when they have it, they receive the treatment an expert determines is in their best interests. That is not bad. The treatment will in an expert objective assessment be good for them. It does commit some wrong in going against their wishes, but usually temporarily. It is far from clear that the wrong in such a case is sufficiently serious that we can justify denying beneficial treatment to patients who should get it.

To conclude this section, the presumption of capacity seems implausible as a presumption of fact, and unjustifiable as a matter of principle.

5.3.4 Blurring the Capacity/Non-capacity Line

Much more could be said about this understanding of autonomy, but as will already be clear it is wrong to regard autonomy or capacity as an 'all or

---

[59] Berghams, Dickenson, and Ter Meulen, 'Mental Capacity: In Search of Alternative Perspectives', 251.
[60] E. Vogelstein, 'Competence and Ability' (2014) 28 *Bioethics* 235, 235.
[61] M. Gunn, 'The Meaning of Incapacity' (1994) 2 *Medical Law Review* 8, 9.

nothing' thing.[62] It is much better to regard capacity as on a scale.[63] A considered autonomous decision, based on full knowledge of the facts and reflecting a person's underlying and enduring values, might be thought to be deserving of greater moral weight than the decision based on mistakes or which is inconsistent with the values they live their life by.[64] In short, not all autonomous decisions deserve the same level of protection.[65]

Yet under the approach traditionally adopted by the Mental Capacity Act 2005 there is no room for giving different weights to autonomy. Bev Clough[66] argues that this causes the current approach to mental capacity to be under- and over-inclusive:

> It may be over-inclusive in that it wrongly focuses on those with certain cognitive impairments, such as those with learning disabilities or dementia, and stigmatises them through a lens of disability and incapacity. However, the Act may be under-inclusive in that others who are in abusive relationships, or who are subject to oppression and domination, are left outside of the legal purview because their decisions are deemed to be autonomous as they are not tainted by the presence of a cognitive impairment.

Once a person is found to have capacity, their decision is respected as much whether they are close to the borderline of incapacity or as richly autonomous as a person may wish. This causes problems in a range of cases. Consider, for example, *Re MB*,[67] where due to a needle phobia a woman refused to consent to a Caesarean section which she wanted and was necessary in order to save her life and that of the foetus. The Court of Appeal stated that to force the injection on her against her wishes would be to infringe her autonomy, although it was permissible in that case because she lacked capacity to refuse the injection and it would be in her best interests to receive it. But was this a correct classification of her autonomous wishes?

A better analysis is that MB had contradictory wishes: to have the Caesarean section operation, but not to have the injection. To not give her the injection would respect one decision but thwart the other. In such a case, if we are seeking to protect the principle of autonomy, the court should seek to ascertain, between the two conflicting decisions, which is closer to the individual's sense of identity. In *Re MB*, if such an approach was taken surely the desire to

---

[62] B. Clough, 'Disability and Vulnerability: Challenging the Capacity/Incapacity Binary' (2017) 16 *Social Policy and Society* 469.

[63] P. Bielby, 'Not "Us" and "Them": Towards a Normative Legal Theory of Mental Health Vulnerability' (2019) 15 *International Journal of Law in Context* 51.

[64] J. Craigie, 'Capacity, Value Neutrality and the Ability to Consider the Future' (2013) 9 *International Journal of Law in Context* 4.

[65] S. Gilmore and J. Herring, '"No" is the Hardest Word: Consent And Children's Autonomy' (2011) 23 *Child and Family Law Quarterly* 3; J. Coggon and J. Miola, 'Autonomy, Liberty and Medical Decision-Making' (2011) *Cambridge Law Journal* 523.

[66] Clough, 'Disability and Vulnerability: Challenging the Capacity/Incapacity Binary', 469.

[67] [1997] 2 FCR 541.

remain alive and give birth to a healthy baby was more important to her than the wish to avoid the prick of a needle.[68] The issue could be put in these terms: should her wishes and beliefs as experienced over a considerable time be given less weight than the momentary decision to reject the injection in a moment of anguish? A similar issue arises in relation to addicted patients who may wish to use a substance and not wish to be addicted.[69]

Where there are conflicting wishes, it can help to distinguish between P's first-order desires and their second-order appropriation of, or identification with, the desires. The problem is that the MCA is effectively unable to account for circumstances where P's decision may not be motivated by their authentic own values, wishes or desires. In other cases, it not possible to determine whether P's desires are 'authentic' and chosen. This can be particularly relevant in cases where P is anorexic. If we are seeking to follow P's autonomous wishes does this mean listening to the P who existed before they developed the condition or the P as they are now. Which is the 'real' P?

These questions are not really dealt with by the MCA. Under the Act, it is sufficient for P to understand the information and use it to make a decision. It provides no mechanism for determining whether their values or preferences are those that have been adopted by the decision maker. An obvious case could be someone in an abusive relationship, in which the abuser has come to have utter control over their victim. Less dramatically, P has values and has reached a decision which is consistent with some of their values and not others. This is, of course, common. The best-known scenario is where a person satisfies their short-term desire over a longer term goal. Dieters or those trying to quit smoking, for example, will inevitably experience a clash between a carefully thought out decision, to diet or quit smoking, and an immediate desire, to eat or smoke.

Identifying these cases, however, can be extremely difficult. We are all inevitably influenced by our family and broader society. How we view ourselves and what we value in life are conceptions of the value that are influenced, caused or constituted by our social relationships and social conditions. Social-relational factors are essential in the development of our capacity for autonomous decision making.[70] We are probably overconfident, if anything, of being actually capable of shaking off the shackles of our relational and social context to form values genuinely 'of our own'. The truth is that all our decisions are impacted to some extent by outside factors, and they do not neatly break down into decisions which are 'ours' and therefore capacitous and decisions which are imposed upon us and so not capacitous.

[68] J. Herring, 'The Caesarean Section Cases and the Supremacy of Autonomy' in M. Freeman and A. Lewis (eds.) *Law and Medicine* (Oxford University Press, 2000).
[69] A. Andreou, 'Making a Clean Break: Addiction and Ulysses Contracts' (2008) 22 *Bioethics* 25.
[70] J. Herring, *Relational Autonomy and Family Law* (Springer, 2014).

To have capacity and be autonomous one must understand the relevant information to make the decision. However, much depends here on what constitutes 'relevant information'. That in turn will often depend on how one interprets the question to be decided. Consider, for example, the question in *A Local Authority* v. *Mr and Mrs A*[71] of whether Mrs A had capacity to make a decision about contraception. While she understood the fact contraception stopped her becoming pregnant, she did not understand that if she did become pregnant given her history it was nearly inevitable that any child born to her would be removed at birth. She wanted to have and care for a child and so chose to stop taking the contraception. The finding that she had sufficient understanding to make the decision must be questioned. It should be remembered that the outcome of the decision is that she is going to undergo the pain and discomfort of pregnancy and birth, followed by the agony of having her children removed. We are justifying this in the name that this respects her autonomy. But her choice in this case was very different from the outcome that arose. Again, we see here the law opting for a narrow interpretation of capacity, meaning that a person's decision is respected without it being an autonomous decision in a rich sense. While that may be appropriate in relation to decisions over minor issues, to rely on it when the decision involves a major aspect of a person's well-being is unjustified.

As this section has sought to demonstrate, although we might like to think there is a clear line between which decisions are made with capacity and which are not, in fact it is an extremely blurry line. Those seeking to respect autonomy face an uphill task in dividing the autonomous from the non-autonomous and in some cases in deciding which of two decisions is the most autonomous.

5.3.5 Solving the Problem

Enough has been said in this section (and more examples could have been used) to show that it is overly simplistic to simply rely on the principle 'we should respect the decision of the patient'. Complex cases are nearly always those where the patient has conflicting wishes either currently or between their wishes now and their longstanding values.

Generally, the courts seem reluctant to find a person to lack capacity. This raises the concerning possibility that a court would determine that because a person has been found to have capacity, the court cannot intervene to protect them (despite genuine concern as to their autonomy). For example, in *PC* v. *York*,[72] although the Court of Appeal claimed to be respecting PC's autonomy by not interfering in her decision, as they themselves admitted, her decision was based on a fundamental misunderstanding of the facts. Respecting a decision based on a major mistake is not respecting autonomy. It is also a

---

[71] [2010] EWHC 1549 (Fam).
[72] [2013] EWCA 478.

failure of the legal system to comply with its obligations under the Human Rights Act 1998 and the European Convention on Human Rights to take reasonable steps to protect vulnerable adults from violence and harm, as set out in Chapter 3. So what can be done?

One response might be to suggest we should seek to promote the decision-making of everyone. Ginerva Richardson uses the UN Convention on the Rights of Persons with Disabilities (CRPD) to make this point:

> Under the CRPD, the approach is very different. The emphasis has moved from substitute to supported decision-making. Decisions are no longer to be made, however benignly, on behalf of the person with disability; instead she is to be supported and encouraged to make her own decisions. In its purest form there is no point beyond which legal capacity is lost. There is no binary divide. Article 12 of the Convention provides:
>
> (1) "States Parties reaffirm that persons with disabilities have the right to recognition everywhere as persons before the law."
> (2) "States Parties shall recognize that persons with disabilities enjoy legal capacity on an equal basis with others in all aspects of life."
>
> These two paragraphs can be read as requiring the law to give the same status and respect to decisions made by people with mental disabilities, however great the impact of those disabilities on their decision-making, as it gives to the decisions made by others. *Legal* capacity should not be dependent on *mental* capacity.[73]

This argument that we should respect people's decisions whether or not they have mental capacity promotes a strong non-discriminatory approach. We should not distinguish between the rights and respect due those with capacity and without capacity. There is an obvious appeal to such an approach. But it should be acknowledged that this argument is not based on the principle of autonomy. As argued in previous sections, a person who lacks capacity lacks the capacity to direct their lives. So the argument in favour of respecting their views must lie in other values. I have suggested these might be liberty, dignity or pluralism.[74] Such an approach may well sit well with the concept of the relational self. It will recognise that our vulnerability means that we all lack full capacity, that no one is in a position to make a decision on behalf of someone else. Making decisions together with those around us might be the best we can expect.

5.3.6 Conclusions on Capacity

This section has highlighted the fiction presented by the model of autonomy as it is commonly presented.[75] The traditional notion of autonomy promotes the

---

[73] G. Richardson, 'Mental Capacity in the Shadow of Suicide: What Can the Law Do?' (2013) 9 *International Journal of Law in Context* 87.

[74] J. Herring, 'Entering the Fog: On the Borderlines of Mental Capacity' (2008) 83 *Indiana Law Journal* 1619.

[75] Herring, *Relational Autonomy and Family Law*.

concept of an isolated patient deciding for himself what is in his best interests (the image of 'the male in the prime of his life'[76]), whereas in fact we live lives based on interdependent relationships.[77] It assumes that we can say straightforwardly 'this is my life' and I can do what I want with it, ignoring the deep interconnections explored in Chapter 2. We need therefore to recognise that for most patients the question is not simply 'what is best for me?', but rather, 'given the responsibilities I owe to those in relationships with me and the responsibilities owed to me by others, what is the most appropriate course of action?'[78] We need a vision of autonomy that promotes the values of love, loyalty, friendship and care.[79] We need to examine people's choices in light of the relationships within which they live and the feelings of worry, concern for others and obligation that they may have.[80] We need too to recognise our deeply flawed decision-making processes and understanding of the world. The pretence that we make our decisions based on detailed knowledge, using values we have chosen for ourselves, and in a rational way, needs to be set aside. A more helpful model is relational autonomy, as explored in Chapter 1.

In a helpful discussion on relational autonomy, Natalie Stoljar[81] considers a woman deciding whether to take hormone replacement therapy for menopausal symptoms. Such a woman is likely to be given all the relevant medical facts:

> However, the decision-making process will likely be influenced by factors in addition to a weighing up of the medical evidence that is presented to the woman, including her education, race, and class; her conception of herself and her unique experience of menopause; cultural norms such as that looking young is attractive and valued whereas looking old is unattractive and devalued; the attitude of family members to the symptoms of menopause; the support of family members for the woman's decision; and so on. The complexity of all these factors and the uncertainty experienced by the woman in weighing them up may lead to diminished self-trust. Informed consent, as an opportunity concept, is inadequate to ensure that agents *exercise* their preference formation with the required subject-referring attitudes. The process of preference formation that we call informed consent is therefore not sufficient for autonomy.

With these concerns in mind she advocates the following:

> Taking relational autonomy seriously suggests that in addition to securing informed consent, health care providers have an important role to play in

[76] A. Donchin, 'Understanding Autonomy Relationally' (2001) 26 *Journal of Medicine and Philosophy* 365.
[77] Herring, 'The Caesarean Section Cases and the Supremacy of Autonomy', 278.
[78] R. West, *Caring for Justice* (New York University Press, 1997).
[79] C. Mackenzie and N. Stoljar (eds.) *Relational Autonomy* (Oxford University Press, 2000).
[80] S. Dodds, 'Choice and Control in Feminist Bioethics' in C. Mackenzie and N. Stoljar (eds.) *Relational Autonomy* (Oxford University Press, 2000), 213.
[81] Stoljar, 'Informed Consent and Relational Conceptions of Autonomy', 375.

promoting patient autonomy. Providers must be alert to the social conditions that affect patients' capacities for autonomous reasoning. For example, internalized norms may undermine an agent's sensitivity to the options that are available to her; and cultural or family expectations may erode a patient's "self-referring attitudes" and lead to diminished self-confidence and self-esteem. The provider must therefore take positive steps to counteract these effects, for instance, encourage imaginative reflection on different options and create the conditions in which patients truly feel authorized to speak for themselves.

This kind of approach which acknowledges our connections with others, our need to consult and work with others when making our decisions and our flawed decision making abilities provides reasons for respecting the decisions reached. But does not need to rely on the artifice that we can act autonomously.

5.4 Best Interests

Under the Mental Capacity Act 2005, if it is found that P lacks capacity then a decision about them can be made based on an assessment of their best interests.[82] The concept of best interests is understood in a broad sense. The *Mental Capacity Act 2005: Code of Practice* states:

> When working out what is in the best interests of the person who lacks capacity to make a decision or act for themselves, decision-makers must take into account all relevant factors that it would be reasonable to consider, not just those that they think are important. They must not act or make a decision based on what they would want to do if they were the person who lacked capacity.[83]

For the purposes of this book, the key issue is that the concept of best interests is focused on P's best interests, and the interests of others cannot be taken into account.[84] Section 4(7) states that in determining P's best interests the decision maker must:

> ... take into account, if it is practical and appropriate to consult them, the views of –
>
> ...
>
> (b) anyone engaged in caring for the person or interested in his welfare
>
> ...
>
> as to what would be in the person's best interests.

---

[82] Mental Capacity Act 2005, s 4.

[83] Department for Constitutional Affairs, *Mental Capacity Act 2005: Code of Practice* (The Stationery Office, 2007), para 5.7.

[84] Mental Capacity Act 2005, s 4. See further J. Manthorpe, J. Rapaport and N. Stanley, 'Who Decides Now? Protecting and Empowering Vulnerable Adults' (2007) 37 *British Journal of Social Work* 557.

This makes it clear that carers, friends and family members can be consulted over what they believe to be in P's interests. However, the decision maker should not take into account their own interests. The only way this might be possible is if it can be 'dressed' up as being about the benefit of the individual. So, if a carer says 'if my views on this issue are not followed, I will cease to care for this person, and that will cause them to suffer', then her views will be given weight. It would often not be in the best interests of the person lacking capacity to be left without a carer. However, if the carer were to say 'the burden of care will be greatly eased if my views are followed and doing so will not really harm the individual, but if my views are not followed, despite my disappointment I will make sure the individual does not suffer', then their views do not appear to be relevant. That is because they do not directly relate to the well-being of the person lacking capacity. Remarkably, this means that if a decision would enormously ease the burden for the carer but slightly harm P it cannot be made. So, imagine a case where a daughter has to travel 100 miles each day to visit her mother in a care home. A place opens up in a care home close to where the daughter lives, but the evidence suggests that the move would be slightly disconcerting for P. Then the move could not be made.

The flaw in this approach is that it imagines we can hermetically seal the interests of P and consider them separately from the interests of those with whom they are in relationship. As will be clear from the earlier chapters in this book, I argue that is artificial and undesirable. The decision of *Re Y (Mental Patient: Bone Marrow Donation)*[85] provides a revealing example of how the best interests test operates ineffectively because of the individualised approach towards best interests. A 25-year-old woman (Y) lacked capacity and lived in a community home, where she was regularly visited by her mother. Y's sister suffered from a bone disorder and her only prospect of recovery was if a bone marrow donor could be found. The only suitable donor who could be found was Y. The sister sought a declaration that the harvesting of Y's bone marrow be authorised. Connell J granted the declaration. The donation would be in Y's best interests. It was explained that Y's mother was very important to Y's welfare. Y was anxious due to the sister's illness. If the sister died this would have a severe impact on the mother's health and this would, in turn, impact on Y's welfare. It was, therefore, in the interest of Y's welfare to donate the marrow. The physical discomfort and invasion caused by the donation were outweighed by the emotion and psychological benefits of her relationship with her mother. My argument will be not that the result reached was incorrect, but that the reasoning is weak. The same reasoning could be used if Y's sister needed cosmetic surgery and that using tissue from Y would help the surgery go well, if that gave the mother pleasure and therefore helped her care for

---

[85] [1997] 2 FCR 172.

Y. To exclude from the reasoning the fact that a life would be saved seems to ignore the elephant in the room.

I will argue in this section that best interests should be understood in a relational way.[86] In other words, that instead of asking 'what is in the interest of P' we ask 'what will promote a good caring relationship for the network of caring relationships of which P is part'. Of course, in relational self terms these are asking the same question.

In support of this claim I would make the following points:

(i) There is in the case law increasing acceptance of the idea that when considering P's best interests the decision maker should pay particular attention to the factors mentioned in section 4(6) MCA:

    (a) the person's past and present wishes and feelings (and, in particular, any relevant written statement made by him when he had capacity),

    (b) the beliefs and values that would be likely to influence his decisions if he had capacity, and

    (c) the other factors that he would be likely to consider if he were able to do so.

I argue that a consideration of these factors should include a consideration of the interests of those with whom P is in relationship. There are very few people who live utterly selfish lives and do not consider the interests of others. Most people want good things for those they love. Indeed, many people are willing to make considerable sacrifices in their own well-being for the good of those they love.

(ii) Best interests and virtue.

When we think of best interests we should think of this in the broad sense.[87] As Butler-Sloss P in *JS v An NHS Trust* stated, the Court should define best interests 'in the widest possible way'.[88] The *Code of Practice* gives a good example:

> The Act allows actions that benefit other people, as long as they are in the best interests of the person who lacks capacity to make the decision. For example, having considered all the circumstances of the particular case, a decision might be made to take a blood sample from a person who lacks capacity to consent, to check for a genetic link to cancer within the family, because this might benefit someone else in the family. But it might still be in the best interests of the person who lacks capacity. 'Best interests' goes beyond the person's medical interests.[89]

---

[86] J. Herring, 'The Place of Carers' in M. Freeman (ed.) *Law and Bioethics* (Oxford University Press, 2008), 225.

[87] For a detailed discussion of this argument see J. Herring and C. Foster, 'Welfare Means Rationality, Virtue and Altruism' (2012) 32 *Legal Studies* 480.

[88] [2002] EWHC 2734 (Fam), para 60.

[89] Department of Constitutional Affairs, *Mental Capacity Act 2005: Code of Practice* (The Stationery Office, 2007), para 5.48.

This highlights the point that when we are considering best interests we are thinking about what is a good life for someone: what makes their life go well. We might consider here what a person would like to be known for and what gives them pleasure. I would argue that this includes a degree of altruism and strong relationships. We would not normally say that a person who lived a life marked by selfishness who did not have close relationships had had a good life. A person who was known to be kind, generous and ready to help their friends would be seen as having a good life. So, we can say in deciding what is in a person's best interests, considering the interests of those they are in relationship with is entirely appropriate. It will be in their best interests to be appropriately altruistic. It might be said that it would not be in the best interests of a person lacking capacity for every decision made about them to consider only their needs. No one actually lives their lives only considering their own interests and placing no weight on the interests of others. Such a way of life would be neither rewarding nor beneficial.[90] No one would want to be cared for in a relationship in which one person's interests counted for nothing. The relationship of caring does, and should, involve give and take. It is not in either party's best interests to be in a relationship which is utterly oppressive of one.[91] It is, therefore, argued that when considering the best interests of an incompetent person such an assessment must consider their well-being in the context of their relationships. This might involve making decisions which in a narrow way do not explicitly promote P's welfare or even slightly harm it, if that is a fair aspect of a caring relationship which is a necessary part of P's well-being.

In fact, this argument has some support in the case law. In *Re G(T)*,[92] the Court had to consider the position of a woman who lacked capacity to make decisions for herself. One of her children was in great need. The question was whether some of the woman's money should be given to her. As the judge noted, at one level the question may appear clear because the giving of the money would not help Mrs G. However, he disagreed with that conclusion:

> the word "interests" in the phrase "best interests" is not confined to matters of self-interest or, putting it another way, a court could conclude in an appropriate case that it is in the interests of P for P to act altruistically. It seems unlikely that the legislature thought that the power to make gifts should be confined to gifts which were not altruistic or where the gift would

[90] J. Piliavin and H.-W. Charng, 'Altruism: A Review of Recent Literature and Research' (1990) 16 *Annual Review of Sociology* 27 discusses the nature of altruism.

[91] For a development of this approach in relation to parents and children, see J. Herring, 'The Human Rights Act and the Welfare Principle in Family Law – Conflicting or Complementary?' (1999) 11 *Child and Family Law Quarterly* 223.

[92] [2010] EWHC 3005 (COP).

confer a benefit on P (or the donor of the lasting power of attorney) by reason of that person's emotional response to knowing of the gift.[93]

The judge noted that under section 4(6)(b) and (c) the Court was required to consider matters P would be likely to consider if she had capacity. These could include altruism.

(iii) Interconnection.

I argue that it is impossible to consider P's well-being without considering the interests of those in close relationship with them. The interests of the two are intertwined. As the US President's Council on Bioethics puts it:

> As a simple rule of thumb, caregivers should do the best they can do; they are never compelled to do what they cannot do, but they are obligated to see how much they can do without deforming or destroying their entire lives. But in practice, this rule of thumb rarely leads to any fixed rules, because every person faces different demands and has different capacities. And inevitably, we cannot do our best simultaneously in every area of our life: that is to say, we cannot do our best for everyone all the time; we cannot be there for everyone all the time; we cannot devote resources to everyone equally all the time. To be a caregiver is to confront not only the limitations of the person with dementia who relies upon us entirely, but our own limitations as human beings who are more than just caregivers or who are caregivers in multiple ways for multiple people.[94]

> As we discussed in Chapter 3, in relationships of care the line between 'carer' and 'cared for' breaks down and their relationship is marked by interdependency. What is good for one is good for another. A harm to the one will be a harm to another.[95]

So can we be more precise about how the interests of carers should be taken into account? It is suggested that the key is to examine the decision at issue in the context of the relationship between two people. How does this decision fit in with the giving and taking involved in this relationship? This will mean that carers will not be treated 'as objects to be manipulated as part of patient care'.[96] There will be decisions that looked at in isolation can be seen as favouring one party or another. However, if they are reasonable within the context of the caring relationship, they can be seen as an acceptable part of a relationship which is in the welfare interests of both parties. Of course, it is extremely difficult, if not impossible, to imagine that a decision that severely harms either the carer or the dependant could be seen as justified in the context of a relationship.[97]

---

[93] Ibid., para 35.

[94] President's Council on Bioethics, *Taking Care* (President's Council on Bioethics, 2004), 198.

[95] D. Gibson, *Aged Care: Old Policies, New Solutions* (Cambridge University Press, 2005).

[96] M. Minow, 'Who's the Patient?' (1994) 53 *Maryland Law Review* 1173.

[97] For a different view see P. Lewis, 'Procedures That Are against the Medical Interests of Incompetent Adults' (2002) 22 *Oxford Journal of Legal Studies* 575.

5.5 Personhood

One of the 'great debates' in medical law and ethics is over the concept of personhood. The terminology is potentially misleading because we are not discussing a biological term but an ethical one. In short, personhood captures the idea of the 'highest moral status'. If a being has personhood they belong to the category of 'highest moral status' (or at least highest moral status that we know about). In practical terms, it means this: if there was a fire in a house and you could rescue a person or a non-person you should rescue the person. So you should rescue your child (a person) before your computer (a non-person). Similarly, for lawyers, if there was a case which required us to balance the interests of a person and a non-person the law should prefer those of the person. The concept of human rights is used to indicate there are special rights attaching to persons that other beings do not have. Meat eaters believe it is acceptable to kill animals (whom most regard as non-persons) to feed humans (whom most regard as persons) but not to kill a person to feed an animal. You can see why the subject is so important in medical law. It is at the heart of the debates over whether a foetus has a 'right to life' and whether a person in PVS should be kept alive.

It is helpful to add a few more things about the concept of personhood before exploring the different ways of defining personhood. Personhood is typically seen as being a threshold and range concept. This means that if a being falls below the threshold it lacks the moral status of personhood, even though it may have some attributes of moral value and have interests deserving of protection. So a conclusion that, for example, a dog is not deserving of the status of a person does not mean the dog has no interests or no moral status; it simply lacks the very high status that is attached to being a person. The argument that personhood is a range concept means that all those who cross the threshold for being a person are equally entitled to all the claims attached to personhood. No distinction is drawn between the moral status of those who only just cross the threshold and those who undoubtedly cross it.

One theme underpinning the debate is the idea of human equality: all persons are equal.[98] This means that we should not draw a distinction between the moral worth of different people. This argument has strong appeal. It is profoundly objectionable to claim that a person is more morally valuable than another on account of their wealth, sex or race. Indeed, many of the horrors of the human race have been predicated on such a belief. Personhood is at the heart of the belief that, to adapt the wording of the American Constitution, 'All persons have been created equally'.

The literature on personhood is extensive, but there are two primary understandings of the concept: those which emphasise mental capabilities

[98] J. Waldron, *One Another's Equals: The Basis of Human Equality* (Harvard University Press, 2017).

and those which emphasise species membership. These take a similar approach. They list the factors which are determinative of personhood and use these to ascertain whether a being has or does not have personhood. Even among those who agree on the criteria there is still plenty of scope for debate over the extent to which a capability need be shown, and the response to an entity which has the potential to develop the capacity but does not currently possess it. I will develop these before promoting a third, which is indicated by the concept of relational personhood.

5.5.1 Mental Capacities

A popular school of thought is that a range of mental capabilities, involving cognition, self-consciousness, autonomy and practical rationality, generate the claims of personhood. David Wasserman, Adrianne Asch and Jeffrey Blustein[99] suggest a typical list might be the following:

> self-consciousness, awareness of and concern for oneself as a temporally-extended subject; practical rationality, rational agency, or autonomy; moral responsibility; a capacity to recognize other selves and to be motivated to justify one's actions to them; the capacity to be held, and hold others, morally accountable.

The precise formulations as to the key criteria differ and might include self-awareness; a being who can value its own existence; or a being who can experience themselves as one whose lives can get better or worse. John Locke suggested that a person is 'a thinking intelligent being, that has reason and reflection, and can consider itself as itself, the same thinking thing in different times and places'.[100]

It is not difficult to appreciate why these factors are emphasised. They seem very readily to explain how human beings differ from, say, pieces of furniture, plants or other animals (or most other animals). But that is in danger of assuming what we are seeking to prove. If we look to identify characteristics that distinguish human beings from other beings and then claim these indicate personhood that is not much of an argument.

However, there are reasons why you might think that autonomy, self-awareness and agency have considerable moral value. Modern forms of utilitarianism seek to promote the meeting of preferences and goals but that assumes that a person has that capacity to formulate such goals and preferences. Much contemporary ethical writing emphasises autonomy as a central value, but autonomy is normally associated with the capacity to make

---

[99] D. Wasserman, A. Asch and J. Blustein, 'Cognitive Disability and Moral Status' in *Stanford Encyclopedia of Philosophy*, https://plato.stanford.edu/entries/cognitive-disability/ [accessed 1 February 2019].

[100] J. Locke, *An Essay Concerning Human Understanding*, ed. P. Nidditch (Clarendon Press, 1975, originally published 1694), 335.

decisions for oneself. A table cannot be wronged as one cannot act against its wishes. Indeed, the table cannot have wishes. There can be no interference in its right to autonomy if it cannot formulate what it wants.

The emphasis on autonomy and agency is important for philosophers who emphasise the importance of the 'chosenness' of a particular act. We might believe, for example, that the best example of a morally good act is one where a person is faced with the option of doing good or doing bad, weighs up the moral arguments and then acts on the good. A dog, say, may do something good (e.g. share a bone with another dog) but we assume this is 'brute animal instinct', rather than a rational judgement to prefer the good over the bad. I would disagree with this assessment that it is rational thought that makes a decision good, but I will explain why later.

One of the appeals of mental capabilities is that cognitive attributes are inherent to the person. They do not depend on biological or social environments. The prisoner locked in solitary confinement and treated with no regard to their dignity can still can claim personhood because they have self-awareness, understanding and autonomy. If personhood claims did not rest in an individual's innate abilities, such a person's status will be precarious. They may gain or lose it depending on the social environment they are in.

It should be noted that the mental capabilities approach is by no means closed to the idea that being other than humans could have personhood. As James Rachels argues: 'if we think it is wrong to treat a human in a certain way, because the human has certain characteristics, *and a particular non-human animal also has those characteristics*, then consistency requires that we also object to treating the non-human in that way'. Some non-human animals might have the kind of capacities for independent thought, self-awareness and the like that are seen as the marker for personhood. Peter Singer has discussed a gorilla (Koko) who was able to understand over 1,000 communications signs. Plenty of other examples could, no doubt, be found. Most supporters of the mental capacity approach will be unconcerned by this point. If animals do have these capacities then we should readily accept that those animals deserve the status of personhood.

Having very briefly summarised the cognitive capacity approach I will now look at the three primary challenges that face it.

5.5.2 Challenges to the Mental Capacities Approach

The first and most significant challenge is that the approach may mean that there are some human beings who are not people. This would be those with significant cognitive impairments and, perhaps, babies and children. It is possible to deal with babies and children by using an argument based on potential (although they do not currently have the morally valuable attributes, they have the potential to have them). That, however, seems to suggest that babies have no moral value per se, only based on the older people they will become. In any event, the potentiality argument is not available for those with profound cognitive impairment.

There are plenty of people for whom the idea that a human being with a profound cognitive impairment is not a person is so repugnant that the arguments must be rejected. The idea, for example, that a human being with limited mental capacity might have the same moral status as a dog, with which they have equivalent mental functioning, is abhorrent.

There are, however, highly respected philosophers who are prepared to accept that conclusion. Jeff McMahan concludes (in language which would be found offensive to many) 'allowing severely retarded human beings to die, and perhaps even killing them, are ... less serious matters than we have believed'.[101] Those sympathetic to such a view argue that our unwillingness to treat a human being with profound mental impairment in the same way as a non-human animal is 'speciesism': an irrational preference for one's own species, equivalent to racism or sexism. They might argue if a human and a dog have the same mental capabilities we need something more than their shape and appearance to justify a moral distinction. Helga Kuhse and Peter Singer have no difficulty in accepting that a child with Down's syndrome may be of less value than a 'normal child'. Discussing whether a Down's syndrome child should be given a live saving operation they write:

> Even allowing for the more optimistic assessments of the potential of Down's syndrome children, this potential cannot be said to be equal to that of a normal child. The possible benefits of successful surgery in the case of a Down's syndrome child are, therefore ... less than the possible benefits of similar surgery in a normal child.[102]

Despite the eminence of these authors and the publicity attached to their views, it should be acknowledged that they are very much a minority in academic writing and perhaps even more so among the general public. But there is no denying the drive of their logic.

The second argument against the mental capabilities approach is that it appears to undermine the claim of equality: that all human beings are equal. As just mentioned, it means that some human beings are denied the status of personhood. But, leaving them aside, even with those who are persons there might be arguments that the mental capabilities approach challenges the claim to equality. If what is of moral value are the mental capacities mentioned then inevitably some people will exhibit these to a greater degree than others. Some people have high states of self-awareness, are more rational or can exercise more richly autonomous decisions than others. If such qualities are what

[101] J. McMahan, *The Ethics of Killing* (Oxford University Press, 2003), 230.
[102] H. Kuhse and P. Singer, *Should the Baby Live? The Problem of Handicapped Infants* (Oxford University Press, 1985), 143.

generate moral value, how then can we avoid the conclusion that some people are of higher moral value than others?

Lawyers might have a way out of that difficulty for supporters of this approach. That is that we constantly are using categories and attaching legal significance to all in that category, regardless of the extent to which they satisfy the requirements to be in that category. For example, the individual waking up with the most dreadful hangover on the morning of their eighteenth birthday is as much an adult for the purposes of the law as the person excitedly reading a telegram from the Queen congratulating them on their one hundredth birthday. So, we might say that all those in the category of personhood are equally entitled to the rights and moral status of personhood, whether they have the requisite capabilities in abundance or whether they just scraped through, just as all those over eighteen are given the status of adults in English law.

The problem is that this response is not entirely satisfactory. It might suggest that equality is just a legal fiction. Although the law assumes that all eighteen-year-olds have the mental capacity of adults, we know that is not really true; it is just that the law treats them as having that capacity. But we do not think the idea of human equality is a 'legal fiction'. We don't believe 'people are not actually equal (e.g. clever people are more morally valuable than stupid people); but we should treat them the same'. We think they are actually more morally valuable. But the mental capabilities approach does not give us a reason for reaching that conclusion.

The third problem with the mental capabilities approach is that it assumes mental capabilities are of the highest moral value. But why are rationality and autonomy necessarily of moral worth? Simo Vehmas objects that the emphasis on mental capabilities is 'intelligentist'.[103] It discriminates against those with 'less intelligence' than others with no moral justification. That, he suggests, is as bad as treating people differently based on their race or physical abilities. Vehmas questions whether intelligence is an objective concept. He writes:

> Intelligence is essentially a normative concept, reflecting the concept of what kind of being a human should be; how s/he should think and act, and in this sense it is more normative than a concept referring to a physical state.

He notes, for example, that for centuries very few people could read or write and those with learning difficulties would not therefore be 'identified' because in a different society they could operate as well as most others. It is, in other words, social expectations and requirements that render some 'intellectually disabled' and others not.

As Vehmas points out, defining personhood in terms of intelligence means making the intellectually disabled an 'other' and judging them in terms of 'our' experience, instead of valuing them in terms of their own experience. Such a

---

[103] S. Vehmas, 'Discriminative Assumptions of Utilitarian Bioethics Regarding Individuals with Intellectual Disabilities' (1999) 14 *Disability & Society* 37–52.

view may be supported with an acknowledgement of the lack of understanding of how the brain works and when it might or might not be enabled to perform tasks. These observations may be reinforced by concerns over the measurement of intellect.

Even more significantly for the purposes of the personhood debate, Vehmas argues that virtue need not be connected to intelligence:

> positive and virtuous traits of character are often characteristic of individuals with intellectual disabilities as well: honesty, courage, persistence, love, a lack of pretence and other similar virtues which individuals with intellectual disabilities are often more able to embrace than normal individuals due to the lack of intellectual reflection; we normal individuals often prevent our moral virtues from becoming actualised by the practice of our intellectual skills.[104]

Certainly, those lacking sophisticated mental capacity can show considerable affection and love. As one parent states:

> Those of us with a Down's Syndrome child (our son, Robert, is almost 24) often wish that all our children had this extraordinary syndrome which defeats anger and malice, replacing them with humor, thoughtfulness and devotion to friends and family.[105]

Further, it is often incorrectly assumed that those with 'higher cognitive functioning' use this to make decisions. Many of our decisions are a result of emotional reactions, imbedded prejudice and so forth, which have little to do with cognitive function. The exhausted parent changing the nappy in the early morning may be showing considerable love and care, even if 'virtually on auto-pilot'. The lifeboat team sacrificing their lives for a stranded sailor may be responding instinctively, rather than making a rational, 'autonomous' decision to be brave. A lack of mental capacity may be one way of falling short of the rational autonomous ideal, but is it any more significant than any others?

5.5.3 Membership of a Human Community

The primary approach taken by those who oppose the mental capabilities approach is to argue that membership of the human species is what generates moral personhood. Eva Feder Kitay[106] argues 'Being human is a sufficient condition for the stringent moral obligations we have to humans.' Bernard Williams,[107] writing in support of species preference, imagines a scenario in

---

[104] Ibid., 51.

[105] Quoted in P. Singer, 'Specisism and Moral Status' in E. Feder Kittay and L. Carlson (eds.) *Cognitive Disability and Its Challenge to Moral Philosophy* (John Wiley & Sons, 2010), 340.

[106] E. Feder Kittay, 'The Moral Significance of Being Human' [2017] *Proceedings and Addresses of the American Philosophical Association* 19.

[107] B. Williams, 'The Human Prejudice' in B. Williams (ed.) *Philosophy as a Humanistic Discipline* (Princeton University Press, 2006), 66.

which aliens conquer the planet and claim to be superior to humans and so entitled to dominate them. Williams suggests that if any human accepted the argument of the aliens, we would ask legitimately, 'Whose side are you on?' He claims we are entitled to say: 'We're humans here, we're the ones doing the judging; you can't really expect anything else but a bias or prejudice in favor of human beings.' To similar effect, Alice Crary[108] argues that in deciding what is valuable about human beings, we need to determine what is valuable about all human beings.

5.5.4 Problems with the Membership of Human Community Approach

The first problem is to explain why it is that membership of the human species generates a moral claim. Jeff McMahan claims 'that there is nothing in or invariably correlated with membership in the human species that can be the basis of our moral equality'.[109] Similarly, Peter Singer[110] is quick to reject the Williams argument mentioned earlier based on the analogy with the Martians. He points out the racist might believe that people of the same race should agree their race is superior to others, but it does not make that claim right. He rejects the argument that simply belonging to a species is itself what generates moral worth.

There are two responses that might be made to this kind of argument. One is to point to the products and achievements of the human race. We might point to artistic endeavours (great music, great architecture) or morally valuable pursuits (a national health service) or intellectual achievements (mathematics) and claim these are the products of the human community which are morally valuable and all members of that community are entitled to moral credit for that.

That argument has some appeal. James Rachels[111] rejects such an argument, claiming that a severely impaired individual has merely a biological link with other people, but no link to the morally valuable endeavours of human civilisation. Further, we can imagine a society which regarded those with severe cognitive impairment as a serious burden on society and shut them off in large institutions, literally 'out of sight and out of mind'. Would those with severe cognitive impairment in such a society cease to have personhood?

The second is to claim that, as John Finis does, 'to be a person is to belong to a kind of being characterized by rational (self-conscious, intelligent) nature'.[112] This criterion, he believes, provides a way for valuing all human beings,

[108] A. Crary, *Inside Ethics* (Harvard University Press, 2016).
[109] J. McMahan, 'Challenges to Human Equality' (2008) 12 *Journal of Ethics* 81.
[110] P. Singer, 'Speciesism and Moral Status' (2009) 40 *Metaphilosophy* 567.
[111] J. Rachels, *Creating from Animals: The Moral Implications of Darwinism* (Oxford University Press, 1990).
[112] J. Finnis, 'The Fragile Case for Euthanasia: A Reply to John Harris' in J. Keown (ed.) *Euthanasia Examined* (Cambridge University Press, 1995), 76.

including those who have profound mental impairments. He explains this by saying that there are two ways a human being can claim the status for all human beings even if they lack the criterion. First, if they have the capacity for it. So, if we accept rational self-governance generates a higher moral status, we should value a child who has the capacity for that and whomever we can expect to develop that capacity deserves the protection associated with personhood. Second, if a person is 'internally directed toward the development of such capacity' they deserve value. This indicates that even if a human being with profound impairment lacks the mental capacity or even the capacity to develop it, if their body and mind are directed to that capacity they have moral status. Jeremy Waldron makes this point well by pointing out that if an ape has an IQ of 60 we are impressed, but if a person has an IQ of 60 we see that as a tragedy.[113] We can value them for what they would be had not the tragedy occurred. Here Waldron is drawing on a broadly Aristotelian idea that our species sets the idea for us. Humans should not seek to be dog-like or tree-like; they should be human like. However, he appears to assume that rationality (or at least IQ) is a central aspect of being human-like, something which I would reject.

There is a major concern that in arguments of this kind a disabled person is being valued not for what they are but rather for what they could be, and doing so fails to recognise their inherent worth and undermines equality. One person is valued for their characteristics, but another is valued for what characteristics they might have had, had tragedy not struck. Is it possible to take such a view and still maintain that we value them equally? This view holds that we can imagine a person separately from their disability. If we tried to consider what a 'Chinese Donald Trump' would be like we would come up against the problem that had Donald Trump been born and lived in China he would be a very different person. Similarly, comparing the Down's Syndrome child to the child they would have been had they not had Down's Syndrome is to compare two utterly different, perhaps unimaginable, beings.

5.5.5 Developing a Relational Account of Personhood

My objection to both the standard approaches to defining personhood is that both rest on a particular understanding of an ideal person. The standard approaches take the 'able independent, rational male' as the model around which the approach to personhood is based. Whether it be the possession of those capabilities, the goods that communities of such people typically possess

---

[113] J. Waldron, 'Hard and Heart-Breaking Cases' The Gifford Lectures 2015 www.ed.ac.uk/arts-humanities-soc-sci/news-events/lectures/gifford-lectures/archive/2014-2015/jeremy-waldron/lecture-six [accessed 2 March 2019].

or the potential or 'natural instinct' towards those capabilities, the ideal is used to determine the value of personhood. But we need to challenge this ideal.[114]

First, we need to recognise it is just that, an ideal. An ideal few, if any of us, reach. As I argued in the first chapter, vulnerability is a universal and inevitable aspect of the human condition. The human self is profoundly relational. People are in their very nature interdependent and vulnerable. It flows from this that the basic moral value of humans is not found in their individual capabilities or in their membership of the species, but rather in their relationships. So it argues the question 'is X a person?' is problematic because we can only conceive of X in the context of their relationships. We can say that X and Y are people if their relationship reveals the moral qualities that we look for in human relationships. But we cannot imagine an isolated person and assess their capabilities, as such a person does not exist. It is their relationships, rather than any inherent characteristics, which have moral value and are deserving of special moral status.

We reach then the position that our value lies not in our selves as isolated egos but in our caring relationships. As Hans Reinders[115] puts it:

> Being loved by someone is what matters most in our lives. What we do not often think about, however, is the logic of this statement, and this logic is what I ask you to contemplate for a moment. If "being loved" is the most important thing in our lives, then the most important thing is something we cannot do by ourselves or on our own. It's not a goal we can strive for, it is not something we can achieve. To be loved by someone implies that the most important thing in our lives is something we can only receive as a gift.

I am not committed to a view that only humans can be persons. I do not know if other animals can have (for example) an interest in the emotional well-being of others, a keenness to respond to emotions of others, a degree of empathy, a spontaneous impulse to share with others or a responsiveness to touch of the kind key to being a party to a caring relationship. If other animals do show these abilities then personhood could be granted to them.

The importance of relationships demonstrates that our intellectual abilities are not key to personhood. Our relationships are not based on intellectual interaction (although they can be). The rush of warmth for the new-born baby is not the recognition of a kindred mind. Many of the deepest manifestations of relationships are not intellectual in nature. For example, many people find sexual relations to be a particularly profound way to express a very deep connection (although they need not be). There are points at which words fail and only a hug will do. The shared grin, the gentle touch, the wild dancing together: these transcend words and intellectual capacity. Intellectual

---

[114] C. Rogers, *Intellectual Disability and Being Human* (Routledge, 2016).

[115] H. Reinders, 'The Power of Inclusion and Friendship' (2011) 15 *Journal of Religion, Disability and Health* 431.

interaction is only part of what makes a relationship and need not be a central part of it. Do people seek intellectual capacity in their friends or rather humour, joy or kindness? It is understandable that an academic, considering what is valuable in life, will highlight academic and intellectual skills. But there is so much more to life than our minds, and it is well known to those involved in relationships with people with mental impairment. Eva Kittay writes of her relationship with her daughter Sesha, who in traditional terms has very limited cognitive ability:

> You know her humanity in every movement, every look, every response. You know it when you see her thrill to music, giggle at something she finds funny, or reach out her arms to embrace you; when she puts down her head shyly or beams when complimented. She has the feel and touch and smell of a human being. And above all, she is my daughter.[116]

As that last sentence indicates, it is through the human caring relationship that Eva and Sesha can claim personhood.

If you are with me this far and you agree that relationships of care are the core values of moral value, then cases of children and those lacking capacity are hardly 'marginal cases' which it can be problematic to fit within the model of human value. Quite the opposite: their relationships become the paradigmatic for what is good about personhood.

In a fascinating record of a conversation between Eva Feder Kittay and Peter Singer, Eva tries to respond to Singer's argument that her daughter Sesha should be regarded as having a similar moral status to a pig:

> The first thing I have to do when you ask me that question, is I have to get over . . . a feeling of nausea. It's not that I'm not able to answer it intellectually, it's that I can't even get to the point emotionally, where I can answer that question.
>
> . . . there is so much to being human. There's the touch, there's the feel, there's the hug, there's the smile . . . there are so many ways of interacting . . . [T]his is why I just reject . . . [the] . . . idea that you [should] base moral standing on a list of cognitive capacities, or psychological capacities, or any kind of capacities. Because what it is to be human is not a bundle of capacities. It's a way that you are, a way you are in the world, a way you are with another.

This quote raises many of the themes of this section. I expect Feder Kittay's heartfelt objection to Singer's arguments was based on the fact that, as I have argued, we are defined and constituted by our relationships. He was claiming that a central relationship for Feder Kittay was equivalent to that with a pig. But worse, his arguments reveal a narrow perception of what is of value. Eva and Sesha's relationship is marked by care, of a kind where they can respond

---

[116] E. Feder Kittay, 'The Moral Significance of Being Human' [2017] *Proceedings and Addresses of the American Philosophical Association* 19.

to each other, meet each other's needs and respect each other. It is their relationship which should be protected by personhood.

So, returning to the core question: what makes you a person? Some philosophers emphasise autonomy as rationality, but as we saw in the section on mental capacity, we greatly exaggerate our abilities to be rational and autonomous. Anyway, it is not clear that these are linked to moral goodness. The autonomous and the rational can do great evil. What generates moral value is our love and care with each other. So our value is not found internally but in relationships of care with others.

5.5.6 Pregnancy

The discussion we have had on personhood has a very practical application in the law on pregnancy. As is well known, the debates over abortion and the regulation of pregnancy often turn on the status of the foetus. Indeed, in an excellent recent analysis, Kate Greasley[117] makes a powerful argument that despite all the other arguments that can be raised about abortion they do genuinely come down to the status of the foetus. For the purposes of this chapter, I will assume this is correct. As is well known, the two primary schools of thought on the status of the foetus are that the foetus is a person from the moment of conception and that the foetus becomes a person later when it acquires the attributes of personhood (birth, on many accounts).

If we take the view that the foetus is a person from the moment of conception, abortion becomes very difficult to support. Greasley argues it cannot be. Once we recognise the foetus is a person we have duties to protect it and not to kill it through abortion, unless there is some overwhelming justification.

On the other hand, if we say that the foetus is not a person until birth and before then has no, or very few, interests, then we have difficulties with cases of miscarriage and termination of pregnancy through a criminal assault or negligence. Then we are left telling the pregnant woman that the end of the pregnancy is the loss of something of little moral value or just part of her body. Neither of these seems accurate to capture the experience.

I will argue here that a relational approach offers us a much better way to understand pregnancy. The error in much writing has been that we need to understand the foetus in terms of its individual characteristic. I argue that the foetus can only be understood in terms of relationship and interconnection. The biological reality is that pregnancy is a relationship of profound interconnection. There is no clear point at which foetal tissue ends and the woman's tissue begins. They share fluids and space. The health and well-being of the

---

[117] K. Greasley, *Arguments about Abortion* (Cambridge University Press, 2017).

woman profoundly affect the foetus and vice versa.[118] As Iris Marion Young puts it:

> [p]regnancy challenges the integration of my body experience by rendering fluid the boundary between what is within, myself, and what is outside, separate. I experience my insides as the space of another, yet my own body.[119']

The interconnection between the two shows that the standard individualised approach is particularly inappropriate in relation to the foetal status.

The relational approach argues that rather than asking what rights or responsibilities are owed to an individual in response to their status, we ask what responsibilities and rights are owed in relation to a relationship. In terms of the personhood debate, this means that the question is not whether the foetus has moral value on its own, nor indeed the pregnant woman on her own, but rather to ask about the moral status of the relationship between woman and foetus and what legal response is appropriate to a relationship of that kind.[120] In short, where a relationship is marked by care I would advocate the law should allocate rights and responsibilities to ensure that relationship is upheld and maintained.[121] Where, however, that relationship is not marked by care, then it does not have moral value and the law should enable parties to find other caring relationships. The relational approach to personhood differs from the standard approach by not focusing on the capacity or attribute of an individual and giving them status, but rather focusing on relationships and considering whether there is moral value there.

This means that a wanted pregnancy can be seen in a completely different way to an unwanted pregnancy. A wanted pregnancy is one marked by care and should be protected by the criminal law. We should use the criminal law to acknowledge the severity of the wrong where a woman is attacked and her pregnancy terminated against her will. We should acknowledge miscarriage as a major loss and provide services and support in such cases. Employment and health law should protect the wanted pregnancy as deserving of protection. However, in the case of an unwanted pregnancy the relationship is not marked by care and love. In fact, it might be impeding relationships of care. The termination of the relationship is required so that caring relationships may be preserved or sought out. Abortion should, therefore, be readily available.[122]

---

[118] See J. Herring and P-L. Chau, 'My Body. Your Body. Our Bodies' (2007) 15 *Medical Law Review* 34 for a discussion of the biology.

[119] I. M. Young, *On Female Body Experience* (Oxford University Press, 2005), 49.

[120] This argument is developed more fully in C. Foster and J. Herring, *Personhood, Identity and the Law* (Springer, 2017).

[121] J. Herring, *Caring and the Law* (Hart, 2013), chapter 2.

[122] This argument is more fully developed in J. Herring 'Ethics of Care and the Public Good of Abortion' (2019) *University of Oxford Human Rights Hub Journal* 1.

5.6 Conclusion

This chapter has explored the significance for medical law of taking a relational self approach. I have focussed on looking at some key topics: the nature of the body; the concept of legal capacity; the best interests test; and the concept of personhood. I have argued that in all of these examples understanding the self in a relational way has opened up richer and more realistic ways of understanding our health, bodies and what is important to us. In the next chapter we will look at family law and the legal responses to our intimate relationships.

6

Family Law and the Relational Self

6.1 Introduction

Family law seems the ideal place to find a law emphasising the importance of relationships. However, as we will see, in fact, family law reveals the complexities of regulating relationships and the debates over the nature of the self at the heart of this book. Although family law does focus on relationships, there is a lack of clarity about which relationships it seeks to regulate; how individuals interests are balanced and understood in terms of the responsibilities of the relationships; and the role of the law in response to a relationship. As with the other chapters in this book, I cannot attempt to set out every consequence for adopting a more relational approach to family law and I will select some key themes: the concept of the family in family law; financial orders on relationship breakdown; the concept of parenthood; the nature of parental responsibility; and the resolution of disputes over children. I will not attempt to set out the law in detail in these areas,[1] rather my primary focus will be on setting out what a relational approach might bring to them.

6.2 The Family of Family Law

Family lawyers and family studies theorists have long debated the nature of the family.[2] There is no correct answer to that question because so much depends on what the category is being used for. For family lawyers, much depends on what the role for family law is. For example, if you understand family law as being about facilitating and supporting certain approved forms of intimate life then this will clearly impact on your understanding of what a family is. Martha Minow and Mary Lyndon Shanley have helpfully set out three primary models that could be used as the foundational values for family law.[3]

---

[1] For that, see, J. Herring, *Family Law* (Pearson, 2019).

[2] For an excellent recent contribution see A. Brown, *What Is the Family of Law?* (Hart, 2019).

[3] M. Minow and M. Lyndon Shanley, 'Relational Rights and Responsibilities: Revisioning the Family in Liberal Political Theory and Law' (1996) 11 *Hypatia* 4.

6.2.1 The Community Model

The 'community model' seeks to promote a particular kind of relationship. An important role of family law under this model is to provide structures and privileges to those kinds of relationships and to encourage others to adopt that relationship status. For a long time, marriage has been the central focus of family law. The traditional image of the family was that it was a private association: the husband, wife, children and perhaps servants. The husband/father had authority over the wife, children and servants. The home was his domain and the role of the state was to enable and support the paterfamilias in his task. The role of the wife was to manage the household and the physical and emotional care of the children. The role of the state was to support and preserve that structure.

In recent times, family law has extended its remit beyond marital relationships to include cohabiting ones and indeed the notion of marriage has changed with equal marriage.[4] Nevertheless, there is still a hierarchy of families in family law: the top position being taken by opposite-sex married couples, with same-sex married couples[5] and civil partners next, then unmarried opposite sex couples and then unmarried same-sex couples below them. The sexual marriage relationship is the ideal and other relationships are judged by comparison with them. If they are sufficiently similar they may be accepted as a family for the purposes of the law. Hence we see the regular statutory description of unmarried couples as 'a couple living together as if they were married'. For example, in Section 1 A Inheritance (Provision for Family and Dependents Act) 1975 a cohabitant of a deceased can apply if:

the person was living –

(a) in the same household as the deceased, and
(b) as the husband or wife of the deceased.

Here we see marriage as being the gold standard a cohabiting couple must 'mimic' if they are to be accepted as alternative relationships.

Of course, there is no need for this model to adopt a marriage-based model of what constitutes the preferred model of a family, and more progressive versions can be promoted. Indeed, it would be possible for the community to favour diversity in family forms and promote a wide range of family forms. What, however, it seems supporters of this model would need to demonstrate is that there are good reasons why society should favour a particular form of relationship as an object for legal regulation over others.

---

[4] Marriage (Same Sex Couples) Act 2013.
[5] For an explanation of why same-sex spouses are seen as lesser than opposite sex spouses see J. Herring, 'Why Marriage Needs to Be Less Sexy' in J. Miles, P. Mody and R., Probert (eds.) *Marriage Rights and Rites* (Hart, 2015), 277.

6.2.2 The Contractual Model

A 'contractual' model would protect the values of autonomy and decry attempts by the state to promote particular kinds of relationships. Instead, the state should allow and encourage people to develop their own understanding of family law by drafting contracts to regulate their relationship. In short, this view would see the precise family structure as irrelevant to the wider community. Lenore Weitzman asserts that 'there is a serious question as to whether the state has any legitimate interest interfering with contracts regarding non-commercial sexual relations between consenting adults'.[6]

The role of family law under this model is to allow couples to determine for themselves what form and regulation for their relationship is appropriate and to provide them with the legal mechanisms to give effect to their choices. The appeal of this approach is that there would be no attempt to privilege particular kinds of relationships over others. In effect, family law would become a branch of contract law where the agreements between the parties would be key. Most supporters of this model would accept that, as is normal in contract law, there would be some restrictions on terms which were contrary to public policy or grossly unfair to one party. So, for example, it is commonly assumed a family contract would need to ensure there was adequate support for children.[7]

6.2.3 Rights-Based Model

The third model is the 'rights-based model', where family law is designed to protect human rights principles. Similarly to the second model, it would see family law as essentially a branch of another area of law, but here human rights law, rather than contract law, governs the area. Supporters are likely to emphasise that family life is an area where human rights are subject to potential challenge. In particular, rights to protection for freedom from violence, gender non-discrimination and privacy might be particularly pertinent. This approach might appeal particularly to feminists who are concerned that the history of community models will mean women's interests are subsumed within an understanding of family life which is said to benefit the community, despite its harms to women.

6.2.4 Caring Family Law

I do not find any of these three over-arching approaches entirely adequate. They fail to capture the profound link between our relationships and our

---

[6] L. Weitzman, 'Marriage Contracts' (1974) 62 *California Law Review* 1169, 1275.
[7] Minow and Lyndon Shanley, 'Relational Rights and Responsibilities: Revisioning the Family in Liberal Political Theory and Law', 4.

identity and interests. As argued throughout this book, the self is constituted through our relationships. As Mary Shanley[8] notes, 'law shapes the way we conceptualise human relationships, we should make sure that the "tale told by law" reflects an understanding of the importance of communal interdependence to both individuals and society'.

This makes the contractual model which imagines two autonomous independent people negotiating the content of their relationship a false image. Similarly, the rights-based model is based on an assumption that we can identify severable individual interests, which can be kept apart. This point was emphasised in Chapter 3. The community model focuses on the goods done to the community by the relationship, but fails to take into account the interactive and interdependent nature of the relationships between a community and a relationship: the network of relationships that constitute a community and are constituted by the community. I suggest a model of Caring Family Law produces the most effective understanding of how families and family law should be understood.

At the moment, family law is centred on sexual relationships. The concept of the nuclear heterosexual family, with two parents of opposite sex and their children, still has a powerful hold over family law as the ideal into which all other would-be families must fit. Indeed, the ecclesiastical origins of family law reveal the obsession of the church to restrict the circumstances in which sexual behaviour was permissible and the role played by marriage in that. Yet still today, remarkably, sexual relationships are at the heart of the law's understanding of marriage. No better example of this can be the fierce campaigns in many countries to allow equal marriage. In England, the Marriage (Same-Sex Couples) Act 2013 struggled in its attempts to fit same-sex couples into the heterosexual paradigm of marriage. Workable definitions of adultery, consummation and presumptions of parenthood for same-sex couples could not be found, it was said. 'Equal marriage' became 'equal but different', with difference between opposite-sex marriage and same-sex marriage in relation to grounds for nullity and divorce; and different parentage rules. Further, in defining who is a man and a woman for the purposes of the law on marriage, the capacity of the person to engage in heterosexual intercourse is the key criterion.[9] The law has proved unable to shake off the heterosexist assumptions about what a marital relationship looked like.

I argue in this chapter that family law should be reconceived as a system of law to promote and protect caring relationships. In fact, many of the tools currently used by family law are entirely appropriate; it is that they are simply

---

[8] M. Shanley, 'Unencumbered Individuals and Embedded Selves: Reasons to Resist Dichotomous Thinking in Family Law' in A. Allen and N. Regan (eds.) *Debating Democracy's Discontent: Essays on American Politics, Law, and Public Philosophy* (Oxford University Press, 1998), 229.

[9] Herring, 'Why Marriage Needs to Be Less Sexy'.

mis-targeted at sexual relationships when they should be focused on caring relationships.

I would argue that what might make a relationship worthy of promotion by the state is care and mutual support, rather than sex. To be blunt, society does not really gain much from a couple having sex, however pleasurable it may be for the participants! However, the state does benefit from care, particularly where it involves a person whose needs would otherwise fall on the state. It is such relationships that should receive the support of the state. Whether the relationship has a sexual side is a red herring.

It might be argued that given the fluid nature of care, we can use sex as a proxy for care. However, that is a very weak argument. Nowadays, sexual relationships often take place in the context of casual relationships. Any assumption that sex is a sign of commitment looks terribly old-fashioned. Certainly, care can clearly take place outside a sexual relationship.

And if sex is not a good marker of commitment or intimacy, why should it be of any legal significance?[10] The only answer seems to be that society has an interest in ensuring that sex takes place in order to produce a sufficient number of children. However, the vast majority of sexual encounters do not produce children. Further, at least currently in Western Europe, it is the care of children that poses far greater challenges than their production.[11] If the law or state is to promote certain kinds of relationship through family law, it should do so for caring relationships, rather than sexual ones.[12,13] The focus of state support and legal confirmation should not be marriage-like sexual relationships, but rather those in which care is provided and received. This would make the primary focus of family law in some ways narrower (there might be some marriages in which there was insufficient caring of dependency to justify legal support), while there would be other relationships of care not currently covered (e.g. an adult caring for an older dependent relative) which would be covered. It would move closer to adopting Iris Marion Young's[14] definition of a family: 'as people who live together and/or share resources necessary to the means for life and comfort; who are committed to caring for one another's physical and emotional needs to the best of their ability'.

I would see no requirement that the people live together, to be in a valuable caring relationship. There would, however, need to be a significant amount of

[10] This is not to say I think the Burdens should not pay inheritance tax. That is an issue which raises broader issues about inheritance taxation policy: J Herring, *Older People in Law and Society* (Oxford University Press, 2009), ch 9.

[11] L. Kessler, 'Community Parenting' (2007) 24 *Washington University Journal of Law and Policy* 47.

[12] J. Herring, 'Caregivers in Medical Law and Ethics' (2008) 25 *Journal of Contemporary Health Law and Policy* 1.

[13] M. Fineman, *The Autonomy Myth* (New Press, 2004); L. Murry and M. Barnes, 'Have Families Been Rethought? Ethic of Care, Family and "Whole Family" Approaches' (2010) 9 *Social Policy and Society* 533.

[14] I. Young, *Intersecting Voices* (Princeton University Press, 1997), 106.

care and that would require considerable amounts of time spent together. I propose the following definition of the unit which would be the focus of family law: people providing each other with a substantial amount of care in a relationship marked by commitment. Note that this includes no need for a sexual element. Nor does it restrict a family to two people and certainly has no restrictions based on the gender of the people.

I will argue that the law needs to protect and promote caring relationships and ensure a fair sharing of the benefits and burdens of those relationships and a regulation of disputes which arise within them. This reflects the three primary functions for a care-based family law:[15]

1. Valuing. Relationships marked by care and which provide meaning to the individuals are of central value to society. The law has a role in promoting and valuing those relationships.
2. Protecting. To protect people from abuse within an intimate relationship. While caring relationships are core to the well-being of societies and the individuals they create, they create dangers of physical, emotional and financial abuse and we need to ensure that there are effective protections from these.
3. Resolving. To resolve disputes between people in a relationship, which reflects the values of the relationship, and ensure the resolution promotes caring relationships.

These three functions are linked. By providing an effective framework for resolving disputes and protecting the parties from abuse, the law makes it attractive to enter these relationships and hence they are promoted. The unifying approach of the law is to recognise that the state has a major interest in promoting caring relationships both in terms of its own interests and to protect those in caring relationships. As Jennifer Nedelsky[16] argues, the state must attend to:

> conditions that foster people's capacity to form caring, responsible and intimate relationships with each other – as family members, friends, members of a community, and citizens of a state.

This structure is not just important for the couple themselves. As Brinig and Nock[17] argue, the availability of state-supported forms of relationship provides a benefit for society and individuals:

> The normative expectation of permanence and unconditional love is the basis for collective trust that the relationship in question will function in its prescribed way. For couples, that means that others will trust that they will pursue intimacy in socially recognized (i.e., normative) ways. For parents, that means trusting

[15] J. Eekelaar, *Family Law and Social Policy* (Weidenfeld & Nicholson, 1984), 24–26.
[16] J. Nedelsky, 'Property in Potential Life: A Relational Approach to Choosing Legal Categories' (1993) 6 *Canadian Journal of Law and Jurisprudence* 343.
[17] M. Brinig and S. Nock, 'Covenant and Contract' (2000) 12 *Regent University Law Review* 9, 11.

that they will provide an environment within which children can flourish. In return for conforming to community norms, that is, people in relationships are given various legal and other supports that further encourage and promote the relationship.

Of course, the legal structure is only part of what is needed to provide effective support for caring relationships. No doubt, the support and approval of their friends, community or faith is of far greater significance than any legal or state recognition. Nevertheless, the state has a role in fostering the circumstances in which dependent relationships receive recognition and support. Martha Minow and Mary Lyndon Shanley[18] make a powerful point:

> while loving and committed relationships might presumably exist without the state, there are in fact no family or family-like relationships that are not shaped by social practices and state action.

Family law, and particularly marriage as it currently stands, seems unfit for the job of promoting and protecting relationships which are valuable to the community, and relationships which require a system of legal support and regulation.[19] Clare Chambers[20] summarises the primary criticisms of it:

> Practical, empirical harms to women resulting from marriage include the contingent facts that marriages tend to reinforce the gendered division of labour, which itself means that women earn less and are less independent than men; that they reinforce the idea that women do most of the housework, even if they work outside the home, which saps their energies and dignity; and that domestic violence may be exacerbated by marital concepts of entitlement and ownership.

To some extent, these criticisms may be seen as unfair. The law does relatively little to regulate the content of marriage. It is true that, traditionally, marriage was a heterosexist patriarchal institution and it would be possible to have a marriage today which reflected those values. But the law is flexible enough to permit a marriage which is equal, feminist and/or queer. In other words, the kinds of undesirable features of traditional marriage highlighted by Chambers may not be caused by the law on marriage, although they may be facilitated by it. Certainly, I very much doubt that if marriage was abolished tomorrow, we would experience a sudden shift to relationships marked by equality, mutual respect and freedom from abuse. It is patriarchal forces, rather than the legal structure, which are the root of the problem.

Indeed, assuming the nature of intimate relationships remains marred by the features Chambers identified, if we did not have forms of legal intervention we would lose the power of the law to remedy those disadvantages at the end

---

[18] Minow and Lyndon Shanley, 'Relational Rights and Responsibilities: Revisioning the Family in Liberal Political Theory and Law', 4.

[19] Herring, 'Why Marriage Needs to Be Less Sexy'.

[20] C. Chambers, 'The Marriage Free State' (2013) 113 *Proceedings of the Aristotelian Society* 123, 124.

of the relationships through court orders. Leaving relationships unregulated would cause significant harms. That is because, as highlighted in Chapter 3, caring relationships create burdens and these are not equally distributed among society or within family relationships. And we cannot leave these harms to be resolved by couples through agreements, as there is no guarantee that contracts would ensure sufficient protection of those who lose out in caring relationships. Also, there would be no public recognition of the value of care work through contracts. More importantly, the nature and kind of dependencies that are generated in intimate relationships cannot be addressed in a contract. There is the difficulty of predicting what will happen during a relationship; the impact on a couple of the decisions that are made. A couple intending to raise a couple with equal division of child care, while continuing their careers, may have their plans thwarted by the birth of a child with a disability; an injury to one of the parents; a health crisis of another family member; a 'once in a lifetime' job opportunity for one of the partners; and so on. It is simply impossible to predict and set out in advance all the permutations and possibilities for a couple. As Martha Minow and Mary Lyndon Shanley[21] write:

> The model of the individual on which proposals for contracts-in-lieu-of marriage and contract pregnancy rests – that of a self-possessing individual linked to others only by agreement – fails to do justice to the complex inter dependencies involved in family relations and child rearing.

As we shall see shortly, the only effective way of responding to the unfairness created by caring relationships is to respond to them retrospectively.

To conclude, if we look at what kind of relationships family law should respond to, I argue it should be caring relationships. This is for two key reasons. First, it is caring relationships which deserve the recognition and support of the law because it is them, rather than sexual relationships, which are of significant value to the state. Second, because the kind of things family law does, redistributing property on divorce, recognising abuse within relationships and resolving disputes, are needed in cases of caring relationships. Sexual relationships do not, per se, create the kinds of problems which family law is targeted at resolving.

6.3 Remedying Unequal Distribution of Relational Advantages or Disadvantages

Within caring relationships, there can be an unfair distribution of the economic gains and losses. This is not necessarily a result of the decision of the parties but the rewarding of certain kinds of activity by society. In traditional

---

[21] Minow and Lyndon Shanley, 'Relational Rights and Responsibilities: Revisioning the Family in Liberal Political Theory and Law', 4.

terms, it is the 'money maker' who will be in a strong financial position at the head of the relationship and the 'child carer' who is in a weak position. The law can offer a remedy to these disadvantages on the breakdown of the relationship. If the law does not do that the costs of care lie where they fall and that will be predominantly women.

The law governing financial orders on divorce is controversial and there have been arguments that we should abolish or limit redistributory orders on divorce or dissolution. However, if we imagined a world in which there were no financial orders available, we would thereby be creating a world in which everyone was encouraged to be financially self-sufficient. It would be a foolish parent who gave up employment to care for a child or ailing relative. They would be putting themselves at grave financial risk. If the relationship broke down they would be in a financially disadvantageous position. It would be much more sensible for them to rely on paid care for their children. There are some who would regard that as a good thing.[22] But to many the vision of a world of mass day care, the discouragement of personal care and encouragement for financial independence is a horror. If undertaking personal care is an option that we wish to preserve we must have a system that does not render the undertaking of family care and home making financially very risky.

The evidence is clear that relationships can impact significantly on the finances of couples. In a thorough review of the evidence, two leading experts in the field, Hayley Fisher and Hamish Low,[23] conclude:

> A wide literature has shown that the financial impact of divorce is greater for women than it is for men across developed countries. Women lose more than men on divorce, regardless of the pre-divorce level of household income ... Men tend to increase their standard of living on divorce, especially low income men.

However, they go on to note that two factors in particular impact on the disadvantage caused by divorce for women: the number of children the couple have (the higher, the greater disadvantage) and the disparity in income between the couple.

For too long, the caring contribution to a marriage was not valued or recognised. As Cynthia Starnes suggests, the law was beset by three myths: 'mothering just happens, mothering is free, and mothering is for babies'.[24] There needs to be a recognition of not only the value but also the necessity of care for ourselves and our community. This point was explored further in Chapter 3.

---

[22] R. Deech, 'Divorce – a Disaster' (2009) 39 *Family Law* 1148.
[23] H. Fister and H. Low, 'Recovering From Divorce: Comparing High and Low Income Couples' (2016) 30 *International Journal of Law, Policy and the Family* 338.
[24] C. Starnes, 'Mothers, Myths, and the Law of Divorce: One More Feminist Case for Partnership' (2006) 13 *William and Mary Journal of Women and Law* 203.

So ensuring that there is a fair distribution of the economic disadvantages and advantages in the relationship is an important way of valuing the care. There are three points in this regard that I would emphasise.

First, is that the law in making orders to equalise the economic consequences of the relationship would reflect the values that typically underpinned such a relationship. According to this view, marriage should be regarded as analogous to a business partnership. The husband and wife co-operate together as a couple as part of a joint economic enterprise. They pool their resources together in their common life. It may be that one spouse is employed and the other works at home, but they work together for their mutual gain just as in a business. Therefore, on divorce each spouse should be entitled to their share of the profits of their enterprise, normally argued to be half each. Shari Motro[25] argues:

> Marriage is not fundamentally about equal contribution of labor. It is about two people joining the risks and rewards of their lives: merging their fates, committing to be 'in the same boat,' to sink or swim together, to contribute unequally at times if that's what it takes to keep the union afloat.

This way of putting the argument is interesting. It is not precisely an agreement to recognise as equal the contributions to the marriage, but rather an agreement to share the joys, slings and arrows of life. These arguments apply to all caring relationships. An intertwining of lives normally leads to sharing of the joys and disadvantages of caring burdens. In some cases, it may be that the relationship can be ended without a court order, because there is a fair share of these. But, often the sharing of the caring is not equal and the disadvantages that result from the relationship will continue well beyond the marriage. It is the intermingling of lives in a caring relationship, especially as it carries undeterminable responsibilities and costs, which justifies the financial re-ordering on separation. There are echoes of this kind of argument in Lord Nicholls's reasoning in *Miller* v. *Miller*[26]:

> [in marriage] the parties commit themselves to sharing their lives. They live and work together. When their partnership ends each is entitled to an equal share of the assets of the partnership, unless there is a good reason to the contrary. Fairness requires no less.

Care is not about counting the hours and pennies. It is a throwing together of lives, without calculating the costs.[27] As Carolyn Frantz and Hanoch Dagan put it:

---

[25] S. Motro, 'Labor, Luck and Love: Reconsidering the Sanctity of Separate Property' (2008) 102 *Northwestern University Law Review* 1623.

[26] [2006] 2 FCR 213, para 16.

[27] A. Alsott, 'Private Tragedies? Family Law as Social Insurance' (2010) 4 *Harvard Law and Policy Review* 3.

The unique goods of "communal" marriage – intimacy, caring, and commitment – are collective in a crucially different way. A mercenary understanding of these goods is hopelessly misguided, corrupting the community ideal of marriage. A self-centered quest to capture these marital goods – cooperating to achieve solely individual ends – will not ultimately be successful. Rather, to secure these unique goods of marriage, what is good for one spouse must affect what is good for the other. This partial fusion, at the core of communal marriage, is achieved when spouses perceive themselves at least partially as a "we," a plural subject, that is in turn a constitutive feature of each spouse's identity as an "I".[28]

Second, it would be an aspect of making relationships attractive, if there was insufficient protection for a party economically disadvantaged by the caring relationship. It is vital that people are not discouraged from entering caring relationships due to the financial risks involved. Lady Hale[29] has asked:

Do we want to encourage responsible families, in which people are able to compromise their place in the world outside the home for the sake of their partners, their children and their elderly or disabled relatives, and can be properly compensated for this if things go wrong? I continue to hope that we do.

It is in society's interest to ensure that care is encouraged, or at least that it is not discouraged.

Third, through financial orders on relationship breakdown, our community is able to recognise the value and importance of care work. It is a ready step to recognise the economic disadvantages that can come from it, the mutuality of caring relationships and that financial abuse does not occur. Joan Williams argues:

If we as a society take children's need for parental care seriously, it is time to stop marginalizing the adults who provide it. The current structure of work is not immutable: it was invented at a particular point in time to suit particular circumstances. Those circumstances have changed.[30]

Part of taking care seriously involves making appropriate orders on separation. As Joan Williams asserts:

Today a man can overinvest in his career secure in the knowledge that if his marriage fails, he can walk away with his wallet and enter another marriage with his financial assets substantially intact. He can put his prior marriage behind him in a way his marginalized wife and children cannot . . . Mothers always have understood that having children decreases future freedom. Fathers need to learn the same lesson. Men today know they can overinvest in work and create a family premised on their absence from daily life, secure in the knowledge that if at any point they want to reverse their priorities, they can walk with their

---

[28] C. Frantz and H. Dagan, 'Properties of Marriage' (2004) 104 *Columbia Law Review* 75, 82.

[29] B. Hale, 'Equality and Autonomy in Family Law' (2011) 33 *Journal of Social Welfare and Family Law* 3, 4.

[30] Ibid.

wallets, get a younger wife and reinvest in a new and improved family, taking with them the asset that embeds not only their market work but their ex-wife's family work as well.[31]

Putting this into application there should be two key principles which underpin the law on financial redistribution. The first is to recognise that the caring responsibilities produced by the relationship will not necessarily end when it is terminated. If caring is a central aspect of this intertwining of lives, then when there are children or other dependants involved, this continues post-relationship. This deals with a further concern from a care-based perspective with the partnership approach, which is that, as Lisa Glennon points out, it only rewards care work performed within the context of the marriage and does not recognise the post-divorce care of children.[32] An approach which puts a caring relationship at its heart can do this. It sees financial orders on divorce as ensuring that the primary purpose of the marriage, the caring of dependants, continues to thrive despite the divorce. A primary purpose of financial orders on separation should be that the caring responsibilities generated through the relationship (e.g. of children) should be enabled to continue. Housing and financial support must, where possible, be ordered, to enable those to continue.

Second, if there are sufficient means to support the future caring responsibilities, there should be a sharing of the resources of the parties, to acknowledge the joint contributions of the parties to the relationship: to accept that in a committed relationship parties bring to it a range of skills, experience and property. They are joined together equally to produce the common life. Just as talents are shared equally, so too should wealth. As Gillian Douglas puts it, a person who enjoys the benefits of care during a marriage cannot claim no responsibilities for its costs:

> Where those gains and benefits are utilized and enjoyed by the recipient, he or she cannot fairly argue that these should simply be treated as windfalls unconnected to the effort – and the commitment – of the care giver.[33]

I fully accept that financial orders on relationship breakdown are only a small part of what is required to properly value care work. The underlying issues are social: a society with gendered inequalities in terms of distribution of child care; housework; wages and access to the employment market; and a society that fails to adequately recognise the value of care work. Given these issues, any attempt to produce a 'fair' law on ancillary relief is doomed to fail. As Maxine Eichner[34] puts it:

---

[31] Ibid., 139–140.

[32] P. Laufer-Ukeles, 'Selective Recognition of Gender Difference in the Law: Revaluing the Caretaker Role' (2008) 31 *Harvard Journal of Law & Gender* 1.

[33] G. Douglas, *Obligation and Commitment in Family Law* (Hart, 2019), 32.

[34] M. Eichner, *The Supportive State: Families, the State, and American Political Ideals* (Oxford University Press, 2011), 301.

Because of this, and the critical role that sound families play in the lives of thriving citizens and a flourishing society, a government committed to human dignity must do more when it comes to families than simply seek to adopt a position of neutrality. It must, instead, actively seek to construct a network of policies that support families and the caretaking and human development functions that they fulfil.

This model is described by Eichner[35] as the 'supportive state'. She argues:

families appropriately bear responsibility for the day-today caring for (or arranging the care for) children and for meeting other dependency needs. Meanwhile, the state bears the responsibility for structuring societal institutions in ways that help families meet their caretaking needs and promote adequate human development. In this way, the supportive state seeks to balance the important goods of caretaking and human development with other important goods that its policies can implicate, including individual autonomy and sex equality.

We explored those issues in a broader context in Chapter 3. Alison Diduck and Helena Orton look forward to a better future where care is valued:

Along with true equality in employment and pay and affordable good quality child care, an adequate valuation of domestic work would mean it would not be necessary that each partner play exactly the same role in wage earning... Roles in marriage could be adopted based on the partners' actual interests and skills. Maintenance on divorce would still sometimes be necessary, then, but it would no longer overwhelmingly be women who require it and it would no longer result in economic disadvantage for the recipient. Maintenance would be seen as a right, expected and earned, rather than as a gift, act of benevolence or based on a notion of women's dependency on men.[36]

6.3.1 Pre-Nuptial Agreements

Considerable attention is now paid to 'pre-nuptial agreements'. In some jurisdictions, they play a major role in determining how property is distributed at the end of the relationship. In England, they seem to be of growing significance. The law is now dominated by *Radmacher* v. *Granatino*,[37] where it was held that it 'should accord respect to the decision of a married couple as to the manner in which their financial affairs should be regulated'.[38] The Court held that:

[t]he court should give effect to a nuptial agreement that is freely entered into by each party with a full appreciation of its implications unless in the circumstances prevailing it would not be fair to hold the parties to their agreement.[39]

---

[35] Ibid., 305.

[36] A. Diduck and H. Orton, 'Equality and Support for Spouses' (1994) 57 *Modern Law Review* 680, 686–687.

[37] [2010] UKSC 42.

[38] Ibid., para 78.

[39] Ibid., para 75.

I would argue that this argument is flawed for two primary reasons.[40]

First, it is hard enough to assess what is a fair distribution of the assets when the facts are known. Trying to predict what will happen in the future is impossible. How can a couple negotiate a fair division of assets when they don't know what life will bring them? One may become seriously disabled, their children may be disabled, the wealth of one could be decimated in a stock market crash: the imponderables are too many. The economically weaker party is also likely to be the one who will suffer most in the event of unexpected occurrences during the marriage, where they involve caring responsibilities. If the child is born disabled or a parent needs extra care, this is most likely to fall on the woman. Relationships are unpredictable and messy. The sacrifices called for can be unpredictable and obligations without limit. Ask any partner caring for their demented loved one. To seek to tie these down at the start of the relationship in some form of 'once and for all' summation of their claims against each other ignores the realities of intimate relationships.[41] We need to ensure a fair sharing of the risks of caretaking.[42] These cannot be predicted in advance and only assessed at the end of a relationship. Lady Hale captured this well in *Radmacher* v. *Granatino*[43]:

> Choices are often made for the sake of the overall happiness of the family. The couple may move from the city to the country; they may move to another country; they may adopt a completely different lifestyle; one of them may give up a well-paid job that she hates for the sake of a less lucrative job that she loves; one may give up a deadend job to embark upon a new course of study. These sorts of things happen all the time in a relationship. The couple will support one another while they are together. And it may generate a continued need for support once they are apart.

Crucially, any attempt to set down the parties' rights and responsibilities is likely to work against the interests of a partner who suffers an unexpected loss or sacrifice. These burdens are likely to fall on women as a result of care work, and so enforcement of pre-nuptial agreements is likely to work to the disadvantage of women particularly.

It may be replied that this argument fails to reflect that in *Radmacher*, as most supporters of pre-nuptial agreements would accept, there is scope for a court to depart from an agreement which is clearly unfair as unexpected events occurred or have left a party in real need. That is true, but it fails to meet the real concern. First, it puts the burden on the disadvantaged person to

---

[40] Inequality of bargaining power when the contract is signed is a further issue, although there are some tools in contract law which could deal with this to some extent.

[41] J. Herring, 'Relational Autonomy and Family Law' in J. Wallbank, S. Choudhry and J. Herring, (eds.) *Rights, Gender and Family Law* (Routledge, 2010) 270.

[42] T. Metz, 'Demands of Care and Dilemmas of Freedom: What We Really Ought to Be Worried About' (2010) 6 *Politics and Gender* 120.

[43] [2010] UKSC 42.

demonstrate their loss. They will need to prove that, for example, the parties had not foreseen that a disabled child would be born or the impact of child care on the wife's career. It is easy to imagine a husband arguing that inevitably people realise there is the risk of disability or that if a child is born it may not be possible for a wife to continue a career. Second, we are not dealing with a class of cases where occasionally unpredictable events occur. In intimate relationships, unexpected events are common. So it seems inappropriate to start with a legal structure based on contract but then permit departure in the event of unexpected events.

My second argument against giving effect to pre-nuptial agreements is that it assumes the financial orders at the end of the agreement are only about the interests of the two parties. There are important broader societal interests which will not be captured in an agreement between the parties.[44] Lady Hale,[45] writing extra-judicially, has pointed out that in the twentieth century the Victorian notion of freedom of contract has been set aside, especially in long-running relationships. She points to the extensive regulation of the employer/employee and landlord/tenant, where the scope for private ordering is very limited. She suggests that these provide a more accurate model than commercial contracts. We do not normally allow people to contract in a way which runs against principles of basic justice or undermines important societal values. Restrictions on the minimum wage, hours of employment and credit agreements demonstrate that we accept that parties should be forbidden from entering contracts which undermine principles we wish to uphold in our society. Discrimination law prohibits parties from entering contracts which are discriminatory. To allow a party to use a pre-marriage contract to take more than their fair share of marital property is likely to lead to results that will in general discriminate against women and those involved in care work. We should not be willing to give effect to contracts that deprive those who have dedicated the relationship to care work an equal share of the family's earnings, any more than we should allow an employer to pay men more than women performing the same job or pay a wage below the minimum wage. Otherwise we are enforcing a contract that de-values childcare and perpetuates gender discrimination.

6.4 Parenthood

In this section I will explore the legal determination of who is the parent of a child. This is significant because parenthood is a status with legal and social significance. It is tied to people's identity and gives parents the rights and responsibilities in relation to their children.

[44] J. Herring, 'Why Financial Orders on Divorce Should Be Unfair' (2005) 19 *International Journal of Law, Policy and the Family* 218; A. Diduck, 'What Is Family Law for?' (2011) 64 *Current Legal Problems* 287.
[45] Hale, 'Equality and Autonomy in Family Law', 3, 14.

Parenthood has traditionally been understood in biological terms. In simple terms, the father is the man whose sperm produced the child, and the mother is the woman whose egg did. This is still true today and indeed the advent of DNA testing has made it easier to determine biological truth, rather than relying on presumptions of genetic connection, as the law used to do. The law has departed from the biological model of parenthood in some cases, most notably in cases of assisted reproduction. Hence under the Human Fertilisation and Embryology Acts 1990 and 2008, egg and sperm donors are not treated as parents of a child, despite the biological link. However, these are seen as exceptions to the general rule[46] which highlights the genetic link.[47]

I would argue that this is misconceived. It should be caring for a child that generates the privileged parental position not a mere biological connection. Before developing that point further it is necessary to put one argument to the side. Many people claim that children have some kind of claim to be entitled to know of their genetic origins. If that is so, which I would question, it is not relevant to the question of the definition of parenthood in the law. That is because access to information about their genetic origins could be provided, without granting that person the status of parent. That is precisely what happens under the Human Fertilisation and Embryology legislation in relation to sperm donors. They are not parents, but children born using donated sperm can access information about the donor.

Returning to the argument that parenthood should be allocated on the basis of a caring relationship, Judith Masson helpfully distinguishes parenting by doing and parenting by being. She explains:

> Parenting by doing acknowledges the reality of looking after children by recognising adult-child relationships. Parenting by being reflects a wish to identify for the child and the state people with responsibility for the child, regardless of the practical role they are playing or want to play in the child's life.[48]

Parental status should be earned by the care and dedication to the child, something not shown simply by a biological link. It is the changing of the nappy, the wiping of the tear and the working out of maths together that makes a parent, not the provision of an egg or sperm. I suggest several reasons for this.

First, we should give parental status to the person who is best placed to meet the rights and responsibilities of being a parent: in other words, the person who it would be in the best interests of the child to be described as parent. That will be the person who knows the child best: the person who is caring for the child day to day.

---

[46] AB v. *Leeds Teaching Hospitals* NHS Trust [2003] EWHC 1034.
[47] For more detail on the legal allocation of parenthood see Herring, *Family Law*, ch 7.
[48] J. Masson, 'Parenting by Being; Parenting by Doing – In search of Principles for Founding Families' in J. Spencer and A. du Bois-Pedain (eds.) *Freedom and Responsibility in Reproductive Choice* (Hart, 2006).

Second, parenthood is responsibility that should be earned. A blood tie may be no more than a brief sexual encounter and is an insufficient basis for asserting claims over a child.[49] As Barbara Bennett Woodhouse claims, there is a danger that the law is 'intent on securing children for adults who claim them' rather than 'seeking to provide adults for children who need them'.[50]

Third, it is desirable for the legal definition of parenthood to match the child's understanding of who their parents are. This is likely to be the person who is carrying out the parental role in the child's life.

Fourth, the current approach of the law is based on the heterosexual married model. The requirement that a child has one father and one mother reinforces that as a norm for parenthood. As we depart from the assumption that this model is the primary game in town, new vistas of what it means to be a parent are opened up.[51] We can start to recognise the network of people that can play a role in a child's life. This includes recognition of the extent to which children care for other children.

Katherine Bartlett suggested that the law should recognise as parents all who

(1) have had custody of the child for at least six months;
(2) are understood to be a parent by the child; and
(3) began their relationship with the child with the support and consent of the child's legal parent.[52]

In a similar vein, Nancy Polikoff argues that legal parents would include 'anyone who maintains a functional parental relationship with a child when a legally recognised parent created that relationship with the intent that the relationship be parental in nature'.[53] It has been argued that this should even apply to those paid for care.[54]

So, to conclude, parenthood should shift from focusing on blood ties to focusing on the caring relationship between child and other. Rights should flow from the relationship with the child, not the blood tie. If this is recognised it has considerable significance. We move away from the idea that a child can have only one parent. Further, in terms of legal rights a range of adults might,

---

[49] J. Wallbank, '(En)Gendering the Fusion of Rights and Responsibilities in the Law of Contact' in J. Wallbank, S. Choudhry and J. Herring (eds.) *Rights, Gender and Family Law* (Routledge, 2009). See further S. Boyd, *Child Custody, Law and Women's Work* (Oxford University Press, 2003).

[50] B. Bennett Woodhouse, 'Hatching the Egg: A Child-Centered Perspective on Parents' Rights' (1993) 14 *Cardozo Law Review* 1747, 1814.

[51] F. Kelly, *Transforming Law's Family: The Legal Recognition of Planned Lesbian Families* (University of British Columbia Press, 2011).

[52] K. Bartlett, 'Re-Thinking Parenthood as an Exclusive Status: The Need for Legal Alternatives When the Premise of the Nuclear Family Has Failed' (1984) 70 *Virginia Law Review* 879.

[53] N. Polikoff, *Beyond (Straight and Gay) Marriage* (Beacon Press, 2008), 23.

[54] P. Laufer-Ukeles, 'Money, Caregiving, and Kinship: Should Paid Caregivers Be Allowed to Obtain De Facto Parental Status?' (2009) 74 *Missouri Law Review* 25.

depending on the context of their particular relationship, have a say in certain areas of the child's life. But the extent and nature of those rights will depend on the relationship.

6.5 Parental Responsibility

In this section I explore the concept of 'parental responsibility'. This is defined in section 3(1), Children Act 1989 (UK): '"parental responsibility" means all the rights, duties, powers, responsibilities and authority which by law a parent of a child has in relation to the child and his property'.

It is not a particularly helpful definition. However, it is reasonably clear what the drafters of the legislation had in mind. They wanted to move away from language referring to the rights of parents to language that instead emphasises their responsibilities. This view was undoubtedly seen as progressive. Children were not objects over which parents had rights, but people they had responsibilities towards. Any rights the parents did have were to be used responsibly to promote the welfare of the child. As Lord Fraser put it in *Gillick* v. *West Norfolk and Wisbech AHA*: 'parents' rights to control a child do not exist for the benefit of the parent. They exist for the benefit of the child and they are justified only in so far as they enable the parent to perform his duties towards the child, and towards other children in the family.'[55] That said, it would be wrong to suggest that there is no scope for parental discretion as to how their responsibilities are carried out. As Baroness Hale has observed, '"the child is not the child of the state" and it is important in a free society that parents should be allowed a large measure of autonomy in the way in which they discharge their parental responsibilities'.[56] The state will only intervene in decisions parents make when either parents cannot agree between themselves on an issue relating to the child or the child is suffering or is likely to suffer significant harm due to their parenting.[57]

I do not want to get into a detailed analysis of the legal nature of parental responsibility, but more explore it as a broader concept in modern society. In particular, how it fits in with the so-called crisis in parenting that we are witnessing. In her book *The Parent Trap*, Maureen Freely refers to the fact that 'as a nation we have become obsessed with fears about damaged children and endangered childhood'.[58] Parents, she argues, are now terrified that they are failing in their responsibilities to their children:

> Never have the odds against good-enough parenting been greater. The standards of performance are rising, just as more mothers are being pushed into work.

---

[55] *Gillick* v. *West Norfolk Area Health Authority* [1985] 3 WLR 830, 853.
[56] *R* v. *Secretary of State for Education and Employment ex parte Williamson* [2005] UKHL 15 [72]).
[57] Children Act 1989, section 31.
[58] M. Freely, *The Parent Trap* (Virago, 2000), 13.

The definitions of neglect and abuse are growing, and now extend to include cohabitation and marriage breakdown. In the present climate, to speak in public as a good-enough parent is to invite someone else to point out how abysmally we've failed. . . . This makes us an insecure and biddable constituency, quick to apologise for our faults and slow to point out where our masters could do better, and the government has taken advantage of our weaknesses to consolidate its power.[59]

Certainly, in the popular media, parents are regularly blamed for raising children in a harmful undesirable way, as exhibited by a wide range of issues from knife crime to screen time.

This bleak picture of parenthood is reinforced by talk of a 'crisis of childhood', with children portrayed as being robbed of their childhood through a range of harmful changes.

This emphasis on the responsibility of parents for the bad behaviour of children has been reflected in the law. Increasingly, authoritarian measures have been used against parents who were seen to be causing anti-social and criminal behaviour by not supplying sufficient levels of parenthood.[60] A good example is Parenting Orders (Magistrates' Courts (Parenting Orders) Rules 2004),[61] which allowed magistrates to require parents to sign parenting contracts, undertake parenting programmes or even attend a residential parenting course.

Another good example is the decision of the Court of Appeal in *Re B-H*.[62] The case involved two teenage girls who, following the separation of their parents, lived with their mother and strongly objected to seeing their father. Vos LJ said: '[i]t is part of the mother's parental responsibility to do all in her power to persuade her children to develop good relationships with their father, because that is in their best interests'.[63] While acknowledging that 'headstrong' teenagers can be 'particularly taxing and 'exceptionally demanding', nevertheless the mother should change her daughters' attitudes. The President of the Family division wrote:

what one can reasonably demand – not merely as a matter of law but also and much more fundamentally as a matter of natural parental obligation – is that the parent, by argument, persuasion, cajolement, blandishments, inducements, sanctions (for example, 'grounding' or the confiscation of mobile phones, computers or other electronic equipment) or threats falling short of brute force, or by a combination of them, does their level best to ensure compliance.[64]

---

[59] Ibid., 201.
[60] V. Gillies, 'From Function to Competence: Engaging with the New Politics of Family' (2011) 16 *Sociological Research* 11.
[61] Statutory Instrument 2004 No 247.
[62] [2015] EWCA Civ 389, [66].
[63] *Re B-H* [2015] EWCA Civ 389, [66].
[64] *Re B-H* [2015] EWCA Civ 389, [66-67].

Much more could be said about this case,[65] but for now three points are worth noting. The first is that the court seems to imagine parents have far more power over their children than might be imagined. How is a mother expected to force teenagers to have a good relationship with someone else? Getting a teenager to do their homework is hard enough; getting them to visit and think positively about someone else is even harder. This is particularly so given that, in this case, the father had treated the children badly in the past. It appears the court is more interested in placing the blame for the breakdown on the mother than anything else. Second, the case ignores the emotional impact on the mother. The breakdown in this case was bitter. The mother had some good reasons to think ill of the father and oppose contact. While accepting that, following the court's decision, it was best for the children to spend time with their father, it might be reasonable to expect the mother not to impede the contact. To expect her to enable the contact to which she was so strongly opposed requires an enormous amount of her. Third, the case loses sight of the children's own autonomy. They, too, had reasons for not wanting to see their father. To assume that the children's views were the responsibility of the mother presents an image of children being completely under the influence of the parents. It denies children's agency and is highly paternalistic. This final point is a general concern about the attitudes towards parenting. The emphasis on parental responsibility for the actions of children, and the significance attached to the need for good parenting, overlooks the agency of children themselves.

This is also revealed in the practice of 'hyper-parenting' and the rapid growth of books and courses designed to teach parents how to be a good parent. Hyper-parents are driven by the belief propagated by politicians and the media that parenting has the power to impact hugely on the well-being of children and that parents need the skills to excel in parenting; they sacrifice everything to ensure their children thrive. They are constantly engaging their children in improving activities to ensure that they 'succeed', by which is meant they perform better than other children. As Alvin Rosenfeld and Nicole Wise write:[66]

> This is happening because many contemporary parents see a parent's funda-
> mental job as designing a perfect upbringing for their offspring, from concep-
> tion to college. A child's success – quantified by "achievements" like speaking
> early, qualifying for the gifted and talented program, or earning admission to an
> elite university – has become the measure of parental accomplishment. That is
> why the most competitive adult sport is no longer golf. It is parenting.

---

[65] J. Herring, 'Taking Sides' (2015) 175 *New Law Journal* 11.
[66] A. Rosenfeld and N. Wise, *Hyper-Parenting: Are You Hurting Your Child by Trying Too Hard?* (St Martin's Press, 2011).

The fetishisation of the ability to genetically engineer children, the desire to control and mould children, and the emphasis of the parents' responsibility for children are all open to technology playing a useful role in 'good parenting', but they are all subject to a single major flaw: they imagine parenthood as a one-way street. Parenthood is something that parents do to children and is designed with the aim of producing good, well-rounded children. The skill of parents is to mould their children to be good citizens, and to be responsible if their children turn out to be otherwise. As Furedi[67] puts it: '[t]raditionally, good parenting has been associated with nurturing, stimulating and socializing children. Today it is associated with monitoring their activities.' Parenting has become a skill set to be learned, rather than a relationship to be lived.

The modern model of parenting described in this section, reinforced by the law, involves children as passive recipients of parenthood. The parent–child relationship is not like that. The modern model overlooks the ways that children 'parent' the adults in their life. Children care, mould, control, discipline and cajole their parents, just as parents do their children. The misdeed of a parent seeking to genetically engineer or hyper-parent their child is not just that the parent is seeking to impose a particular view of what is a good life on their child, although that is wrong. It is the error of failing to be open to change as an adult: failing to learn from children, failing to see that the things you thought were important are, in fact, not. It is failing to find the wonder, fear, loneliness, anxiety, spontaneity and joy of children, and to refind them for oneself.

Parenthood is not about the doing of tasks for which one has been trained, with technological tools. It is not a job to perform with responsibility; it is a relationship. Should we not look for parents who are warm, kind, loving and understanding, rather than well-trained, equipped with technology and hyper-vigilant? This is not least because being a parent is not accomplished by possessing a skill-set in the abstract. It is a specific relation to a particular child. It involves the parent and child working together to define what will make a successful relationship. The child is not a project for parents to design and control. The language of children as a gift is preferable. That is typically seen as a religious claim, but it can be seen as a metaphor.

These points are all the more apparent to those of us whose children do not fall into the conventional sense of 'normal'. The notion of parental control and responsibility for what a child is or does seems absurd in this context. The rule books are long since discarded and it is a matter of finding day by day what works or, more often, what does not work. Parents of disabled children come to know that the greatest success for the child will be a failure by the objective standards of any Government league table or examination board. But such social standards fail to capture a key aspect of parenting – that children can

---

[67] F. Furedi, 'It's Time to Expel the "Experts" from Family Life' *Spiked* 12 September 2011.

cause parents to be open to something more wonderful, particularly when they are more markedly different from a supposed social norm.

Our vision of what is best for our children is too depressingly restrained: a good job, a happy relationship, pleasant health and to be free from disease. Yet the best of lives is not necessarily marked by these things. Ellis[68] writes that parents of disabled children suffer 'the grief of the loss of the perfect child'. This is a sad framing of such parenthood because disability can at least throw off the shackles of what is expected. It takes parents out of the battle of competitive parenting, where the future is not a predictable life course and is all the more exciting for that.

6.6 Disputes over Children

When a court comes to resolve a dispute over the upbringing of children, English law is dominated by the 'welfare principle':

When a court determines any question with respect to –

(a) the upbringing of a child; or
(b) the administration of a child's property or the application of any income arising from it,

the child's welfare shall be the court's paramount consideration.[69]

When considering applications under section 8 of the Children Act 1989, the court must take into account the checklist of factors in section 1(3) in deciding what is in the welfare of the child.[70] The court is required to consider all the different factors and weigh them in the balance, although the court can also take into account other factors not mentioned in the list.[71]

There is much to be said that is beneficial about the welfare principle: it ensures that the focus is on the child and enables an individual assessment of the needs of the child.[72] However, I argue that it is typically understood in an individualistic way and it must be re-imagined in a relational way.

Under the welfare principle, as interpreted by the courts, the interests of adults and other children are only relevant in so far as they might affect the welfare of the child in question.[73] As was stated by the Court of Appeal in Re P (Contact: Supervision),[74] 'the court is concerned with the interests of the mother and the father only in so far as they bear on the welfare of the child'.

---

[68] J. Ellis, 'Grieving for the Loss of the Perfect Child: Parents of Children Born of Handicaps' (1989) 6 *Child and Adolescent Social Work* 259.

[69] Children Act 1989, s 1(1).

[70] Ibid., s 1(4).

[71] Baroness Hale in *Re G (Children) (Residence: Same-Sex Partner)* [2006] UKHL 43, para 40.

[72] J. Herring, 'Farewell Welfare' (2005) 27 *Journal of Social Welfare and Family Law* 159.

[73] See e.g. Lord Hobhouse in *Dawson v. Wearmouth* [1999] 1 FLR 1167.

[74] [1996] 2 FLR 314, 328.

So whether an order is 'fair' or infringes the rights of parents is not relevant; all that matters is whether the order promotes the interests of children. .[75]

However, as this book consistently emphasises, children, as we all do, live in the context of relationships. We cannot separate either the welfare or the rights of children from their parents. Their interests and rights are so intertwined and the parties so inter-dependent that to consider what order will promote the welfare of the child, as an isolated individual, and without consideration of the interests of the parents, as the courts suggest, is simply an impossibility.

A relational approach would require us to consider the child in the network of relationships within which they live. Relational welfare[76] argues that children should be brought up in relationships which overall promote their welfare.[77] Relationships are central to the lives of children and so should be at the centre of decisions about their lives.[78] It is beneficial for a child to be brought up in a family that is based on relationships which are fair and just. A relationship based on unacceptable demands on a parent is not furthering a child's welfare. Indeed, it is impossible to construct an approach to looking at a child's welfare which ignores the web of relationships within which the child is brought up. Supporting the child means supporting the caregiver and supporting the caregiver means supporting the child.[79] So a court can legitimately make an order which benefits a parent, but not a child, if that can be regarded as appropriate in the context of their past and ongoing relationship.

A central aspect of relational welfare is that we need to take a long-term view when considering welfare. The danger with the welfare principle is that it can lead to a snapshot approach being taken. The court looks at the pros and cons of a particular course of action at the time of the hearing and determines the correct result. The problem with this approach is that it focuses the court's attention simply on the current issues and fails to locate it as part of an ongoing relationship between the parties. What has happened to date in the relationship and what will happen in the future between the parties drop out of the picture.[80]

---

[75] J. Herring, 'The Human Rights Act and the Welfare Principle in Family Law – Conflicting or Complementary?' (1999) 11 *Child and Family Law Quarterly* 223.

[76] Ibid. See also J. Bridgeman, 'Children with Exceptional Needs: Welfare, Rights and Caring Responsibilities' in J. Wallbank, S. Choudhry and J. Herring (eds.) *Rights, Gender and Family Law* (Routledge, 2010).

[77] S. Sevenhuijsen, 'An Approach through the Ethic of Care' in A. Carling, S. Duncan and R. Edwards (eds.) *Analysing Families* (Routledge, 2002), 144.

[78] M. Kavanagh, 'Rewriting the Legal Family: Beyond Exclusivity to a Care-Based Standard' (2004) 16 *Yale Journal of Law and Feminism* 83.

[79] Ibid.

[80] L. Rosenbury, 'Feminist Perspectives on Children and Law: From Objectification to Relational Subjectivities' in T. Gal and B. Duramy (eds.) *International Perspectives and Empirical Findings on Child Participation: From Social Exclusion to Child-Inclusive Policies* (Oxford University Press, 2015).

The standard individualised understanding of welfare often works against the interests of mothers. Susan Boyd[81] has written powerfully of the way that the care giving of the mother enables a child to become autonomous, yet the very act of care giving restricts the autonomy of mothers. This is a common feature of family life, that at different points and times in life dreams are not pursued to enable other family members to pursue theirs. Boyd believes the impact of this on women is particularly significant, arguing:

> the still powerful societal expectations that mothers will provide primary care for children, and the strong sense of responsibility that many or most mothers feel towards the wellbeing of their children, the constraints that parenting imposes on female autonomy remain more significant than those on male autonomy.

It is also an overly narrow understanding of welfare to assume that it will promote the welfare of a child to make every decision based on what is best for them. As Charles Foster and I have argued,[82] it is in a person's welfare to live in caring relationships which are mutual and not exploitative, and to develop the virtues of altruism and relationality. A proper understanding of a person's wellbeing can require decisions to be made which will primarily benefit (or appear primarily to benefit) another person. That is because a 'good life' is not just about promoting one's own happiness. A good life is one that involves the cultivation of virtues, deep relationships with others and a meeting of one's responsibilities.

There is an obvious and strong objection to our view. Is it virtuous to have a virtuous decision made on your behalf? Does compelled altruism lose the moral virtue of altruism? The very fact one is incapable of making decisions for oneself might be thought to indicate that one has been robbed of the chance to be virtuous or meet one's responsibilities. Some will say that this argument cannot apply to an adult who permanently lacks capacity and can never hope to develop virtue. I disagree. I would question the assumption that children or adults lacking capacity cannot be virtuous because they lack the capacity to choose. Choice, it is commonly assumed, is central to the notion of a virtue. But can we say that children and those lacking mental capacity are incapable of being virtuous? No. There are two reasons why not.

First, it embodies an unduly narrow understanding of virtue. Virtues are not an expression of rational choice. Anyone dealing with those lacking mental capacity knows that they rarely lack desires, attitudes, sensibilities or expectations that can form the basis of a virtue. In these, and in their cultivation, virtue can be found. The toddler who cuddles the crying friend exhibits compassion and empathy, even if they lack the mental capacity to express it in those terms. The love and care exhibited there is a simple expression of feeling. Those without mental capacity are perfectly capable of expressing

[81] Boyd, *Child Custody, Law and Women's Work*, 2.
[82] C. Foster and J. Herring, *Altruism, Welfare and the Law* (Springer, 2015).

warmth, affection and kindness, even if they lack the capacity to articulate what they are doing.

Second, our assumption that 'we' (the capacitous adults) have the autonomy and strength to be virtuous, while 'they' (the children and those lacking capacity) do not involves not only a misunderstanding of virtue but also an inaccurately inflated view of ourselves. We might like to pretend we are autonomous and strong. The reality is a little less grand. The exhausted carer returning the demented adult to bed in the early hours of the morning may not be exercising rational capacity but is certainly showing capacity. Many of our virtuous activities are not a reflection of rational capacity, at least not primarily so.

So, in deciding how to resolve disputes over children we need to consider children within their relational context. We cannot properly conceive of children without considering the interests of those with whom they are in relationship. The standard approach of promoting the interests of the child requires a false separation of the child from their relational context. Even if we were able to do this, it is not in the interests of a child to be raised in one-sided relationships which are solely about the child. A good upbringing for a child is one in which relationships and the mutual respect and fair distribution of goods and harms of a relationship are shared between the members of the family.

6.7 Conclusion

This chapter has argued that an understanding of the relational self can provide a new and improved framework for family law. It will require a refocussing of family law away from marriage and towards all caring relationships. This will mean that some relationships which are currently at the core of family law (a married couple with no children) might fall outside the remit of the subject. But other relationships which currently fall outside family law will be drawn into its core (e.g. those caring for disabled adults; unorthodox family forms caring for dependants). The chapter has also argued that care should be seen as the core value in financial orders at the end of the caring relationship.[83] Through them we can provide a way of recognising the value of care and, in some cases, ensure a fairer sharing of the costs of care.

This chapter has also called for a refocussing on parenthood from being based on biological connection to being a label that reflects the relationship someone has developed with a child. For some that might be through the process of pregnancy or birth; for others it will be through hands-on care of the child. I have also reflected on the nature of parental responsibility, both in the law and more broadly. I have argued that we need to understand the parent–child relationship as a two-way process. Children are not a project that parents must work on and that parents are responsible for if the child does not

---

[83] To be clear, I am not restricting this to marriage but to any relationship marked by significant levels of care.

emerge as an 'ideal citizen'. Rather, parents must learn from children. We must acknowledge the care that children give parents, just as parents care for their children.

Finally, I promoted relational welfare as an approach to deal with cases where there is a dispute over the upbringing of a child. This involves seeking a solution which will promote caring relationships between the child and those connected to the child. It rejects an approach which asks what order might promote the interests of a child, because we cannot consider the child outside their relational context. Rather, simply put, family law should be about the promotion of care.

7

Criminal Law and the Relational Self

7.1 Introduction

The criminal law is a revealing example of how the law understands the self. This chapter will explore three particular issues to illustrate this. The first is the law's understanding of what is a harm for the purposes of criminal law. It will be argued that this largely focus on harms to the self, understood in a highly individualised way: harms to a person's body or property. The criminal law pays little attention to harms to relationships or emotions. The second is the criminal law's understanding of blame. Here too a highly individualised understanding of blame is used. The assumption is that the defendant and the defendant alone is responsible for their actions. The third is the role of the criminal law in society. This issue will take up the idea of our vulnerable natures requiring a criminal law that upholds and supports our responsibilities to each other. There are, no doubt, plenty of other issues that are raised by criminal law, particularly in relation to sentencing, punishment and criminal procedure, but the three issues which are the focus of this chapter will highlight insights that a relational understanding of the self can offer criminal law.

7.2 Relational Harms

In introducing students to criminal law it is common, if somewhat over-simplistic, to explain that criminal offences are made up of two elements: the harm to the victim and the wrongfulness of the defendant. This reflects the classical separation between the *actus reus* (the physical element) and the *mens rea* (the mental element). When discussing which harms to the victims are included within criminal law, many presentations start with the 'harm principle': The leading exposition of this is provided by John Stuart Mill with his famous essay *On Liberty*. At the heart of his argument is the following:

> The only purpose for which power can be rightfully exercised over any member of a civilized community against his will is to prevent harm to others. His own good, either physical or moral, is not sufficient warrant. He cannot rightfully be

compelled to do or forbear ... because in the opinion of others to do so would be wise or even right.[1]

Harm is important, therefore, in a criminal law analysis because it is harm to the victims that justifies a criminal intervention. And if there is no harm to the victim there should be no criminal offence. This is widely supported, and although there are some debates on the criminalisation of 'harmless wrong-doing', the debates are premised on the assumption that it is normally inappropriate to criminalise non-harmful conduct.

Harm is also significant because it is used to grade offences, explaining which are the more serious. Students of criminal law are presented with a reasonably coherent model of the harms that are the focus of the criminal law. These are crimes against the person, crimes against property and public order offences. Offences against the person are presented as a 'ladder of harms' with a battery (a mere touching of person) being at the bottom, leading up through offences involving actual bodily harm and grievous bodily harm until we reach homicide at the top of the ladder. Typical is this presentation from the University of London Guide to Criminal Law:

> The crimes of violence dealt with in this subject guide are those appearing in the Offences Against the Person Act 1861 (OAPA). These offences form a ladder of relative seriousness starting from, at the bottom of the ladder, assault occasion-ing bodily harm (s.47), to malicious wounding (s.20), up to wounding with intent to cause grievous bodily harm (GBH) (s.18).[2]

This is a clear way of presenting the law to students. No doubt, most students find it an intuitively natural way to grade harms. The more serious the injury to the body of the victim, the more serious the harm. Hence we can see causing a bruise is worse than a slap and so on.

Academic writers have supported this approach. Andrew von Hirsch and Nils Jareborg have produced an influential approach to assessing the gravity of the harm to the victim and focus on the following[3] four kinds of interests:

(1) physical integrity: health, safety and the avoidance of physical pain;
(2) material support and amenity: includes nutrition, shelter and other basic amenities;
(3) freedom from humiliation or degrading treatment;
(4) privacy and autonomy.

We see here a prioritisation of the individual imagined as a static entity. Those things which challenge self-sufficiency, autonomy and independence are

---

[1] J. Mill, *On Liberty* (Cosimo Classics Philosophy, 1991, originally published 1859).

[2] University of London, *Guide to Criminal Law: Offences against the Person* (University of London, 2018), 91.

[3] A. von Hirsch and N. Jareborg, 'Gauging Criminal Harm: A Living-Standard Analysis' (1991) 11 *Oxford Journal of Legal Studies* 1.

identified as the most serious harm to what they call 'the living standard'. They are explicit that they harm an individual:

> While the living standard, thus conceived, includes non-material capabilities, it is restricted to those capabilities that are self-regarding: those that are involved in the quality of a person's *own* life. Altruistic satisfactions and dissatisfactions would not be taken into account. In Sen's words, 'one's misery at the sorrow of another ... is not a reduction in ... the person's living standard'.[4]

Likewise, they deliberately exclude emotional harms because these might 'flow from victimisation' but should not be categorised as a wrong themselves.

Yet in view of the themes of this book it is possible to imagine a different way of understanding a harm. If we are essentially relational beings then the greatest harms are the wrongs done to the relationships that make up our selves. Harms would be described not purely in terms of impact on bodily movement or integrity, but in terms of impact on the caring relationships which are so central to whom we are. To be clear, of course a breach of bodily integrity can have serious impacts on a person's relationships and their relational self. But the wrong should be identified in terms of its relational impact not in terms of its impact on bodily wholeness. I will use three examples to illustrate further these points.

7.2.1 Dhaliwal

In *R* v. *Dhaliwal*,[5] a husband subjected his wife to a sustained campaign of abuse which drove his wife to commit suicide. He was charged with manslaughter but acquitted, confirmed on appeal. The problem for the prosecution was that it was not possible to identify a criminal act that he had done which had caused her to commit suicide. Looked at individually, none of his profoundly unpleasant remarks were not criminal offences. Even though there was evidence of some physical violence, which would be an offence, it could not be shown that any one of the acts of violence had caused her to commit suicide. The sustained campaign of verbal abuse did cause the suicide, but that could not be captured by the traditional tools of legal analysis as an offence.

I would make three points about this case. The first is that the traditional focus of the court is to take a 'snapshot' approach, whereby the wrong is seen in terms of the particular moment of the violent act. Descriptions of the facts in criminal cases will focus on the moment the assault took place. In trials, CCTV footage of the incident will often be the focus of the jury's attention. Yet this isolates the attack from its broader context and the relationship between

---

[4] Ibid., 11, quoting Amartya Sen, *The Standard of Living* (Cambridge University Press, 1987).
[5] *R* v. *Dhaliwal* [2006] EWCA Crim 113.

the parties. In *Dhaliwal*, it was not surprising that a single unpleasant remark made to his wife, viewed in isolation, was not a criminal offence. The failure of the law was the inability to capture the combined effect of all the remarks and behaviour together: to watch the streaming of the relationship, rather than looking at a photograph of the incident, if you like. It was not that the court was not able to appreciate what had happened. Judge LJ stated:

> On the evening on which she committed suicide there was an argument between Mr and Mrs Dhaliwal, in the course of which, as he admitted later, he struck her on the forehead. The bangle he was wearing at the time cut her skin at the point where his blow landed. It seems likely that this assault operated as the immediate trigger which precipitated her suicide. Psychiatric evidence suggested that the "overwhelming primary cause" for the suicide "was the experience of being physically abused by her husband in the context of experiencing many such episodes over a very prolonged period of time."[6]

The failure lay in the substantive criminal law to capture this. The prolonged abuse could not be identified in itself as a legally recognised wrong, only a series of individual attacks. The case lays bare the narrow focus of traditional criminal law.[7]

Second, even though the court acknowledged that emotional harm could be regarded as bodily harm and hence a criminal offence, that was only if it can be medically recognised as a condition. In *R* v. *Dhaliwal*[8] one of the difficulties was it could not be shown that she suffered a specific medical condition. This might seem surprising, as the fact she committed suicide might be thought to indicate a serious mental disturbance. However, the criminal law acknowledges the existence of psychological harm only through the prism of medicine.[9] In this case, not surprisingly, the expert was unable to offer a definite diagnosis (because there had been no opportunity to assess the victim's psychological health; indeed the husband restricted her access to medical professionals) and so the harm was not proved.[10]

Third, it is notable the case pays little attention to the fact the couple were in a close relationship (they were married) and it seems from the narration of the facts that Ms Dhaliwal had little interaction with anyone else outside her marriage. This meant that her relationship with the defendant was a core part of her identity. This was central to an appreciation of the significance of his verbal and physical abuse. It meant her defining relationship was being used as a tool against her. Yet none of this is captured with the analysis of the court in terms of whether there could be actual or grievous bodily harm.

---

[6] Para 9.
[7] M. Burton, 'R v Dhaliwal Commentary' in R. Hunter, C. McGlynn and E. Rackley (eds.) *Feminist Judgments* (Hart, 2010), 258.
[8] *R* v. *Dhaliwal* [2006] EWCA Crim 1139.
[9] *R* v. *Chan Fook* [1994] 1 WLR 698.
[10] Burton, 'R v Dhaliwal Commentary'.

7.2.2 Marital Rape

A striking example of the failure to recognise a relational wrong is the marital rape exemption. This was abolished by the House of Lords in *R* v. *R*.[11] After that decision a husband could be convicted of raping his wife. The previous law played no attention to the reality of the relationship between the parties: the focus was on their legal status. The fact that in many cases the relationship was marked by domestic abuse and the rape was just one feature of that was overshadowed by the dominance placed on the marital status.

One might think that following that decision there is not much more that needs to be said on the topic. However, although no longer part of the substantive law on rape the marital status of the parties is still used in sentencing.[12] A good example of the courts' attitudes in the 1990s is *R* v. *M*,[13] where Lord Taylor explained:

> In the present case we would point out that there is a distinction between a husband who is estranged from his wife and is parted from her and returns to the house as an intruder either by forcing his way in or by worming his way in through some device and then rapes her, and a case where, as here, the husband is still living in the same house and, indeed, with consent occupying the same bed as his wife. We do not consider that this class of case is as grave as the former class.[14]

In *R* v. *Millberry*[15] the Court of Appeal reviewed its approach to cases of relationship rape and noted that the sentence for rape would not necessarily be the same in all cases. It recognised that there might be 'mitigating circumstances', suggesting that:

> Where, for example, the offender is the husband of the victim there can, but not necessarily will, be mitigating features that clearly cannot apply to a rape by a stranger ... [I]t is not to be overlooked, when considering 'stranger rape', the victim's fear can be increased because her assailant is an unknown quantity. Is he a murderer as well as a rapist? In addition, there is the fact ... that when a rape is committed by a stranger in a public place, not only is the offence horrific to the victim it can also frighten other members of the public. This element is less likely to be a factor that is particularly important in a case of marital rape were the parties to the marriage are living together.[16]

---

[11] *R* v. *R* [1992] 1 AC 599. J. Herring, 'No More Having and Holding: The Abolition of the Marital Rape Exemption' in P. Handler, H. Mares and I. Williams (ed.) *Landmark Cases in Criminal Law* (Hart, 2017).
[12] K. Warner, 'Sentencing in Cases of Marital Rape' (2000) 20 *Legal Studies* 592.
[13] (1995) 16 Cr App R (S) 770.
[14] Para 17.
[15] [2002] EWCA Crim 2891.
[16] Para 13.

Phil Rumney, in his 1999 analysis of relationship rape cases, concluded[17] that 'there appears to be little difference in the approach of the courts to marital rape sentencing today from their approach prior to R'.[18]

What has been missing from the courts' analysis is an understanding of how the breach of trust involved in a relationship where the parties is a particular wrong against the victim. There are some cases where this is acknowledged. The Court of Appeal in *Attorney-General's Reference (No 90 of 2009)*[19] increased a sentence of ten years to eighteen in a case of marital rape. This was justified on this basis:

> This is an extreme case of its kind: rape by a husband of his wife from whom he was separated. The facts that we have narrated demonstrate, and the conduct of his defence confirms, that the offender deliberately chose to use sexual inter-course with his wife without her consent as a weapon with which to dominate and humiliate her. This was the woman with whom he had once had a relationship of genuine affection and who had borne him two children. There was a grave breach of trust. The offender used the kind of knowledge that couples have of each other, which he would have acquired during their moments of warm intimacy, about a sexual practice that she found wholly unacceptable. With that knowledge he forced her to submit to it. Apart from the sheer humiliation and horror, she suffered physical pain. Having done that, he added to her degradation by raping her vaginally. The offender's actions were quite merciless.[20]

However, this seems to be regarded as an exceptional case. If the horrific facts of that case are what is required before the courts will acknowledge the gravity of breach of trust, we are still a long way from an adequate acknowledgement that marital rape and rape in other cases where there is a close relationship between the parties has an added inherent wrong.

We need a clear acknowledgment from the courts that where the parties were in a close intimate relationship, such as marriage, this should be an aggravating, rather than mitigating, feature in relation to rape. In the writings and decisions on marital rape the experiences of the victims of rape have been silenced. In *R* v. *R* itself little weight was attached to the experience of women who have experienced marital rape. Remarkably, Glanville Williams' advice was to listen to 'sensible women', rather than the victims of marital rape.[21] Had he listened to those who had experienced it he would have heard of the trauma and turmoil caused by marital rape.[22] The assumption that marital

---

[17] P. Rumney, 'When Rape Isn't Rape: Court of Appeal Sentencing Practice in Cases of Marital and Relationship Rape' (1999) 19 *Oxford Journal of Legal Studies* 243.

[18] *R* v. *PH* [2001] 1 Cr App R (S) 52.

[19] [2009] EWCA Crim 2610.

[20] Para 21.

[21] G. Williams, 'Rape Is Rape' (1991) 142 *New Law Journal* 11.

[22] J. Bennice and P. Resick, 'Marital Rape: History, Research and Practice' (2003) 4 *Trauma, Violence and Abuse* 228.

rape is necessarily less serious than non-marital rape does not fit with the evidence about the impact of marital rape, which indicates high rates of trauma and significant long-term effects.[23] Jennifer Bennice and Patricia Resick argue that marital rape victims suffer more severe post-trauma distress than those raped by strangers.[24] David Finkelhor and Kersti Yllo describe the feelings of one victim of marital rape:[25]

> My whole body was being abused. I feel if I'd been raped by a stranger, I could have dealt with it a whole lot better. When a stranger does it, he doesn't know me, I don't know him. He is not doing it to me as a person, personally. With your husband, it becomes personal. You say, this man knows me. He knows my feelings. He knows me intimately, and then to do this to me – it's such a personal abuse.

As this discussion indicates, it is only with a relational approach that the horror of rape between intimate partners can be acknowledged.

7.2.3 BDSM

Another example of the law's failure to take seriously the relational aspect is the regulation of BDSM.[26] In *Brown*,[27] notoriously the House of Lords upheld the conviction of a group of men engaging in BDSM.[28] It was held that the consent of participants to activities which caused actual bodily harm or grievous bodily harm provided no defence. That decision has been strongly criticised in academic circles.[29] With considerable justification, the judgements of the majority have been said to reflect prejudices of various kinds. The approach taken by the minority, that consensual private BDSM practices should not be criminalised, has found much more favour.

However, I think, particularly in light of the more recent cases, the main-stream acceptance of BDSM should be questioned. In particular, it is crucial to explore the relational context of the case. Consider, for example, the case of *Wilson*, where the Court of Appeal allowed the appeal of a husband who had branded his initials on his wife's buttocks.[30] The Court of Appeal explained that *Brown* could be distinguished and that 'Consensual activity between

---

[23] B. Katz, 'The Psychological Impact of Stranger versus Non-stranger Rape on Victims' Recovery' in A. Parrot and L. Bechhofer (eds.) *Acquaintance Rape – The Hidden Crime* (John Wiley & Sons, 1991).

[24] Bennice and Resick, 'Marital Rape: History, Research and Practice', 228.

[25] D. Finkelhor and K. Yllo, *License to Rape: Sexual Abuse of Wives* (Free Press, 1985), 118.

[26] A full analysis is found in Herring, 'No More Having and Holding: The Abolition of the Marital Rape Exemption'.

[27] [1994] 1 AC 212 (HL).

[28] The acronym is designed to convey practise including bondage and discipline (BD), dominance and submission (DS), sadism and masochism (SM).

[29] S. Cowan, 'To Buy or Not to Buy? Vulnerability and the Criminalisation of Commercial BDSM' (2012) 20 *Feminist Legal Studies* 263.

[30] *R* v. *Wilson* [1997] QB 47.

husband and wife, in the privacy of the matrimonial home, is not, in our judgment, normally a proper matter for criminal investigation, let alone criminal prosecution.'[31] That justification for the outcome was hard to justify. Subsequently, different explanations were offered for the decision: the case was analogous to tattooing[32] or Mr Wilson did not intend to cause pain to his wife.[33] Neither of those is very convincing either and a comparison of *Wilson* and *Brown* seems to provide a conclusive case of the law in this area being driven by irrational prejudice, rather than sound reasoning.

But the decision and the criticism of it I think miss the point. Mr Wilson had branded his initials, W and A, on his wife's buttocks with a hot knife. She went to see the doctor and showed him what had happened. The doctor notified the police, breaching patient confidentiality. The wife refused to give evidence in her husband's defence. We do not know what Mrs Wilson told her doctor, but one of the few situations in which breach of medical confidentiality is permitted is to prevent domestic abuse. Remarkably, in this case, the court accepted the defendant's account that the branding was consensual.[34] However, the branding of one's name on one's partner seems like the nadir for an abuser seeking the ultimate control over his spouse, echoing the marking of slaves by their 'owners'. It has all the hallmarks of coercive control.

Other cases following *Brown* raise similar concerns. In *Emmett*, the defendant poured lighter fuel on his partner's breasts and set them alight, causing severe third degree burns in a 24 cm squared area. He also put a plastic bag over her head and tightened it to the point she could no long endure the pain and was unable to communicate with him. Pouring lighter fuel on someone's chest and setting it alight is not standard BDSM practise, nor is preventing the partner from using the safe word. Nevertheless, the case was presented in court and accepted as a case of consensual BDSM. Although, this time, Brown was followed and consent was held not to be a defence. As in Wilson, the victim went to see her doctor, who informed the police. She refused to give evidence in his defence.[35] Again, the only person who knew her side of the story was the doctor and it is revealing they decided to breach the duty of confidentiality that normally applies to doctor/patient communications and inform the police.[36] While we cannot know the truth, there must be a strong suspicion that this was simply a case of domestic violence to which the defendant gave the only defence he could: she wanted it.

In *Meachen*, the victim had been given a 'date rape drug' and then been anally penetrated by a very large object, causing a serious injury, requiring permanent use of a colostomy bag. He claimed that she consented to this,

---

[31] Ibid., 50.
[32] *R v. Emmett* [1999] All ER (D) 641.
[33] *R v. Dica* [2004] EWCA 1103.
[34] *Wilson* [1997] QB 47.
[35] *Emmett* [1999] All ER (D) 641.
[36] General Medical Council, *Confidentiality* (GMC, 2009).

although yet again the victim gave no evidence to support this. The court accepted that had she consented to this he would have had a defence.[37] The case demonstrates the ease with which an abuser can rely on sado-masochism as a defence. In this case, the use of the drug appears to undermine the claim the case was one of consensual sex.

In *Lock*, also portrayed as a BDSM case, the woman had the words 'Property of Steven Lock' tattooed around her genitals. Lock chained the woman 'like a dog' to his bedroom floor and whipped her repeatedly with a rope.[38] This case has all the hallmarks of the coercive control model of domestic abuse mentioned earlier.

These cases demonstrate the dangers of simply accepting 'consensual BDSM' as a defence at face value. Cheryl Hanna states:

> If consent were allowed as a defense in the S/M context, defense attorneys would have carte blanche to raise it in every sexual assault case where the victim is injured. This would essentially gut rape law jurisprudence as it now stands. So too could defense attorneys raise the S/M defense in many cases of domestic violence, undermining the slow and steady strides the law has made in sanctioning male violence.[39]

In cases in which a domestic abuser is charged with assaulting their partner where there are proven injuries, explaining the injuries as the results of consensual sado-masochism is one of the few defences available to him, and if the victim is too scared to give evidence, it will be a hard defence for the prosecution to rebut. With that in mind, there is a strong case for saying the defence of sado-masochism should not be available, or, at the very least, it must be proved by evidence from the victim. The real issues in the case can only be explored by considering the relational context of the activity. We need to make sure that domestic violence abusers cannot escape being held to account by claiming their actions were consensual BDSM, as I suspect happens too often at the moment. It may require a reversal of burden of proof so that those claiming that BDSM was consensual have to prove it by producing evidence from the alleged victim and demonstrating that their activities were in the context of a mutually respecting, autonomy-enhancing relationship.

This discussion indicates that there are real dangers of BDSM being legalised without a willingness to look at its broader social context. Most academics seem to think that 'consent' and protection of autonomy are sufficient to ensure the defence should be lawful. Only a relational approach can ensure an effective distinction is drawn between BDSM and intimate abuse.

---

[37] *R v Meachen* [2006] EWCA Crim 2414.

[38] B. Kendall, 'Gardener cleared of assault after Fifty Shades of Grey-inspired sadomasochistic sex session' The Independent (22 January 2013).

[39] C. Hanna, 'Sex Is Not a Sport: Consent and Violence in Criminal Law' (2001) 42 *Boston College Law Review* 239, 286.

7.2.4 Acknowledgement of Relational Harms

Despite the points made so far, it must be accepted that the law is just beginning to take account of these relational harms. The Protection from Harassment Act 1997, for example, recognises that a course of conduct which causes harassment can be a criminal offence. Most notably, the offence of 'controlling or coercive behaviour in an intimate or family relationship' has been created in section 76 of the Serious Crime Act 2015:

(1) A person (A) commits an offence if –
    (a) A repeatedly or continuously engages in behaviour towards another person (B) that is controlling or coercive,
    (b) at the time of the behaviour, A and B are personally connected,
    (c) the behaviour has a serious effect on B, and
    (d) A knows or ought to know that the behaviour will have a serious effect on B.
(2) A and B are "personally connected" if –
    (a) A is in an intimate personal relationship with B, or
    (b) A and B live together and –
        (i) they are members of the same family, or
        (ii) they have previously been in an intimate personal relationship with each other.
(3) But A does not commit an offence under this section if at the time of the behaviour in question –
    (a) A has responsibility for B, for the purposes of Part 1 of the Children and Young Persons Act 1933 (see section 17 of that Act), and
    (b) B is under 16.
(4) A's behaviour has a "serious effect" on B if –
    (a) it causes B to fear, on at least two occasions, that violence will be used against B, or
    (b) it causes B serious alarm or distress which has a substantial adverse effect on B's usual day-to-day activities.
(5) For the purposes of subsection (1)(d) A "ought to know" that which a reasonable person in possession of the same information would know.
(6) For the purposes of subsection (2)(b)(i) A and B are members of the same family if –
    (a) they are, or have been, married to each other;
    (b) they are, or have been, civil partners of each other;
    (c) they are relatives;
    (d) they have agreed to marry one another (whether or not the agreement has been terminated);
    (e) they have entered into a civil partnership agreement (whether or not the agreement has been terminated);
    (f) they are both parents of the same child;
    (g) they have, or have had, parental responsibility for the same child.

(7) In subsection (6) –
     "civil partnership agreement" has the meaning given by section 73 of the
        Civil Partnership Act 2004;
     "child" means a person under the age of 18 years;
     "parental responsibility" has the same meaning as in the Children Act
        1989;
     "relative" has the meaning given by section 63(1) of the Family Law Act
        1996.
(8) In proceedings for an offence under this section it is a defence for A to
     show that –
     (a) in engaging in the behaviour in question, A believed that he or she
          was acting in B's best interests, and
     (b) the behaviour was in all the circumstances reasonable.
(9) A is to be taken to have shown the facts mentioned in subsection (8) if –
     (a) sufficient evidence of the facts is adduced to raise an issue with
          respect to them, and
     (b) the contrary is not proved beyond reasonable doubt.
(10) The defence in subsection (8) is not available to A in relation to behav-
     iour that causes B to fear that violence will be used against B.
(11) A person guilty of an offence under this section is liable –
     (a) on conviction on indictment, to imprisonment for a term not
          exceeding five years, or a fine, or both;
     (b) on summary conviction, to imprisonment for a term not exceeding
          12 months, or a fine, or both.

This is a welcome departure from the 'snapshot' approach and appreciation
that the real wrong in coercive control cannot be captured by a consideration
of a separate act.

There are two issues which are worth exploring further. The first is the
requirement that the couple are 'in an intimate personal relationship or live
together as a family'. As explored in Chapter 4, it is welcome that the
legislation acknowledges that the issue is not restricted to family relationships
as traditionally understood, nor that it is limited to those living together.
However, it is hoped that where coercive control is being exercised it will
almost inevitably mean there is an 'intimate personal relationship'. Indeed, it is
hard to imagine coercive control existing save within an intimate personal
relationship. That said, worryingly, subsection 4 makes it clear that a parent
cannot be convicted of this offence in relation to a child. It is a revealing failure
of the law to take children's rights seriously that the law permits parents to
coercively control their children.

Second, it must be shown that the behaviour must have a 'serious effect' on
the victim. This is a rather vague phrase. Subsection 4 defines a serious effect
as a case where the victim fears violence on two occasions or where the victim
suffers 'serious alarm or distress which has a substantial adverse effect on B's

usual day-to-day activities'. This means that if there is a controlling relation-ship but the victim is perfectly happy with the relationship there is no offence. Arguably, if the parties were members of a religion which taught that wives must obey their husbands, the relationship may be controlling, but the wife is happy with that. If she is not suffering a 'serious effect' there may be no offence.

Despite these two areas of concern, the willingness to take this form of relational harm seriously is greatly to be welcomed.

7.3 Consent and the Criminal Law

Our understanding of the nature of the human self has important implications for the role of consent in criminal law. If we start with an image of the self as autonomous, self-sufficient and capable, then we might welcome the standard picture of consent offering a defence to what might otherwise be a criminal charge. D wants to harm V and V should be able to decide whether it will benefit V for D to do so. D's responsibility in such a case is limited to ensuring that V has expressed agreement. However, that all looks very different if we assume that in our natures we are all vulnerable, dependent on others and living in inter-locking caring relationships, with the law designed to maintain good caring relationships. Here we would not be assuming responsibilities for V to look after themselves, but rather responsibilities between us to look out for each other. Philip Petit[40] discussing his theory of republicanism makes some insightful comments on the nature of the wrong from the perspective of the vulnerability:

> The republican theory of suitable protection emphasizes the need to guard against domination, not just interference. You will enjoy suitable protection in a particular choice just to the extent that other individuals or groups do not have access to means of non-deliberative control over that choice. Others may be able to deliberate with you on the basis of sincere, take-it-or-leave-it reasons and influence what you do. But they should not be allowed a power of interfering with the choice, without exposing themselves to an inhibiting risk of punish-ment; they should not be able to block, burden, or deceptively redirect the choice with any degree of impunity. In short, they should not have 'dominating control' over what you choose.

This perspective understands the wrong that can take place where there is consent. It shows that in cases of apparent consent we need to explore carefully the relational context in which it takes place. It means the defendant will have duties to care for the victim even in cases of apparent consent. I will explore these issues further with two examples.

---

[40] P. Petit, 'The Basic liberties' in M. Kramer, C. Grant, B. Colburn and A. Hatzistavrou (eds.) *The Legacy of HLA Hart: Legal, Political and Moral Philosophy* (Oxford University Press, 2008), 201.

7.3.1 Theft

In financial transactions, many people think that generally it is reasonable to expect people to make their own enquiries and determine whether or not it is appropriate to purchase a particular item. If they buy a car and it turns out to be a bad deal, well they only have themselves to blame. Hence we might expect the law on theft, for example, to only apply in a case where property has been removed without the consent of the victim. Surprisingly, that is not the position the law has taken.

The case of *R* v. *Hinks*[41] highlights the issues well. A 38–year-old woman (Karen Hinks) befriended a 53-year-old man (John Dolphin), who was described as of limited intelligence. Over a period of eight months, £60,000 was given to Ms Hinks. Her conviction for theft was upheld. Although it appeared that no threats or deceptions had been used (which would have made the case an easy one), it was felt she had behaved dishonestly in receiving the money. What is notable about the case is the House of Lords' willingness to find that there was theft, even though there was no civil wrong (in other words, the gifts may have been valid under the law of property). Lord Steyn noted the possible differences between civil and criminal law as mentioned earlier in the chapter. He saw this justifying a finding that a criminal offence had taken place, even though there may have been an effective transfer of ownership.[42] He noted that the aims of the criminal and civil law may be different. While a particular transaction might be upheld as valid for the purposes of property law, with its emphasis on the importance of certainty of ownership, the criminal law may legitimately criminalise it if it involves dishonesty. Interestingly, the case has generated considerable criticism from criminal lawyers.

Andrew Simester and Bob Sullivan[43] claim that theft only occurs where there is a breach of property rights, arguing that property offences:

> attack the practices of creating and exchanging property rights. In doing so, they set back the dependability of proprietary entitlements; which, in turn, restricts the ability of property owners to plan their own lives, relying on both the property rights they have already and on the expectation of being able to improve their lives by formulating proprietary transactions in the future.

As they accept, their approach is based on an assumption that the property regime is a reasonably fair one. However, it seems their argument may be claiming too much. Indeed, taken at face value it appears to suggest any breach

---

[41] [2000] UKHL 53.

[42] The case has generated much debate among criminal lawyers. This is summarised in J. Herring, *Criminal Law: Text Cases and Materials* (Oxford University Press, 2018), ch 10.

[43] A. Simester and R. Sullivan, 'On the Nature and Rationale of Property Offences' in R. Duff and S. Green (eds.) *Defining Crimes: Essays on the Special Part of the Criminal Law* (Oxford University Press, 2015), 211.

of a civil obligation is potentially sufficient harm to justify the harm principle. Further, it is hard to see how an individual instance of theft imperils the property regime, especially given the existence of civil remedies.[44]

As the *Hinks* case demonstrates, there is much to be gained from the criminal law not simply focusing on the moment of the crime and defining the wrong in terms of a particular act and state of mind. Rather, we should look at the act within the broader context of the relationship. Only then, for example, can the wrong in *Hinks* be identified. It indicates that dishonesty is not simply a matter of whether there was consent but whether taking advantage by a stronger party to the relationship occurred. Simon Gardner, supporting Gomez and Hinks, explains:

> It is submitted that the quality of dishonest conduct is not necessarily altered by the victim's consent. Consider, above all, cases where the victim consents to the taking, but does so in a state of low-level, non-specific confusion. For example, elderly people are often exploited by rogues who dishonestly overcharge them for work, or underpay them for their treasures. The victim in such a case has consented to the taking, and her consent is not obviously vitiated, but it is very possible to sense that the rogue's conduct should be criminal.[45]

7.3.2 Consent to Sexual Relations

How can we draw the line between sexual behaviour which is exploitative and deserving of criminal sanction and that which is not? There are some cases of rape where it is obvious that there is no consent. The difficult cases turn on whether the exploitative or threatening techniques employed by a defendant mean there is no genuine consent, even though there may have been words or behaviour indicating consent.

To understand the issue it is necessary to say a little more about consent.[46] You do not need a person's consent to perform an act unless you are doing something that is prima facie a harm to them. You do not normally need permission to look at someone because looking at them causes them no harm. Consent becomes relevant when D's act wrongfully harms another person's (V) wellbeing, thereby rendering the act a prima facie wrong. Where an act is a prima facie wrong the actor (D) must provide a reason justifying acting in the way they did. Consent operates as providing a justifying reason. Where V consents to the act, D is entitled to assume that the act is not all things considered contrary to the wellbeing of the victim (V). That is because D is permitted to rely on V's assessment

---

[44] A. Steel, 'The Harms and Wrongs of Stealing: The Harm Principle and Dishonesty in Theft' (2008) 31 *University of New South Wales Law Journal* 712.

[45] S. Gardner, 'Appropriation in Theft: The Last Word' (1993) *Law Quarterly Review* 194.

[46] M. Madden Dempsey, 'Victimless Conduct and the Volenti Maxim: How Consent Works' (2013) 7 *Criminal Law and Philosophy* 11.

that the act is overall in V's best interests. Madden Dempsey explains that in effect where consent is effective, D is entitled to say:

> This is [V]'s decision. He's an adult and can decide for himself whether he thinks the risk is worth it. In considering what to do, I will assume that his decision is the right one for him. After all, he is in a better position than I to judge his own well-being. And so, I will not take it upon myself to reconsider those reasons. Instead, I will base my decision of whether to [harm] him on the other relevant reasons.[47]

This approach only operates where there is full consent. That means that D can reasonably take V to be making an effective assessment of V's best interests. This means that where V is mistaken or pressurised or their thinking is impaired, then their apparent consent will not be sufficient to entitle D to assume that V has made an effective assessment of their best interests. This important point can be developed further.[48]

If V is consenting to an act which is prima facie wrongful, but is doing so under pressure or under a mistake, D cannot be confident the act will promote V's best interests. So if V is, for example, agreeing to sex with D or agreeing to give D her car, but is doing so because V believes D is a former lover she has not seen for many years, whereas in fact D is someone else, D cannot take V's consent as an assessment of her well-being, because it is an assessment based on an error of the factual scenario. There are three important aspects of this approach.

The first is that it reinforces the idea that if D is to wrong V, D has responsibilities to ensure that he or she has good reasons for so acting. The model acknowledges that D can accept V's assessment of V's own well-being, but that consent can only be effective where it can be accepted as that. This is why the mere word 'yes' is not enough for consent. Even though, for example, an intoxicated V may be saying 'yes' it will not give D warrant to assume that V has made an effective assessment of her wellbeing.[49] D must be acting in order to promote V's well-being and not for their own reasons. As discussed in Chapter 2, recognition of our universal vulnerability requires us to watch out for each other.

Second, there is often talk when consent arises (especially in the context of sexual offences) of the victim being to blame for putting themselves in the position where they were liable to be attacked or where D could have thought they were consenting. This is erroneous for many reasons, but one is that it overlooks the fact that D is choosing to do an act which is prima facie wrongful to V. D, therefore, has the responsibility to ensure that they are in fact not wronging V. The fact, for example, that V is so intoxicated she cannot indicate

[47] Ibid., 20.
[48] For the argument that sexual penetration is a prima facie wrong see M. Madden Dempsey and J. Herring, 'Why Sexual Penetration Requires a Justification' (2007) 27 *Oxford Journal of Legal Studies* 467.
[49] J. Herring, 'Consent in the Criminal Law: The Importance of Relationality and Responsibility' in A. Reed and M. Bohlander (eds.) *General Defences in Criminal Law* (Routledge, 2018).

her views, of course, provides D with no justification for wronging V; indeed, it is a particularly strong case of where D has no good reason for wronging V.

Third, when the court is considering whether V's consent provides D with a defence, this involves looking at the encounter between the two people, and how they understood and negotiated the act. This involves not just looking at the moment of sex but the context of the relationship and the broader social environment. Does the interaction indicate that D was seeking to let or enable V to make a free, informed decision about what was in her best interests or was D lying, threatening, pressurising V? The use of deceptions, pressures, manipulations and the like indicate that D was not seeking to use consent as an assessment by V of their wellbeing. Was D giving time and space to make the decision? Was D ensuring they were not labouring under any mistake? Threats are clearly inconsistent with this. D is seeking to manipulate V into agreeing to the act in order to avoid the adverse consequence, rather than making an assessment about the value of the act. Similarly, incentives too are likely to work in this way, particularly where the act is benefiting D. In such a case, we expect that the incentive is offered at the level that D believes is a fair price for what is on offer. When D agrees a price with a prostitute he is little concerned with a calculation of whether the sum involved is such as to make the transaction conducive to V's wellbeing, nor even concerned about whether V determines the sum is sufficient; he is likely to offer a price that reflects the value of the service to him. This indicates that he is not using V's consent in the acceptable way advocated in this chapter.

In this section I have argued that an analysis of the troublesome issue of consent to sexual relations can be greatly enhanced by taking a relational approach. This is based on an acceptance that our relational and vulnerable nature requires us to have responsibilities towards each other. Where one person is doing an act which is a prima facie wrong the other must take care to ensure the consent is an effective assessment by the individual of their wellbeing. This will require positive acts of enabling them to come to that determination. The approach highlights the responsibilities we have towards our fellow vulnerable human beings.

7.4 Exploitation

Some of the issues in the previous section give rise to a larger point. Generally, in the criminal law the focus tends to be on the consent of the victim, rather than the theme of exploitation. The term exploitation has proved difficult to define. A starting definition may be as follows[50]:

> Exploitation is a special kind of moral wrong and arises where a defendant who takes advantage of a person's vulnerability for the defendant's personal gain and/or the victim's loss.

[50] J. Herring, *Vulnerable Adults and the Law* (Oxford University Press, 2016), 185.

This captures the essence of exploitation but it requires quite a bit of unpacking and is far from straightforward.

Robert Goodin[51] argues:

> If A's interests are vulnerable to B's actions and choices, B has a special responsibility to protect A's interests; the strength of this responsibility depends strictly upon the degree to which B can affect A's interests.

This is an interesting analysis of vulnerability because it focuses on the extent to which B is in a position to affect A's interests, rather than any inherent characteristic of B. This is a broad concept of vulnerability because in many transactions one party can affect the interests of the other.

Tea Logar[52] suggests that vulnerability should be limited to cases where the person is in real need:

> vulnerabilities considered relevant for exploitation are usually those that are more or less directly connected to our essential needs, while taking advantage of mere desires is generally not considered exploitative.

The difficulty with Logar's approach is that much then turns on what is an 'essential need'. That seems such a fluid concept that it may not be helpful. It also seems to overlook the human nature of being powerfully influenced by desires that are not 'essential needs'. It also ignores the fact that what might be essential to some people is not to others.

One major issue is whether or not a transaction is exploitative if it is consensual.[53] Stephen Wilkinson[54] argues that a transaction between A and B 'amounts to A's exploiting B if and only if: (a) the distribution of benefit and harm between A and B is (other things being equal) unjust (in A's favour); and (b) B does not validly consent'. The basis of this argument is that otherwise exploitation opens the door to paternalism. Wilkinson claims that it is easy for others to believe that, for example, a person who sells their kidney for £20,000 must be being 'exploited'. Without the consent exception, he suggests, we are in danger of undermining the autonomy of people. I would argue against this.

First, exploitation may in its nature undermine autonomy, even if there is consent. There is only autonomy, according to Raz, if the choices 'must be free from coercion and manipulation by others'.[55] Many forms of exploitation will, therefore, negate autonomy, even if there is consent for legal purposes. This argument was developed in Chapter 6 and will not be repeated here.

---

[51] R. Goodin, *Protecting the Vulnerable* (University of Chicago Press, 1985).

[52] T. Logar, 'Exploitation as Wrongful Use: Beyond Taking Advantage of Vulnerabilities' (2010) 25 *Acta Analytica* 329.

[53] S. Wilkinson, *Bodies for Sale: Ethics and Exploitation in the Human Body Trade* (Routledge, 2003).

[54] Ibid., 173.

[55] J. Raz, *The Morality of Freedom* (Oxford University Press, 1988), 373.

Second, the exploiter is showing the wrong attitude towards consent. If we take the principle of autonomy seriously, we should require people to show respect for other's autonomy. A person who takes unfair advantage of another's vulnerability to obtain a consent may be failing to show due respect for their autonomy.[56] As argued in the previous section on consent to sexual relations, if a person is going to do a prima facie wrongful act to another they have responsibilities to ensure they have good enough reasons to act.[57]

At the heart of exploitation is the concept of taking advantage, but what does that mean.[58] Goodin argues that power-holders have a 'moral responsibility to protect the weaker'. This is notable because it is not only limited to acts which might be seen as wrongful but also to acts that fail to positively take steps to protect a vulnerable person. For example, Alisa Carse and Margaret Little[59] define exploitation as 'an exchange that involves wresting benefit from a genuine vulnerability in a way or to a degree one ought not'.[60]

Jennifer Collins,[61] applying Goodin's approach, gives some examples of what taking advantage might involve:

> Such circumstances could be occasions where D plays for advantage against those who have renounced playing for advantage themselves or against those who are unfit to play. Alternatively, it could be taking advantage if those who D plays against are no match for him, or where D's relative advantage derives from others' grave misfortunes. The power-holder is examined on the basis of whether they have engaged in "fair play" in the context of the norms of the particular relationship.

It has proved surprisingly difficult to define exploitation. It is clear there are several elements at play. Most definitions include some combination of the following elements:

- One party being able to influence the interests of the other party
- One party improperly taking advantage of the other party
- There not being an adequate sharing of the gains and losses flowing from the transaction.

It may be that the difficulty of definition arises because the exploitation is the result of a combination of all three of these, but there is no one level at which these can be set. So in a case where one party has considerable power over another, a relatively small degree of inequality in the sharing of the gains and

[56] Page 74.
[57] Herring, 'Consent in the Criminal Law: The Importance of Relationality and Responsibility'.
[58] Goodin, *Protecting the Vulnerable*.
[59] A. Carse and M. Little (2008) 'Exploitation and the Enterprise of Medical Research' in J. Hawkins and E. Emanuel (eds.) *Exploitation and Developing Countries: The Ethics of Clinical Research* (Princeton University Press, 2008), 38.
[60] R. Sample, *Exploitation: What It Is and Why It's Wrong* (Rowman & Littlefield, 2003).
[61] J. Collins, 'The Contours of Vulnerability' in J. Herring and J. Wallbank (eds.) *Vulnerabilities, Care and Family Law* (Routledge, 2014), 22.

losses is sufficient to make the transaction exploitative. Where, however, there is relatively little power one party has over the other, a more significant inequality in the sharing of the gains and losses needs to be shown.

It is suggested that what may be the most helpful approach is to ask whether the parties showed each other due respect for the vulnerability of the other. Where one party is aware that the other is vulnerable in some sense, this may require them to take special steps to ensure the transaction is fair. We should ask: to what extent was the stronger party legitimately able to say 'I am confident that the other party was able to make a reasonable assessment of whether the transaction was in their best interests.' The greater the pressures, the mistakes and incapacities of the other party, the harder it will be persuade the court of that. A party who contributes to these will find it all the harder to claim they were properly seeking a justification for the transaction.

7.5 Relational Blame and Joint Enterprise

At the heart of vulnerability theory is the claim that it is good for people to join together for common enterprises. Not only good, but essential. Our vulnerability requires us to co-operate together to meet each other's needs. The notion of the rugged individual living the self-sufficient, independent life is an artificial construct. Rather, we need to emphasise the values of mutuality, rationality and co-operation, rather than the traditional emphasis on rights which accentuates privacy, autonomy and independence.

Turning to the criminal law, we see a strong focus on individual responsibility and a suspicion of those who work together with others in enterprises. A good example of this suspicion is Lord Steyn's comment in *Powell and English*:[62]

> The criminal justice system exists to control crime. A prime function of that system must be to deal justly but effectively with those who join with others in criminal enterprises. Experience has shown that joint criminal enterprises only too readily escalate into the commission of greater offences. In order to deal with this important social problem the accessory principle is needed and cannot be abolished or relaxed.

The assumption here is that the 'go it alone' criminal is less dangerous than those who are working with others. Yet joining together is normal. Of course, the terminology of 'gangs' is a pejorative term. A book group, the British Philosophical Society and your local knitting circle team are all gangs in one sense. These gatherings together of like-minded people offer important support and encouragement. They provide a shared identity and mutual help. We must be wary of the law on accomplices being set so wide that people will be

---

[62] [1997] UKHL 45.

discouraged from joining groups, for fear of being found responsible for the acts of others.

That is why the *mens rea* of accomplices is important. In short, if you join a group foreseeing that another member of the group might commit an offence you might be found to have committed an offence. This makes it very dangerous to join together with others. If a member of a religious group is aware another member is using drugs and offers to help and support them as they seek to reduce their dependence and get help for their addiction, are they to be held liable? Are workers for a charity offering support for those with drug addiction potentially liable for encouraging reduction in drug use?[63] This seems absurd simply because we do not see religious groups or charity workers as 'gangs'.

These examples may seem unrealistic, but in the legal textbooks there is much discussion of whether a shopkeeper who sells a kitchen knife to someone they fear might possibly use it for a criminal offence is liable as am accomplice; or the host who serves alcohol at a dinner party aware that some guests have travelled by car and might later commit a driving while intoxicated offence.[64] These demonstrate that the parameters of accomplice liability are in danger of inhibiting behaviour which is beneficial. Or rather that the rules used to convict gang members through joint enterprise and accessorial liability look thoroughly unjust when applied in other contexts.

Lord Bingham in *Hasan*[65] describes the policy of the courts well, 'The policy of the law must be to discourage association with known criminals, and it should be slow to excuse the criminal conduct of those who do so.'

At first sight this might be thought to be a sensible policy, but a moment's thought should show otherwise. For a start, prison officers, probations officers and criminal lawyers breach this advice by associating with known criminals. Religious groups welcoming ex-convicts or support groups assisting those who have left prison to integrate into society will breach this. In fact, given that around a third of British men have a criminal record, Lord Bingham's advice is very hard to follow. Indeed, it does not seem implausible to suggest that good citizens should be encouraged to associate with criminals to help them see the error of their ways and reintegrate within society.

A good example of the concerns in this section is the case of *Brock and Wyner*.[66] Two project workers were 'concerned in the management' of a 'drop-in centre' in Cambridge. The centre was run by Winter Comfort, a charity for homeless people. They were convicted under s. 8(1) of the Misuse of Drugs Act 1971 of being concerned in the management of a premises and

---

[63] P. Glazebrook, 'On being Required to Be a Policeman, Untrained and Unpaid' (2011) 60 *Cambridge Law Journal* 537.

[64] Herring, *Criminal Law: Text, Cases and Materials*, ch 16.

[65] [2005] UKHL 22.

[66] [2001] 2 Cr App Rep 31.

knowingly permitting or suffering drug offences. The project workers were convicted on the basis that they knew or suspected drug dealers visited their drop-in centres and that they had not done all they reasonably could to have prevented them. Although they had taken steps to prevent drug dealing, the Court of Appeal concluded that it was open to the jury to conclude they had not done all they reasonably might. The case demonstrates the need to be very wary about throwing the net of accessorial and joint enterprise liability too widely for fear of discouraging communal and relational activities.[67]

The issues are well illustrated by *R* v. *Stone and Dobinson*,[68] which involved two defendants: John Stone described as below average intelligence, partially deaf and almost blind, and Gwendoline Dobinson, described as 'ineffectual and inadequate'. Stone's 50-year-old sister, Fanny, who was suffering from anorexia nervosa, came to live with them. Fanny regularly refused food and grew very weak. The defendants failed to summon help, despite requests from neighbours. Fanny was later found dead in squalid conditions. The appellants were convicted of manslaughter and their convictions were upheld by the Court of Appeal. The Court of Appeal emphasised the fact they had taken on care of a person who was unable to care for herself and that they had been negligent in the performance of that care.

The decision has proved controversial. The defendants were of low mental capacity. It appears they had enough difficulty looking after themselves, yet alone anyone else. Notably, the Court of Appeal confirmed the use of the negligence standard for cases of this kind. In other words, guilt flowed from the fact their level of care fell below that expected and there was no need to show any kind of intention or recklessness. The fact they had done the best that might be expected of them was irrelevant. The concern here is that the criminal law is being used to impose higher standards than the defendant is capable of. That seems inherently unjust. Even taking the point that these defendants had assumed responsibility for the victim, they cannot be taken to have assumed responsibility to do more than they were capable of.

Further, it seems the real failures were the lack of support from social services and medical professionals. One could imagine a very different telling of this story where the focus was on the failing of the different public authorities to support Stone, Dobinson and the sister. Indeed, in terms of resources, knowledge and expertise were not the authorities in a far better position to intervene than Stone and Dobinson?[69] Was this a case where laws designed to protect one vulnerable person left another vulnerable person open to abuse?

As the discussion of *Stone and Dobinson* suggests, the criminal law too readily identifies a vulnerable person to blame, rather than identifying the

---

[67] Glazebrook, 'On Being Required to Be a Policeman, Untrained and Unpaid', 537.

[68] [1977] QB 354.

[69] J. Herring, 'The Legal Duties of Carers' (2010) 18 *Medical Law Review* 248.

broader social failures. Another example of this is the offence of familial homicide found in section 5 of the Domestic Violence Crime and Victim Act 2004:

(1) A person ("D") is guilty of an offence if –
   (a) a child or vulnerable adult ("V") dies or suffers serious physical harm as a result of the unlawful act of a person who –
      (i) was a member of the same household as V, and
      (ii) had frequent contact with him,
   (b) D was such a person at the time of that act,
   (c) at that time there was a significant risk of serious physical harm being caused to V by the unlawful act of such a person, and
   (d) either D was the person whose act caused [the death or serious physical harm]^2 or –
      (i) D was, or ought to have been, aware of the risk mentioned in paragraph (c),
      (ii) D failed to take such steps as he could reasonably have been expected to take to protect V from the risk, and
      (iii) the act occurred in circumstances of the kind that D foresaw or ought to have foreseen.

The offence was targeted at, say, a mother who was aware her partner posed a risk of violence to her child and yet did nothing to protect the child from harm. If the partner did then go on to kill or cause serious harm to the child she could be prosecuted for the offence. While well intentioned, the offence has given rise to serious concern: in particular, because it has been used to prosecute victims of domestic abuse for failing to protect children from their abusive partner.[70]

To give one example, in May 2005 Rebecca Lewis, aged twenty-one, was sentenced for failing to prevent the murder of her baby Aaron Gilbert at the hands of her partner, Andrew Lloyd, with whom she had lived for six weeks.[71] She was sentenced to six years in prison. Lloyd was sentenced to twenty-four years in prison for murder. The court accepted that Lewis was largely absent during the attacks and was not present at the killing, but held she did know enough to be aware of a risk of death or serious harm. In particular, Lewis knew that Lloyd had flicked Aaron's ears and feet when he cried; had picked him up by his ears and ankles; and had thrown him onto a bed. In sentencing her, the judge said:

> You put your own interests first, above and beyond that of your vulnerable child. You could have stopped the violence that Lloyd was subjecting Aaron to. You could so easily have got the authorities to stop it.

---

[70] For a detailed discussion see J. Herring, 'Familial Homicide, Failure to Protect and Domestic Violence: Who's the Victim?' [2007] *Criminal Law Review* 927.
[71] *BBC News*, 'Mother Allowed Baby Son's Murder', 15 December 2006.

This case seems to inadequately take account of the impact of the domestic violence. At the trial, Lewis had explained that she did not summon help because Lloyd had said he would kill her if she left. For 'putting her interests first' she was given a sentence only a little shorter than the average given for rape. Of particular note is the fact that local services had been told by Lewis's cousin of concerns about the child. The social services wrote a letter asking to make an appointment, but it was sent to the wrong address. The authorities were aware of the dangers the child faced and given their expertise were in a better position than Lewis to foresee what might happen. More importantly, the authorities had the resources to respond to the problems and freedom from fear of reprisals if they did so. Was it really Lewis who was to blame in this scenario?[72] First, the offence imposes an obligation on people to take reasonable steps to protect vulnerable people who are at risk of violence, yet this is imposed on a limited number of people. As we have already seen, in practice this has too often been people who themselves are the victims of domestic abuse and least well-placed to take steps to protect them. The obligation is imposed on a person who is a member of V's household and had frequent contact with him.[73] That would exclude a social worker or other professional who has contact with the person. It is not clear that those living in a violent household are either in a position to foresee what the future holds or are readily able to protect others in the household.

The traditional understanding of responsibility is that you are casually responsible for your own actions, but not those of others (unless they lack capacity). The case of R v. Kennedy[74] demonstrates this well. The drug dealer was responsible for his actions – handing over the drugs – but was not responsible for what the victim did with the drugs (inject himself) or the consequences of that (death). The well-established doctrine of novus actus interveniens establishes that D cannot be held responsible for the free voluntary and informed act of others.[75] That other will be responsible for what they have done. As their Lordships explain:[76]

> The criminal law generally assumes the existence of free will. The law recognises certain exceptions, in the case of the young, those who for any reason are not fully responsible for their actions, and the vulnerable, and it acknowledges situations of duress and necessity, as also of deception and mistake. But, generally speaking, informed adults of sound mind are treated as autonomous

---

[72] L. Clayton-Helm, 'To Punish or Not to Punish? Dealing with Death or Serious Injury of a Child or Vulnerable Adult' (2014) 78 Journal of Criminal Law 477; S. Morrison, 'Should There Be a Domestic Violence Defence to the Offence of Familial Homicide' [2013] Criminal Law Review 826.

[73] R. v. Khan [2009] EWCA Crim 2.

[74] [2007] UKHL 38.

[75] R v. Pagett (1983) 76 Cr App R 279. M. Moore, Causation and Responsibility (Oxford University Press, 2010), ch 2.

[76] Para 14.

beings able to make their own decisions how they will act, and none of the exceptions is relied on as possibly applicable in this case. Thus D is not to be treated as causing V to act in a certain way if V makes a voluntary and informed decision to act in that way rather than another. There are many classic statements to this effect. In his article *"Finis for Novus Actus?"* (1989) 48(3) CLJ 391, 392, Professor Glanville Williams wrote:

"I may suggest reasons to you for doing something; I may urge you to do it, tell you it will pay you to do it, tell you it is your duty to do it. My efforts may perhaps make it very much more likely that you will do it. But they do not cause you to do it, in the sense in which one causes a kettle of water to boil by putting it on the stove. Your volitional act is regarded (within the doctrine of responsibility) as setting a new 'chain of causation' going, irrespective of what has happened before."

This highly individualised understanding of criminal responsibility produces some well-known problems. It means the criminal law struggles to respond to communal crimes. Two well-known examples are criminal liability for corporations' environmental pollution and misogynistic environments. In all of these cases it is not straightforwardly a single person who has caused the harm, but rather the harm is caused as a result of a culture or community atmosphere.[77] As criminal law is based around a model of identifying the individual who has caused the wrong, these situations are not dealt with effectively, or at all, by the law.

Vulnerability theory offers a rather different approach to such questions. As we are dependent on others and are constituted through our relationships, the self is integrated into their social network. It becomes therefore entirely natural to focus on the questions: has our relationship caused a harm? Or has our community caused harms? These questions are natural because we rarely, if ever, act alone. We always act, or nearly always, act through, with and in relations to others. Our acts are given meaning by the response of others and in order to evoke responses in others. This means that the separation between what I do and to what I contribute causally in, through and with others breaks down.

This 'relational liability' approach would see accessorial liability as a norm. All crimes can be understood as the outcome of complex relational webs and societal interactions. The 'lone gunman' is properly the stuff of fiction. We are responsible for the kind of society we live in and the products of our relationships.[78]

Tatjana Hörnle usefully refers to the concept in the German legal academic literature of whether someone has 'dominion over' the offence.[79] She argues

---

[77] C. Wells, *Corporations and Criminal Responsibility* (Oxford University Press, 2011).

[78] L. Farmer, 'Complicity beyond Causality' (2007) 1 *Criminal Law and Philosophy* 151.

[79] T. Hörnle, 'Commentary to "Complicity and Causality"' (2007) 1 *Criminal Law and Philosophy* 143.

that this has the potential to provide 'richer ways of describing the psychological circumstances, and the various differences in the degree of knowledge and willpower that allow control over situations' than a straightforward distinction of who was the principal and who the accessory. This approach recognises that we impact upon others and are impacted upon by them. Our selves and our understandings emerge from our relationships with our communities; just as other selves and our community values emerge from our contributions.[80] There is complex to-ing and fro-ing of influences between the self, relationships and communities.

Jonathan Glover has raised a hypothetical scenario which demonstrates the point well. He contrasts two situations.[81] In the first, thirty thieves descend on a village and each thief finds a villager and steals all their beans. In the second, each thief takes from each villager a single bean. The first case is unproblematic. We can say of each thief that they have rendered a particular villager hungry. In the second, we cannot identify one particular thief who has caused a particular impact on the villagers. Considering people separately, we must conclude that each thief has taken a single bean from a villager, which causes them minimal harm. Christopher Kutz's discussion[82] gives the example particular bite by imagining the villagers die as a result of hunger. As Kutz puts it, looking at the scenario in terms of traditional individual responsibility we either conclude that no thief can be charged with murder as 'no [one] thief directly causes any death, so none might be counted a direct murderer',[83] or we say that each thief has made a significant (or at least not insignificant) contribution to the death and so each thief can be charged with thirty murders. These both seem over- or under-inclusive. Kutz puts it in this way:

> moral responsibility in such situations is best understood not separably, in terms of individual causal relations, but collectively, in terms of what the gang has done. The thieves' responsibility must be understood *inclusively*: each is included in the group that did the wrong, and bears responsibility qua member of that group. The basis of responsibility in such a case is not the difference an individual contributor makes, but the common plan, mediated by each individual's intention to participate in that plan.[84]

The response, as he suggests, is to move beyond thinking of the issue in terms of individuality and discuss how 'we thieves' are responsible and how 'we villagers' are impacted.

---

[80] C. Foster and J. Herring, *Identity, Personhood and the Law* (Springer, 2017), ch 2.
[81] Discussed in C. Kutz 'The Philosophical Foundations of Complicity Law' in J. Deigh and D. Dolinko (eds.) *The Oxford Handbook of Philosophy of Criminal Law* (Oxford University Press, 2016).
[82] Ibid.
[83] Ibid., 156.
[84] Ibid., 157.

The broad argument here is that we are responsible for the kind of relationships and communities that we live with, but that also our relationships and communities impact on us. This is particularly apparent from the literature on gangs.[85] A study by Alleyne, Fernandes and Pritchard[86] found the importance of the rules, rituals and attitudes of the gang on the members' attitudes to violence and how they have a profound impact on individual psychology of the members. Indeed, there is substantial literature showing that gang membership escalates criminal behaviour.[87] The informal social controls that might have been installed through school or other positive criteria are discarded for new norms, in the form of gang rules.[88] James Vigil's[89] study highlights that for young people who join gangs 'the gang norms, its functions, and its roles help shape what a person thinks about himself and others, and the gang provides models for how to look and act under various circumstances'. Young people are pushed into gang membership by threats from outside but are also drawn in by the attractions that gang membership can offer, such as higher social status, friendship and solidarity. Hence those with lower self-esteem and weaker bonds to social networks such as schools and families are more likely to be drawn to gangs with criminal purposes.[90] Gang members profoundly impact on each other's behaviour, emotions and acts.[91]

So in a general sense and in relation to gangs we need to find a more sophisticated way of capturing the wrongs that emerge from our communal, social and relational contexts. In Antje du Bois-Pedain's excellent article[92] on accessorial liability, she explores the psychological literature which explains how group membership can challenge concepts of responsibility:

> not only does the direct agent in some crowd situations not relate to his actions as actions for which he is responsible – he has no sense of ownership of them – but that the very actions themselves are more extreme than the group members would be minded to perform outside the group context. This has been explored in research on group polarisation.

This kind of examination of the issue shows the inadequacy of orthodox ways of thinking about this issue. One is to consider the 'common purpose' of the

---

[85] J. Densley, *How Gangs Work: An Ethnography of Youth Violence* (Palgrave Macmillan, 2013).
[86] E. Alleyne, I. Fernandes and E. Pritchard, 'Denying Humanness to Victims: How Gang Members Justify Violent Behavior' (2014) 17 *Group Processes and Intergroup Relations* 750.
[87] S. Battin, K. Hill, R. Abbott, R. Catalano and D. Hawkins, 'The Contribution of Gang Membership to Delinquency beyond Delinquent Friends' (1998) 36 *Criminology* 93.
[88] E. Alleyne, and J. Wood, 'Gang Involvement: Social and Environmental Factors' (2011) 60 *Crime and Delinquency* 547.
[89] J. Vigil, *Barrio Gangs: Street Life and Identity in Southern California* (University of Texas Press, 1988), 421.
[90] R. Dukes, R. Martinez and J. Stein, 'Precursors and Consequences of Membership in Youth Gangs' (1997) 28 *Youth and Society* 139.
[91] Ibid.
[92] A. Du Bois-Pedain, 'Violent Dynamics: Exploring Responsibility-Attribution for Harms Inflicted during Spontaneous Group Violence' (2016) 6 *Oñati Socio-legal Series* 1053.

group and to argue that an accomplice adopts the group's goals as their own and hence can be responsible for them.[93]

Although the approach is not entirely without merit, it fails to capture the dynamic process in which a person in a group may contribute to and be caught up by the common purpose. The association view may capture a little crudely what is happening. Members of a gang formulate and produce through their relationships common cultural values that can create an often-formulated vision. On joining a gang, one may not simply become associated with the common purpose, but with changing it and being changed by it. So Kutz's[94] idea of a collective action may imagine too much of a coherent image of what is an imprecise, dynamic and unclear picture.

A useful analogy may be the concept of corporate culture. Writing in connection with corporate responsibility, Susanne Beck[95] writes:

> Most socially important – and dangerous – decisions are not reached by individuals but by collectives; the way modern societies change depends on which kind of corporations acquire social power, their internal regulations and values, and the way they are integrated into existing regulative structures. And, while the power of collectives has expanded, the power of individuals has decreased. Individuals are members of different collectives, their behavior regulated by divergent normative systems, and their intentions assimilated by collective goals. All these developments can be observed worldwide thereby increasing the need for global regulation.

These points are well made and can be applied to gangs as much as to corporations. The attempt to use the tools of criminal law to capture the responsibility for corporate culture seems entirely appropriate to gang culture.

This suggests that we need to move away from offences which express the wrong in individual terms and identify a principle and an accomplice to ones which recognise the communal nature of the wrong.

As Lindsay Farmer points out in his important recent book *Making the Modern Criminal Law,*[96] the criminal law has as its subject the autonomous, reasoning individual who is guided by norms and can be held to account for their conduct if they breach those norms. That, he argues, disguises the complexity of responsibility. Arlie Loughnan[97] argues that once a deeper study of criminal responsibility is undertaken, it will 'allow for multiple stories about criminal responsibility to emerge, with interest in what might be found in the

---

[93] A. Rogers, 'Accomplice Liability for Unintentional Crimes: Remaining within the Constraints of Intent' (1998) 31 *Loyola of Los Angeles Law Review* 1351.

[94] C. Kutz, 'Acting Together' (2000) 61 *Philosophy and Phenomenological Research* 1.

[95] S. Beck, 'Corporate Criminal Responsibility' in M. Dubber and T. Hörnle (eds.) *The Oxford Handbook of Criminal Law* (Oxford University Press, 2011), 335.

[96] L. Farmer, *Making the Modern Criminal Law* (Oxford University Press, 2017).

[97] A. Loughnan, 'The Meta-Significance of Criminal Responsibility' (2017) 4 *Critical Analysis of Law* 35.

intricacies or margins of the criminal law, in its messy reality or operation, if not on the face of its "principles."'

As Norris asks:

> Legal categories presuppose an individual subject in whom responsibility is fixed by mental characteristics relating to the cognitive control of actions. These characteristics establish what seems to be a discrete, fixed, stable individual subject, but what if subjects are not like that? What if identity ... [is] located in significant measure beyond the individual in the social realm, and [is] therefore fluid and changing?[98]

Norrie is right to question this assumption, and the literature on gang membership shows this. The assumption that we have one individual who chooses to commit the offence as principle and another choosing to assist or encourage them ignores the complex group dynamics at play.

This section has sought to open up our understanding of criminal responsibility and accountability in cases of joint enterprise. As Lindsay Farmer[99] has argued:

> there are a variety of forms of collective involvement in wrongdoing that cannot easily be reduced to the model of one person causing another to act.

This section has argued that vulnerability offers some interesting challenges to standard legal approaches to joint enterprise. By claiming that we are all vulnerable and dependent on others to meet our physical, emotional and definitional needs, it raises questions about how to respond to criminal groups. I have sought to develop three claims in particular. The first is that the law must ensure it does not encourage collaborating or joining together with others. That is a natural and inevitable thing. Second, a proper understanding of the nature of relationships should cause us to see the current criminal responses as being under-inclusive in failing to capture our responsibilities towards those we are in relationship with and over-inclusive in attaching too much responsibility to individual actors. I have explored, briefly, ways in which analogies might be drawn with corporate responsibility doctrine to deal with gangs. Finally, I have argued we need to be much more open to using the defence of duress in joint enterprise cases, acknowledging the significance that personal relationships have for people and therefore the potential that they be used for threats.

7.6 Conclusion

This chapter has sought to explore the significance of criminal law for taking a relational approach. It highlighted four particular areas, by way of example.

---

[98] A. Norrie, *Crime, Reason and History* (Cambridge University Press, 2000), 12.
[99] Farmer, 'Complicity beyond Causality', 151.

It has argued that an understanding of the significance of relationships to our identities should shift our focus away from highlighting bodily injuries as the primary example of a criminal wrong, to focusing on harms to caring relationships. Second, it has argued that we need to understand consent in a relational way, seeing it as an interchange between vulnerable people that acknowledges their responsibilities to each other. Third, I have sought to unpack the concept of exploitation as a form of relational wrong which is insufficiently utilised in the criminal law. Finally, I have sought to suggest that our understanding of responsibility within the criminal law is unduly individualistic. A relational approach can also foster a more sensitive assessment of our responsibilities for our actions and the actions of others as members of communal endeavours. It can lead to us discovering a role of the criminal to acknowledge our deeply vulnerable and interdependent natures.

Concluding Thoughts

Who are we? What is important to us? What makes us who we are? These are some of the deep questions addressed in this book. Such questions might be seen as too 'airy fairy' for lawyers to seek to address. Yet I have argued it is essential that they do.

This book has argued that the law is based around a clear, but false, understanding of what it is to be a person: an individualised one. The individualistic understanding of the self is based on seeing human beings as generating their own identities, ideas and values. It emphasises the importance of allowing people the freedom to plan their own lives. It places legal rules around a norm of a self-sufficient, independent person. Hence we see the values of autonomy, privacy and bodily integrity as central human rights. In short, the right not to be bothered is a core human right.

Of course, the law recognises exceptions to this. We have special rules to govern those unfortunates who cannot live up to the norm of the law: children, those lacking mental capacity and 'vulnerable adults'. However, these inter-ventions are typically designed to enable these people to leave their wretched state and become independent and autonomous 'like the rest of us'.

Yet that is an impoverished view of what it is to be human. Joy is not found in rational thought. The controlled, autonomous life is an utterly boring one. Individual projects are little fun. Virtually no one actually lives their life as a hermit dedicated to self-absorption. No one plans for a life with no regard to others. We seek out families, friends, children, fellow travellers to share our journey together.

The language we use is language given to us by our carers. Our descriptions of objects and feelings emerge from our relationships in early age. Our senses of who we are and where we belong come from those relationships. Our ideas are those developed with and based on the ideas of others. Anyone who believes they are an original thinker is deceiving themselves. Even the most brilliant idea is developed from and dependant on earlier ideas.

I suspect that for nearly everyone the most wonderful thing that has ever happened to them, and the very worst thing that has ever happened to them, has been in relational terms. We think, live and establish our identity through our relationships.

It is the failure of the law to appreciate the importance of relational values that has caused some of its abject failures: the lack of protection for those in abusive relationships, explored in Chapter 4; the failure to protect and reward caring relationships, discussed in Chapter 3; a criminal law which can spot the cut to the finger but not the damage to the soul caused by abuse, as examined in Chapter 7; a family law which seems obsessed with the sexual practices of couples, while being blind to the importance of care work, as explained in Chapter 6; and a medical law which absurdly assumes we are competent to make decisions for ourselves, rather than acknowledging our vulnerable, irrational incapacity, as considered in Chapter 5.

This book has called for a re-imagining of what law could be like if it took the concept of the relational self seriously. It would be a law which saw the sustenance, support and reward for caring relationships as a central goal. It would be law which recognised that we cannot consider the rights and interests of individuals separately from each other, but needs to focus on enabling caring relationships to develop. A law which would recognise our deep universal vulnerability, requiring legal protections and state provisions and which recognised that powerful social forces mean that some people are very well provided for by the state and others are not. A law that appreciated that the abuse of a relationship to undermine and destroy another person was the most profound of wrongs, the prevention of which should be a key role for the law. A law that recognises that on our own we humans are of little moral or scientific interest, but that in a relationship of care and love we can produce wonders.

Index

Accomplices, 185
actus reus, 167
altruism, 60, 126–127, 164
animalism, 4
anthropology, 1
Aristotle, 5
Asch, Adrianne, 129
autonomy, 16, 36, 38, 46

Baier, Annette, 12
Bartlett, Katherine, 157
Bauman, Zygmunt, 64
BDSM, 173
Beauchamp, Tom, 25
Beck, Susanne, 193
Bennett Woodhouse, Barbara, 157
bereavement, 13
Berlin, Issiah, 17
best interests, 125
Bielby, Phil, 35
birth certificate, 114
Blustein, Jeffrey, 129
bodies, 4–7, 20–22, 27, 32, 42, 52, 55, 58, 63, 66,
    100, 102–108, 140
bodily integrity, 3–4, 20, 23, 169, 196
Boyd, Susan, 164

Cameron, David, 25, 69
capacity test, 109
Cartesian Dualism, 4, 6
Case, Amelia, 41
Chambers, Clare, 147
children., 95
Childress, James, 25
Choudhry, Shazia, ix, 96
Clapton, Jayne, 22
class, 89–90
Clough, Bev, 118

Code, Lorraine, 9
coercive control, 81, 174
Collins, Jennifer, 184
Collins, Stephanie, 54
Conly, Sarah, 116
Consent, 180
contract law, 3, 36–37, 67, 143, 154
contracts, 143
crime, 2
criminal law, 15, 23
Cushing, Pamela, 55

Dagan, Hanoch, 150
de Beauvoir, Simone, 7
Diduck, Alison, 38, 153
dignity, 41
Dillon, Robin, 53
disability studies, 1
disability, 13, 19, 62
disabled people, 20, 30
Dodds, Susan, 27, 30, 37, 44, 52
domestic abuse, 74
domestic violence, 174
Douglas, Frederick, 29
Douglas, Gillian, 60, 152
Drobac, Jennifer, 115
du Bois-Pedain, Antje, 192
Dutton, Mary Ann, 82–83, 91
Dworkin, Ronald, 111

Eekelaar, John, 61, 87
Eichner, Maxine, 47, 153
embryo, 108
emotional harm, 86, 167, 169
emotions, 59
empathy, 41, 59
Engster, Daniel, 26–27, 54
Equal marriage, 142, 144

ethics, 1
exploitation, 182

familial homicide, 188
family law, 141
Farmer, Lindsay, 193–194
Feder Kittay, Eva, 21, 57–58, 66, 137
feminism, 69
feminist, 3
Ferrante, Elena, 11
financial orders on divorce, 149
Fine, Michael, 55
Fineman, Martha, 24, 29, 32–35, 42–43, 47, 62, 68, 70
Fisher, Berenice, 50
Fisher, Hayley, 149
Foster, Charles, ix, 139, 164
Frantz, Carolyn, 150
Frazer, Elizabeth, 92
Freely, Maureen, 158
Friedman, Marilyn, 87
Frye, Marilyn, 94

gangs, 185
Gardner, Simon, 180
Garland-Thomson, Rosemarie, 22
gaslightighting, 82
Gavison, Ruth, 92
Geertz, Clifford, 10
Gefenas, Eugenijus, 26
genetic origins, 156
Gergen, Kenneth, 10, 12
Giddens, Anthony, 75
Gilligan, Carol, 55, 61
Glendinning, Caroline, 55
Glennon, Lisa, 152
Glover, Jonathan, 191
Goldscheid, Julie, 92
Goodenough, Oliver, 115
Goodin, Robert, 38–39, 183
Goodman, Lisa, 83, 91
Greasley, Kate, 138
grief, 41, 59
Gunn, Michael, 117

Harding, Rosie, 16, 28, 54
Harris, Bridget, 83
Harris, John, 19
Held, Virgina, 53, 56, 60, 67
Hester, Marianne, 82, 95
Heumann, Judy, 65

Himmelweit, Susan, 71–72
Ho, Anita, 112
Holloway, Wendy, 58
Hörnle, Tatjana, 190
human equality, 128, 132
Hurst, Samia, 31
Hutchings, Kimberly, 92
hyper-parenting, 160

Intersectional analysis, 13
intimate abuse, 74, 76
Istanbul Convention, 76, 96

Jareborg, Nils, 168
Joas, Hans, 2
Johnson, Michael, 82

Kant, 8, 59
Karpin, Isabel, 103
Katz, Larissa, 102
Kelly, Christine, 64
Kirschner, Suzanne, 12
Kitzinger, Jenny, 43
Kutz, Christopher, 191

L'Arche communities, 55–56
Lasch, Christopher, 11
Lawless, John, 18
Lefley, Harriet, 50
Lévinas, Emmanuel, 30
Lewis, Tanya, 55
liberty, 36
Lindemann, Hilde, 12, 14
Lindemann, Kate, 30
Logar, Tea, 183
Loughnan, Arlie, 193
Low, Hamish, 149
Lyndon Shanley, Mary, 141, 147–148

Mackenzie, Catriona, 19, 27, 30, 44
Maclean, Mavis, 107
Madden Dempsey, Michelle, ix, 79, 90, 92
Marion Young, Iris, 94, 122, 145
marital rape, 171
Masson, Judith, 156
McMahan, Jeff, 131, 134
mens rea, 167, 186
Mill, John Stuart, 167
Minow, Martha, 141, 147–148
Morris, Jenny, 63

Motro, Shari, 150
Myhill, Andy, 90

Naffine, Ngaire, 7, 11
Natalie Stoljar, 19, 122
Neal, Mary, 31
Nedelsky, Jennifer, 15, 112, 146
Noddings, Nel, 62
Norrie, Alan, 194
Nussbaum, Martha, 2

Olsen, Eric, 5
Orton, Helena, 153
Ownership, 101

parental responsibility, 78, 141, 158–160, 165, 176
parenthood, 144
pater familias, 68
Patriarchy, 14, 16, 19, 79–80, 89–94, 96
personhood, 41, 128
Peter Beresford, 54
Peter Singer, 130–131, 134, 137
Pettit, Philip, 17, 178
philosophy, 1
Plato, 6
pluralism, 17
Polikoff, Nancy, 157
pregnancy, 138
pre-nuptial agreements, 151
presumption of innocence, 46, 114, 117
property, 101

race, 89, 128
Rachels, James, 130, 134
racism, 14, 131
rape, 180
rationality, 6, 8–9, 12, 15, 23, 41, 129, 132, 135, 138, 185
Reinders, Hans, 136
relational autonomy, 18–19
relational harms., 176
relational liability, 190
Relational welfare, 163
Respect, 53
responsibilities, 53, 60
Richardson, Ginerva, 121

Rogers, Wendy, 27, 30, 44, 116
Rosenfeld, Alvin, 160

Schroeder, Doris, 26
second persons, 12
self-sufficiency, 14, 18, 28, 42, 45, 168
Selma Sevenhuijsen, 48, 71
sexuality, 6, 13, 89, 93
Shakespeare, 42
shared vulnerability, 36
Shildrick, Margrit, 40
Simester, Andrew, 179
Smith, David, 15
Sociology, 1
Solomon, Andrew, 21
soul, 6
Stark, Evan, 81–82, 88, 91
Sullivan, Bob, 179

Tadros, Victor, 84
theft, 179
theology, 1
Tronto, Joan, 50–51, 58, 65, 72
Trump, Donald, 135
trust, 23, 87
Twigg, Julia, 52

Ungerson, Clare, 52
Uwechia Nzegwu, Nkiru, 16

Vehmens, Simo, 132
virtue, 164
von Hirsch, Andrew, 168

Waldron, Jeremey, 135
Wall, Jesse, 4
Wasserman, David, 129
Weitzman, Lenore, 143
West, Robin, 59
Wilkinson, Stephen, 183
Williams, Fiona, 33
Williams, Joan, 151
Winance, Myrian, 22, 63
Wise, Nicole, 160
Woodlock, Delanie, 83
Woods, Richard, 64
work and skill exception, 100